ALL GLORY TO ŚRĪ GURU AND GAURĀṄGA

ŚRĪMAD BHĀGAVATAM

of

KṚṢṆA-DVAIPĀYANA VYĀSA

गोप्यस्तपः किमचरन् यदमुष्य रूपं
लावण्यसारमसमोर्ध्वमनन्यसिद्धम् ।
दृग्भिः पिबन्त्यनुसवाभिनवं दुरापम्
एकान्तधाम यशसः श्रिय ऐश्वरस्य ॥१४॥

gopyas tapaḥ kim acaran yad amuṣya rūpaṁ
lāvaṇya-sāram asamordhvam ananya-siddham
dṛgbhiḥ pibanty anusavābhinavaṁ durāpam
ekānta-dhāma yaśasaḥ śriya aiśvarasya

(p. 246)

BOOKS by
His Divine Grace
A. C. Bhaktivedanta Swami Prabhupāda

Bhagavad-gītā As It Is
Śrīmad-Bhāgavatam, cantos 1-10 (30 vols.)
Śrī Caitanya-caritāmṛta (17 vols.)
Teachings of Lord Caitanya
The Nectar of Devotion
The Nectar of Instruction
Śrī Īśopaniṣad
Easy Journey to Other Planets
Kṛṣṇa Consciousness: The Topmost Yoga System
Kṛṣṇa, The Supreme Personality of Godhead (3 vols.)
Perfect Questions, Perfect Answers
Teachings of Lord Kapila, the Son of Devahūti
Transcendental Teachings of Prahlāda Mahārāja
Teachings of Queen Kuntī
Kṛṣṇa, the Reservoir of Pleasure
The Science of Self-Realization
The Path of Perfection
Search for Liberation
Life Comes from Life
The Perfection of Yoga
Beyond Birth and Death
On the Way to Kṛṣṇa
Geetār-gan (Bengali)
Vairāgya-vidyā (Bengali)
Buddhi-yoga (Bengali)
Bhakti-ratna-bolī (Bengali)
Rāja-vidyā: The King of Knowledge
Elevation to Kṛṣṇa Consciousness
Kṛṣṇa Consciousness: The Matchless Gift
Back to Godhead magazine (founder)

A complete catalog is available upon request.

Bhaktivedanta Book Trust
3764 Watseka Avenue
Los Angeles, California 90034

ŚRĪMAD BHĀGAVATAM

Tenth Canto

"The Summum Bonum"

(Part Seven—Chapters 36–44)

With the Original Sanskrit Text,
Its Roman Transliteration, Synonyms,
Translation and Elaborate Purports

The Great Work of

His Divine Grace
A. C. Bhaktivedanta Swami Prabhupāda
Founder-*Ācārya* of the International Society for Krishna Consciousness

Continued by

His Divine Grace
Hridayananda dāsa Goswami Ācāryadeva

Sanskrit Editing by

Gopīparāṇadhana dāsa Adhikārī

THE BHAKTIVEDANTA BOOK TRUST
Los Angeles • London • Paris • Bombay • Sydney • Hong Kong

Readers interested in the subject matter of this book
are invited by the International Society for Krishna Consciousness
to correspond with its Secretary:

International Society for Krishna Consciousness
3764 Watseka Avenue
Los Angeles, California 90034

First Printing, 1986: 5,000 copies

Printed in Singapore

Library of Congress Cataloging in Publication Data (Revised)

Purāṇas. Bhāgavatapurāṇa. English and Sanskrit.
Śrīmad-Bhāgavatam.

Includes bibliographical references and indexes.
Contents: Canto 1. Creation (3 v)— Canto 2. The cosmic manifestation (2 v)— Canto 3. The status quo (4 v)— Canto 4. The creation of the fourth order (4 v)— Canto 5. The creative impetus (2 v)— Canto 6. Prescribed duties for mankind (3 v)— Canto 7. The science of God (3 v)— Canto 8. Withdrawal of the cosmic creations (3 v)— Canto 9. Liberation (3 v)— Canto 10. The summum bonum (14 v)— Canto 11. General history (5 v)— Canto 12. The age of deterioration (2 v)
Cantos 10 (v 4–14), 11 and 12 by Hridayananda Goswami Ācāryadeva, completing the great work of His Divine Grace A. C. Bhaktivedanta Swami Prabhupāda; Sanskrit editing by Gopīparāṇadhana dāsa Adhikārī.
1. Purāṇas. Bhāgavatapurāṇa—Criticism, interpretation, etc. 2. Chaitanya, 1486-1534. 3. Vaishnavites—India—Biography.
I. Bhaktivedanta Swami, A. C., 1896-1977.
II. Hridayananda Goswami, 1948-
III. Gopīparāṇadhana dāsa Adhikārī, 1950-
IV. Title.
BL1140.4.B432E5 1972 294.5'925 73-169353
ISBN 0-89213-141-1 (Canto 10, v. 7) AACR2

Table of Contents

CHAPTER THIRTY-EIGHT

Akrūra's Arrival in Vṛndāvana

CHAPTER THIRTY-NINE

Akrūra's Vision

CHAPTER FORTY
The Prayers of Akrūra

CHAPTER FORTY–ONE
Kṛṣna and Balarāma Enter Mathurā

CHAPTER FORTY-TWO
The Breaking of the Sacrificial Bow

CHAPTER FORTY–THREE
Kṛṣṇa Kills Kuvalayāpīḍa

CHAPTER FORTY–FOUR
The Killing of Kaṁsa

Appendixes

Preface

nama oṁ viṣṇu-pādāya kṛṣṇa-preṣṭhāya bhū-tale
śrīmate bhaktivedānta-svāmin iti nāmine

I offer my most respectful obeisances at the lotus feet of His Divine Grace A. C. Bhaktivedanta Swami Prabhupāda, who is very dear to Lord Kṛṣṇa on this earth, having taken shelter at His lotus feet.

namas te sārasvate deve gaura-vāṇī-pracāriṇe
nirviśeṣa-śūnyavādi-pāścātya-deśa-tāriṇe

I offer my most respectful obeisances unto the lotus feet of His Divine Grace A. C. Bhaktivedanta Swami Prabhupāda, who is the disciple of Śrīla Bhaktisiddhānta Sarasvatī Ṭhākura and who is powerfully distributing the message of Caitanya Mahāprabhu and thus saving the fallen Western countries from impersonalism and voidism.

Śrīmad-Bhāgavatam, with authorized translation and elaborate purports in the English language, is the great work of His Divine Grace Oṁ Viṣṇupāda Paramahaṁsa Parivrājakācārya Aṣṭottara-śata Śrī Śrīmad A. C. Bhaktivedanta Swami Prabhupāda, our beloved spiritual master. Our present publication is a humble attempt by his servants to complete his most cherished work of *Śrīmad-Bhāgavatam*. Just as one may worship the holy Ganges River by offering Ganges water unto the Ganges, similarly, in our attempt to serve our spiritual master, we are offering to him that which he has given to us.

Śrīla Prabhupāda came to America in 1965 at a critical moment in the history of America and the world in general. The story of Śrīla Prabhupāda's arrival and his specific impact on world civilization, and especially Western civilization, has been brilliantly documented by His Divine Grace Satsvarūpa dāsa Goswami. From Śrīla Satsvarūpa's authorized biography of Śrīla Prabhupāda, called *Śrīla Prabhupāda-līlāmṛta*, the reader can fully understand Śrīla Prabhupāda's purpose, desire and mission in presenting *Śrīmad-Bhāgavatam*. Further, in Śrīla Prabhupāda's own preface to the *Bhāgavatam* (reprinted as the Foreword in this volume), he clearly states that this transcendental literature will provoke a cultural revolution in the world, and that is now underway. I do not wish to be redundant in repeating what Śrīla Prabhupāda has so eloquently stated in his preface, nor that which has been so abundantly documented by Śrīla Satsvarūpa in his authorized biography.

It is necessary to mention, however, that *Śrīmad-Bhāgavatam* is a completely transcendental, liberated sound vibration coming from the spiritual world. And, being absolute, it is not different from the Absolute Truth Himself, Lord Śrī Kṛṣṇa. By understanding *Śrīmad-Bhāgavatam*, consisting of twelve cantos, the reader acquires perfect knowledge, by which he or she may live peacefully and progressively on the earth, attending to all material necessities and simultaneously achieving supreme spiritual liberation. As we have worked to prepare this and other volumes of *Śrīmad-Bhāgavatam*, our intention has been always to serve faithfully the lotus feet of our spiritual master, carefully trying to translate and comment exactly as he would have, thus preserving the unity and spiritual potency of this edition of *Śrīmad-Bhāgavatam*. In other words, by strictly following the disciplic succession, called in Sanskrit *guru-paramparā*, this edition of the *Bhāgavatam* will continue to be throughout its volumes a liberated work, free from material contamination and capable of elevating the reader to the kingdom of God.

The purport is that we have faithfully followed the commentaries of previous *ācāryas* and exercised a calculated selectivity of material based on the example and mood of Śrīla Prabhupāda. One may write transcendental literature only by the mercy of the Supreme Personality of Godhead, Śrī Kṛṣṇa, and the authorized, liberated spiritual masters coming in disciplic succession. Thus, we humbly fall at the lotus feet of the previous *ācāryas*, offering special gratitude to the great commentators on the *Bhāgavatam*, namely Śrīla Śrīdhara Svāmī, Śrīla Jīva Gosvāmī, Śrīla Viśvanātha Cakravartī Ṭhākura and Śrīla Bhaktisiddhānta Sarasvatī Gosvāmī, the spiritual master of Śrīla Prabhupāda. We also offer our obeisances at the lotus feet of Śrīla Vīrarāghavācārya, Śrīla Vijayadhvaja Ṭhākura and Śrīla Vaṁśīdhara Ṭhākura, whose commentaries have also helped in this work. Additionally, we offer our humble obeisances at the lotus feet of the great *ācārya* Śrīla Madhva, who has made innumerable learned comments on *Śrīmad-Bhāgavatam*. We further offer our humble obeisances at the lotus feet of the Supreme Personality of Godhead, Śrī Kṛṣṇa Caitanya Mahāprabhu, and to all of His eternally liberated followers, headed by Śrīla Nityānanda Prabhu, Advaita Prabhu, Gadādhara

Prabhu and Śrīvāsa Ṭhākura, and to the six Gosvāmīs, Śrīla Rūpa Gosvāmī, Śrīla Sanātana Gosvāmī, Śrīla Raghunātha dāsa Gosvāmī, Śrīla Raghunātha Bhaṭṭa Gosvāmī, Śrīla Jīva Gosvāmī and Śrīla Gopāla Bhaṭṭa Gosvāmī. Finally we offer our most respectful obeisances at the lotus feet of the Absolute Truth, Śrī Śrī Rādhā and Kṛṣṇa, and humbly beg for Their mercy so that this great work of *Śrīmad-Bhāgavatam* can be quickly finished. *Śrīmad-Bhāgavatam* is undoubtedly the most important book within the universe, and the sincere readers of *Śrīmad-Bhāgavatam* will undoubtedly achieve the highest perfection of life, Kṛṣṇa consciousness.

In conclusion, I again remind the reader that *Śrīmad-Bhāgavatam* is the great work of His Divine Grace A. C. Bhaktivedanta Swami Prabhupāda, and that the present volume is the humble attempt of his devoted servants.

Hare Kṛṣṇa

Hridayananda dāsa Goswami

Foreword

We must know the present need of human society. And what is that need? Human society is no longer bounded by geographical limits to particular countries or communities. Human society is broader than in the Middle Ages, and the world tendency is toward one state or one human society. The ideals of spiritual communism, according to *Śrīmad-Bhāgavatam,* are based more or less on the oneness of the entire human society, nay, of the entire energy of living beings. The need is felt by great thinkers to make this a successful ideology. *Śrīmad-Bhāgavatam* will fill this need in human society. It begins, therefore, with an aphorism of Vedānta philosophy, *janmādy asya yataḥ,* to establish the ideal of a common cause.

Human society, at the present moment, is not in the darkness of oblivion. It has made rapid progress in the fields of material comforts, education and economic development throughout the entire world. But there is a pinprick somewhere in the social body at large, and therefore there are large-scale quarrels, even over less important issues. There is need of a clue as to how humanity can become one in peace, friendship and prosperity with a common cause. *Śrīmad-Bhāgavatam* will fill this need, for it is a cultural presentation for the respiritualization of the entire human society.

Śrīmad-Bhāgavatam should be introduced also in the schools and colleges, for it is recommended by the great student-devotee Prahlāda Mahārāja in order to change the demoniac face of society.

kaumāra ācaret prājño
dharmān bhāgavatān iha
durlabhaṁ mānuṣaṁ janma
tad apy adhruvam artha-dam

(*Bhāg.* 7.6.1)

Disparity in human society is due to lack of principles in a godless civilization. There is God, or the Almighty One, from whom everything emanates, by whom everything is maintained and in whom everything is merged to rest. Material science has tried to find the ultimate source of creation very insufficiently, but it is a fact that there is one ultimate source of everything that be. This ultimate source is explained rationally and authoritatively in the beautiful *Bhāgavatam*, or *Śrīmad-Bhāgavatam*.

Śrīmad-Bhāgavatam is the transcendental science not only for knowing the ultimate source of everything but also for knowing our relation with Him and our duty toward perfection of the human society on the basis of this perfect knowledge. It is powerful reading matter in the Sanskrit language, and it is now rendered into English elaborately so that simply by a careful reading one will know God perfectly well, so much so that the reader will be sufficiently educated to defend himself from the onslaught of atheists. Over and above this, the reader will be able to convert others to accepting God as a concrete principle.

Śrīmad-Bhāgavatam begins with the definition of the ultimate source. It is a bona fide commentary on the *Vedānta-sūtra* by the same author, Śrīla Vyāsadeva, and gradually it develops into nine cantos up to the highest state of God realization. The only qualification one needs to study this great book of transcendental knowledge is to proceed step by step cautiously and not jump forward haphazardly like with an ordinary book. It should be gone through chapter by chapter, one after another. The reading matter is so arranged with the original Sanskrit text, its English transliteration, synonyms, translation and purports so that one is sure to become a God-realized soul at the end of finishing the first nine cantos.

The Tenth Canto is distinct from the first nine cantos because it deals directly with the transcendental activities of the Personality of Godhead, Śrī Kṛṣṇa. One will be unable to capture the effects of the Tenth Canto without going through the first nine cantos. The book is complete in twelve cantos, each independent, but it is good for all to read them in small installments one after another.

I must admit my frailties in presenting *Śrīmad-Bhāgavatam*, but still I am hopeful of its good reception by the thinkers and leaders of society on the strength of the following statement of *Śrīmad-Bhāgavatam* (1.5.11):

tad-vāg-visargo janatāgha-viplavo
yasmin prati-ślokam abaddhavaty api
nāmāny anantasya yaśo 'ṅkitāni yac
chṛṇvanti gāyanti gṛṇanti sādhavaḥ

His Divine Grace
A. C. Bhaktivedanta Swami Prabhupāda
Founder-Ācārya of the International Society for Krishna Consciousness

PLATE ONE: **Kṛṣṇa Kills Ariṣṭa, the Bull Demon**

The huge bull demon, Ariṣṭa, came to the cowherd village of Gokula, making the earth tremble as he tore it apart with his hooves. When the cowherd men and ladies saw the demon and heard his ear-splitting bellowing, they were struck with terror. They all rushed to Govinda for shelter, crying, "Kṛṣṇa! Kṛṣṇa!" The Lord calmed them, saying, "Don't be afraid," and then called out to Ariṣṭa as follows: "You fool! What do you think you're doing, you wicked rascal, frightening the cowherd community when I am here just to punish corrupt miscreants like you!" Thus provoked, Ariṣṭa pawed the ground with one of his hooves and then furiously charged Kṛṣṇa. But the Lord seized the demon by the horns and threw him back eighteen paces. Then Ariṣṭa got up and, breathing hard and sweating all over his body, again charged Kṛṣṇa in a mindless rage. As Ariṣṭa attacked, the Lord grabbed him by the horns and knocked him to the ground with His foot. Then Kṛṣṇa thrashed him as if he were a wet cloth, and finally He yanked out one of the demon's horns and struck him with it until he lay dead. (*pp. 2-9*)

PARIHA

PLATE TWO: **Nārada Muni Visits Kaṁsa**

Nārada Muni, the exalted sage among the demigods, always desires to facilitate the pastimes of the Lord. Being a great mystic, Nārada knew that with the killing of the bull demon, Kṛṣṇa had nearly completed his pastimes in Vṛndāvana, and thus the sage visited Kaṁsa in Mathurā to set

the stage for the Lord's next series of pastimes. Nārada told Kaṁsa, "Yaśodā's child was actually a daughter, and Kṛṣṇa is the son of Devakī. Also, Balarāma is the son of Rohiṇī. Out of fear, Vasudeva entrusted Kṛṣṇa and Balarāma to his friend Nanda Mahārāja, and it is these two boys who have killed your men." *(pp. 11-20)*

PLATE THREE: **The Horse Demon Attacks Kṛṣṇa**

The demon Keśī, sent by Kaṁsa, appeared in Vraja as a great horse. Running with the speed of the mind, he tore up the earth with his hooves. The hairs of his mane scattered the clouds and the demigods' airplanes throughout the sky, and he terrified everyone present with his loud neighing. When Lord Kṛṣṇa saw how the demon was frightening his village of Gokula, He came forward to meet him. Keśī was searching for Kṛṣṇa to fight, so when the Lord stood before him and challenged him, the horse responded by roaring like a lion. Keśī charged Kṛṣṇa in extreme rage, his mouth gaping as if to swallow up the sky. Rushing with furious speed, the unconquerable and unapproachable horse demon tried to strike the lotus-eyed Lord with his two front legs. (*pp. 37-40*)

PLATE FOUR: **Akrūra Comes Upon Kṛṣṇa's Lotus Footprints**

As Akrūra meditated deeply on Lord Kṛṣṇa in pure devotion, he reached the cowherd village of Gokula as the sun was setting. In the cow pasture he suddenly saw the prints of Kṛṣṇa's lotus feet, whose pure dust the rulers of all the planets in the universe hold on their crowns. Those footprints, distinguished by such marks as the lotus, barleycorn and elephant goad, made the ground wonderfully beautiful. Akrūra became increasingly agitated by ecstasy as he beheld the wonderful sight, and because of his pure love for Kṛṣṇa his bodily hairs stood on end and his eyes filled with tears. He jumped down from his chariot and exclaimed, "Ah, this is the dust from my master's feet!" (*pp. 76-78*)

PLATE FIVE: **Lord Kṛṣṇa Departs for Mathurā**

When the *gopīs* saw their beloved Kṛṣṇa sitting on the chariot that would take Him to Mathurā, they became extremely agitated by their imminent separation from Him. They said, "Let us directly approach Mādhava and stop Him from going. What can our elders do to us now? We

are already so wretched that we have nothing to lose." Then, forgetting all shame, they cried out, "O Govinda! O Dāmodara! O Mādhava!" But even as the *gopīs* cried out in this way, Akrūra began to drive the chariot. Then Kṛṣṇa somewhat pacified the *gopīs* with his glances and consoled them with this loving promise: "I will return." (*pp. 101-114*)

PLATE SIX: **Kṛṣṇa and Balarāma Enter Mathurā**

As Lord Kṛṣṇa and Lord Balarāma walked down the main road of Mathurā, *brāhmaṇas* approached Them along the way and honored Them with presentations of yogurt, unbroken barleycorns, pots full of water, garlands, fragrant substances such as sandalwood paste, and other items of worship. And from the roofs of the mansions along the road the women of the city exclaimed, "Oh, what severe austerities the *gopīs* must have performed to be able to regularly see Kṛṣṇa and Balarāma, who are the greatest source of pleasure for all mankind!" (*pp. 168-169*)

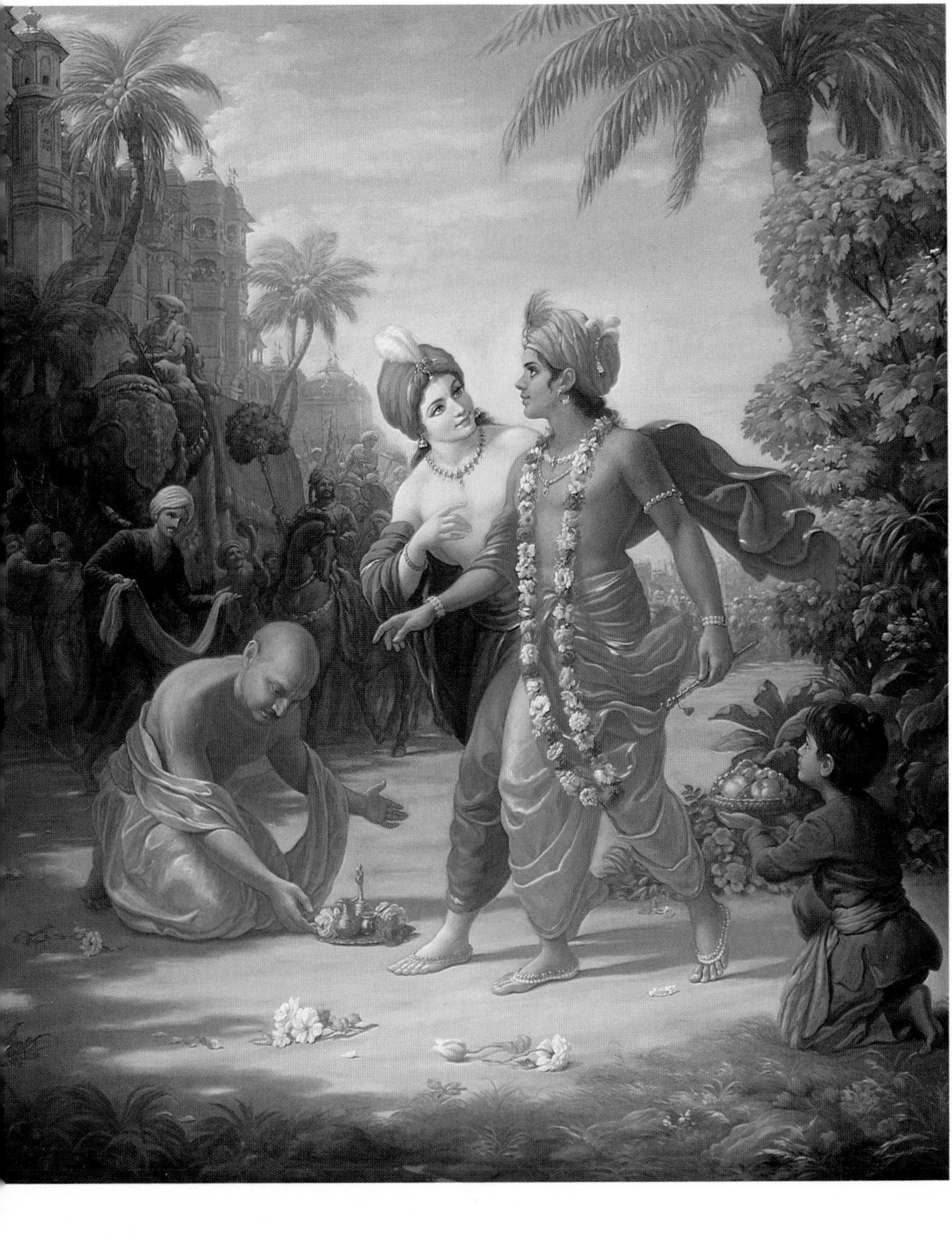

PLATE SEVEN: **Kṛṣṇa Kills the Washerman and Takes His Clothes**

As He walked down the main road in Mathurā, Kṛṣṇa saw a washerman approaching who had been dyeing some clothes for King Kaṁsa. The Lord asked him for the finest garments he had, promising him a benediction if he complied. But the arrogant washerman became angry and said: "You impudent boys! You're accustomed to roaming the mountains and forests, and yet You would dare put on such clothes as these! These are the King's possessions You're asking for!" As the washerman raved on, Kṛṣṇa became angry, and then merely with His fingertips He beheaded the brute. Kṛṣṇa and Balarāma then put on some of the garments that especially pleased Them, and the cowherd boys also took their pick of the fine clothes. (*pp. 170-173*)

PLATE EIGHT: **Killing Kaṁsa's Men with the Broken Bow**

Lord Kṛṣṇa entered the arena and saw the amazing bow, which resembled Lord Indra's. A large company of men were guarding it and respectfully worshiping it. But Kṛṣṇa pushed His way forward and, despite the guards' attempts to stop Him, easily picked it up with His left hand. In a fraction of a second He had strung it, and then He powerfully pulled the string and snapped the bow in half, just as an excited elephant might break a stalk of sugar cane. The resounding *crack* filled the earth and sky in all directions, striking terror into the heart of Kaṁsa. The enraged guards then took up their weapons and surrounded Kṛṣṇa and Balarāma, shouting, "Grab Him! Kill Him!" But the Lords took up the two halves of the bow and struck down the aggressors. (*pp. 194-197*)

PLATE NINE: **The Elephant Kuvalayāpīḍa Confronts Kṛṣṇa**

When Lord Kṛṣṇa reached the entrance to the wrestling arena, He saw the elephant Kuvalayāpīḍa blocking His way at the urging of his keeper. After securely binding up His clothes and tying back His curly locks, the Lord addressed the elephant-keeper with words as grave as the rumbling of a cloud: "O driver, driver, move aside at once and let Me pass! If you don't, this very day I will send both you and your elephant to the abode of Yamarāja!" (*pp. 211-212*)

PLATE TEN: **The Wrestling Match**

Kṛṣṇa paired off with Cāṇūra, and Balarāma with Muṣṭika. Seizing each other's hands and locking legs with each other, the opponents struggled powerfully, eager for victory. They each struck fists against fists, knees against knees, head against head, and chest against chest. Each fighter contended with his opponent by dragging him about in circles, shoving and crushing him, throwing him down and running before and behind him. As they forcefully lifted and carried each other, pushed each other away and held each other down, the fighters appeared to be hurting even their own bodies in their great eagerness for victory. (*pp. 238-241.*)

PARIKSIT DĀSA
'86

PLATE ELEVEN: **The Killing of Kaṁsa**

The invincible Lord Kṛṣṇa quickly and easily jumped up onto the high royal dais. Kaṁsa, seeing the Lord approaching like death personified, instantly rose from his seat, took up his sword and shield, and began moving quickly from side to side like a hawk in the sky. But the irresistibly powerful Kṛṣṇa seized Kaṁsa just as Garuḍa might capture a snake. The Lord grabbed him by the hair and knocked off his crown, and then he threw him off the elevated dais onto the wrestling mat. Finally Kṛṣṇa jumped down and, straddling the king, began to strike him over and over again. Simply from the blows of Kṛṣṇa's fist, Kaṁsa lost his life. (*pp. 259-261*)

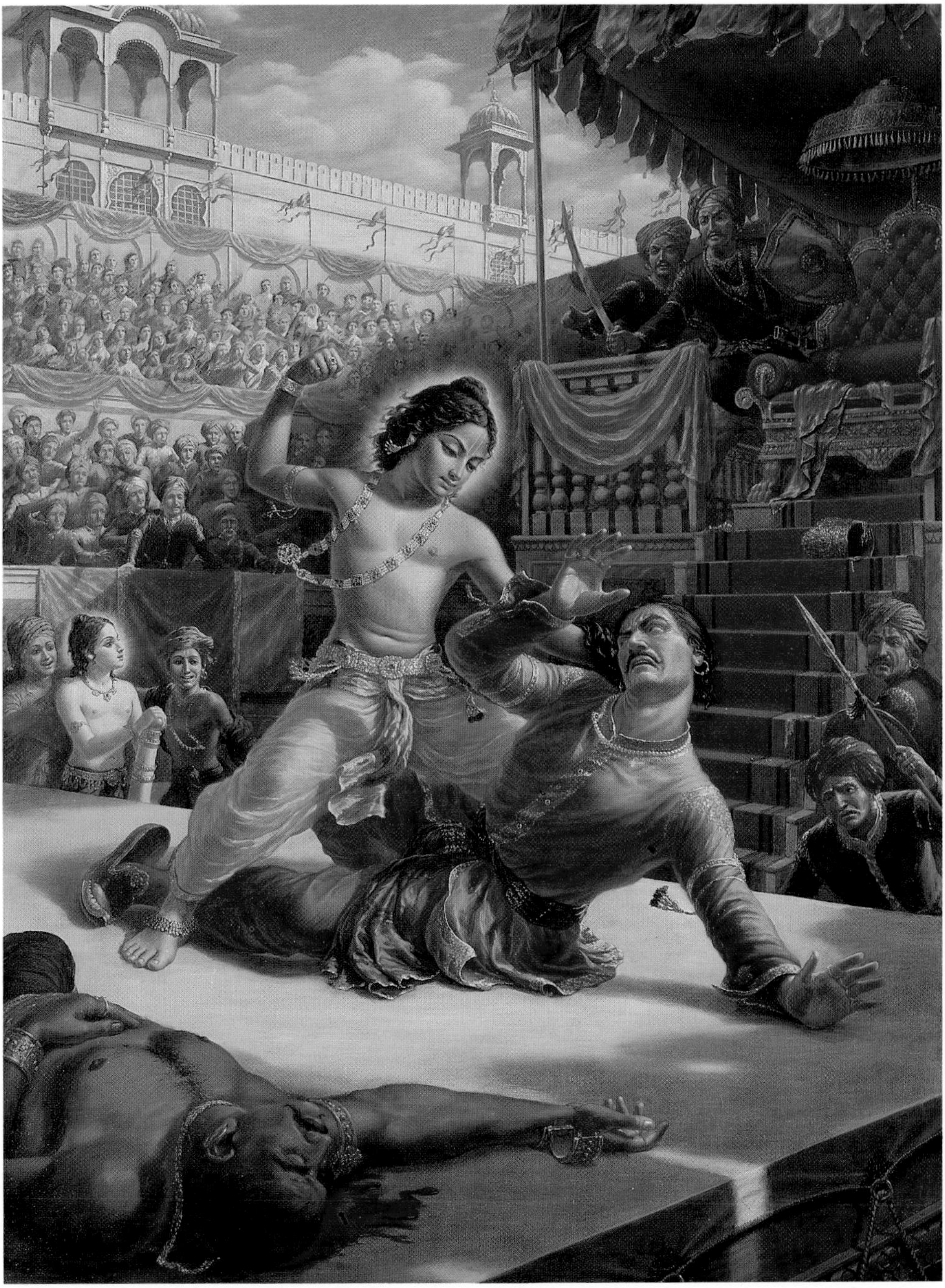

"That literature which is full of descriptions of the transcendental glories of the name, fame, form and pastimes of the unlimited Supreme Lord is a transcendental creation meant for bringing about a revolution in the impious life of a misdirected civilization. Such transcendental literature, even though irregularly composed, is heard, sung and accepted by purified men who are thoroughly honest."

Oṁ tat sat

A.C. Bhaktivedanta Swami

Introduction

"This *Bhāgavata Purāṇa* is as brilliant as the sun, and it has arisen just after the departure of Lord Kṛṣṇa to His own abode, accompanied by religion, knowledge, etc. Persons who have lost their vision due to the dense darkness of ignorance in the age of Kali shall get light from this *Purāṇa*." (*Śrīmad-Bhāgavatam* 1.3.43)

The timeless wisdom of India is expressed in the *Vedas*, ancient Sanskrit texts that touch upon all fields of human knowledge. Originally preserved through oral tradition, the *Vedas* were first put into writing five thousand years ago by Śrīla Vyāsadeva, the "literary incarnation of God." After compiling the *Vedas*, Vyāsadeva set forth their essence in the aphorisms known as *Vedānta-sūtras*. *Śrīmad-Bhāgavatam* (*Bhāgavata Purāṇa*) is Vyāsadeva's commentary on his own *Vedānta-sūtras*. It was written in the maturity of his spiritual life under the direction of Nārada Muni, his spiritual master. Referred to as "the ripened fruit of the tree of Vedic literature," *Śrīmad-Bhāgavatam* is the most complete and authoritative exposition of Vedic knowledge.

After compiling the *Bhāgavatam*, Vyāsa imparted the synopsis of it to his son, the sage Śukadeva Gosvāmī. Śukadeva Gosvāmī subsequently recited the entire *Bhāgavatam* to Mahārāja Parīkṣit in an assembly of learned saints on the bank of the Ganges at Hastināpura (now Delhi). Mahārāja Parīkṣit was the emperor of the world and was a great *rājarṣi* (saintly king). Having received a warning that he would die within a week, he renounced his entire kingdom and retired to the bank of the Ganges to fast until death and receive spiritual enlightenment. The *Bhāgavatam* begins with Emperor Parīkṣit's sober inquiry to Śukadeva Gosvāmī: "You are the spiritual master of great saints and devotees. I am therefore begging you to show the way of perfection for all persons, and especially for one who is about to die. Please let me know what a man should hear, chant, remember and worship, and also what he should not do. Please explain all this to me."

Śukadeva Gosvāmī's answer to this question, and numerous other questions posed by Mahārāja Parīkṣit, concerning everything from the nature of the self to the origin of the universe, held the assembled sages in rapt attention continuously for the seven days leading up to the king's death. The sage Sūta Gosvāmī, who was present in that assembly when Śukadeva Gosvāmī first recited *Śrīmad-Bhāgavatam*, later repeated the *Bhāgavatam* before a gathering of sages in the forest of Naimiṣāraṇya. Those sages, concerned about the spiritual welfare of the people in general, had gathered to perform a long, continuous chain of sacrifices to counteract the degrading influence of the incipient age of Kali. In response to the sages' request that he speak the essence of Vedic wisdom, Sūta Gosvāmī repeated from memory the entire eighteen thousand verses of *Śrīmad-Bhāgavatam*, as spoken by Śukadeva Gosvāmī to Mahārāja Parīkṣit.

The reader of *Śrīmad-Bhāgavatam* hears Sūta Gosvāmī relate the questions of Mahārāja Parīkṣit and the answers of Śukadeva Gosvāmī. Also, Sūta Gosvāmī sometimes responds directly to questions put by Śaunaka Ṛṣi, the spokesman for the sages gathered at Naimiṣāraṇya. One therefore simultaneously hears two dialogues: one between Mahārāja Parīkṣit and Śukadeva Gosvāmī on the bank of the Ganges, and another at Naimiṣāraṇya between Sūta Gosvāmī and the sages at Naimiṣāraṇya forest, headed by Śaunaka Ṛṣi. Furthermore, while instructing King Parīkṣit, Śukadeva Gosvāmī often relates historical episodes and gives accounts of lengthy philosophical discussions between such great souls as Nārada Muni and Vasudeva. With this understanding of the history of the *Bhāgavatam*, the reader will easily be able to follow its intermingling of dialogues and events from various sources. Since philosophical wisdom, not chronological order, is most important in the text, one need only be attentive to the subject matter of *Śrīmad-Bhāgavatam* to appreciate fully its profound message.

The translators of this edition compare the *Bhāgavatam* to sugar candy—wherever you taste it, you will find it equally sweet and relishable. Therefore, to taste the sweetness of the *Bhāgavatam*, one may begin by reading any of its volumes. After such an introductory taste, however, the serious reader is best advised to go back to Volume One of the First Canto and then proceed through the *Bhāgavatam*, volume after volume, in its natural order.

This edition of the *Bhāgavatam* is the first complete English translation of this important text with an elaborate commentary, and it is the first widely available to the English-speaking public. The first thirty volumes (Canto One through Canto Ten, Volume Three) are the product of the scholarly and devotional effort of His Divine Grace A. C. Bhaktivedanta Swami Prabhupāda, the world's most distinguished teacher of

Indian religious and philosophical thought. His consummate Sanskrit scholarship and intimate familiarity with Vedic culture and thought as well as the modern way of life combine to reveal to the West a magnificent exposition of this important classic. After the departure of Śrīla Prabhupāda from this world in 1977, his monumental work of translating *Śrīmad-Bhāgavatam* has been continued by his disciple His Divine Grace Hridayananda dāsa Goswami Ācāryadeva.

Readers will find this work of value for many reasons. For those interested in the classical roots of Indian civilization, it serves as a vast reservoir of detailed information on virtually every one of its aspects. For students of comparative philosophy and religion, the *Bhāgavatam* offers a penetrating view into the meaning of India's profound spiritual heritage. To sociologists and anthropologists, the *Bhāgavatam* reveals the practical workings of a peaceful and scientifically organized Vedic culture, whose institutions were integrated on the basis of a highly developed spiritual world view. Students of literature will discover the *Bhāgavatam* to be a masterpiece of majestic poetry. For students of psychology, the text provides important perspectives on the nature of consciousness, human behavior and the philosophical study of identity. Finally, to those seeking spiritual insight, the *Bhāgavatam* offers simple and practical guidance for attainment of the highest self-knowledge and realization of the Absolute Truth. The entire multivolume text, presented by the Bhaktivedanta Book Trust, promises to occupy a significant place in the intellectual, cultural and spiritual life of modern man for a long time to come.

—The Publishers

CHAPTER THIRTY-SIX

The Slaying of Ariṣṭa, the Bull Demon

This chapter describes how Kṛṣṇa killed Ariṣṭāsura and how Kaṁsa reacted when he learned from Nārada that Kṛṣṇa and Balarāma were the sons of Vasudeva.

The demon Ariṣṭa wanted to kill Kṛṣṇa and Balarāma, and thus he assumed the form of a huge bull with sharp horns. Everyone in Kṛṣṇa's cowherd village became terrified when Ariṣṭāsura approached it, but the Lord pacified them, and when the bull demon charged Him He seized him by the horns and threw him about six yards. Though weakened, Ariṣṭa still wanted to attack Kṛṣṇa. Thus, dripping with sweat, he charged the Lord once again. This time Kṛṣṇa grabbed his horns, threw him to the ground and thrashed him like a pile of wet clothing. The demon vomited blood and gave up his life. Then Kṛṣṇa and Rāma, while being honored by the demigods and cowherd boys, returned to the village.

A short time later Nārada Muni, the great sage among the demigods, came to see King Kaṁsa. He informed the King that Kṛṣṇa and Balarāma were not Nanda's sons but rather Vasudeva's. It was out of fear of Kaṁsa that Vasudeva had put the two boys under Nanda's care. Furthermore, said Nārada, Kaṁsa would meet his death at Their hands.

Kaṁsa shook with fear and anger when he heard all this, and in great agitation he began thinking of how to destroy Kṛṣṇa and Balarāma. He called for the demons Cāṇūra and Muṣṭika and instructed them to kill the two brothers in a wrestling match. Then he spoke to Akrūra, who was expert at executing his duties. Taking Akrūra by the hand, Kaṁsa persuaded him to go to Vraja to bring the two boys to Mathurā. Akrūra agreed to carry out Kaṁsa's order and then returned home.

TEXT 1

श्रीबादरायणिरुवाच

अथ तर्ह्यागतो गोष्ठमरिष्टो वृषभासुरः ।
महीं महाककुत्कायः कम्पयन् खुरविक्षताम् ॥१॥

śrī-bādarāyaṇir uvāca
atha tarhy āgato goṣṭham
ariṣṭo vṛṣabhāsuraḥ
mahīṁ mahā-kakut-kāyaḥ
kampayan khura-vikṣatām

śrī-bādarāyaṇiḥ uvāca—Śrī Śukadeva Gosvāmī said; *atha*—next; *tarhi*—then; *āgataḥ*—came; *goṣṭham*—to the cowherd village; *ariṣṭaḥ*—named Ariṣṭa; *vṛṣabha-asuraḥ*—the bull demon; *mahīm*—the earth; *mahā*—great; *kakut*—having a hump; *kāyaḥ*—whose body; *kampayan*—making tremble; *khura*—by his hooves; *vikṣatām*—torn.

TRANSLATION

Śukadeva Gosvāmī said: The demon Ariṣṭa then came to the cowherd village. Appearing in the form of a bull with a large hump, he made the earth tremble as he tore it apart with his hooves.

PURPORT

According to the *Śrī Viṣṇu Purāṇa,* Ariṣṭāsura entered Kṛṣṇa's village at twilight, as the Lord prepared to dance with the *gopīs:*

prodoṣārdhe kadācit tu
rāsāsakte janārdane
trāsayan sa-mado goṣṭham
ariṣṭaḥ samupāgataḥ

"Once, midway through the period of dusk, when Lord Janārdana was eager to perform the *rāsa* dance, Ariṣṭāsura madly entered the cowherd village, terrifying everyone."

TEXT 2

रम्भमाणः खरतरं पदा च विलिखन्महीम् ।
उद्यम्य पुच्छं वप्राणि विषाणाग्रेण चोद्धरन् ।
किञ्चित्किञ्चिच्छकृन्मुञ्चन्मूत्रयन् स्तब्धलोचनः ॥२॥

rambhamāṇaḥ kharataraṁ
padā ca vilikhan mahīm
udyamya pucchaṁ vaprāṇi
viṣāṇāgreṇa coddharan
kiñcit kiñcic chakṛn muñcan
mūtrayan stabdha-locanaḥ

rambhamāṇaḥ—bellowing; *khara-taram*—most harshly; *padā*—with his hooves; *ca*—and; *vilikhan*—scraping; *mahīm*—the ground; *udyamya*—raising upward; *puccham*—his tail; *vaprāṇi*—the embankments; *viṣāṇa*—of his horns; *agreṇa*—with the tips; *ca*—and; *uddharan*—lifting and tearing up; *kiñcit kiñcit*—a little; *śakṛt*—stool; *muñcan*—releasing; *mūtrayan*—urinating; *stabdha*—glaring; *locanaḥ*—his eyes.

TRANSLATION

Ariṣṭāsura bellowed very harshly and pawed the ground. With his tail raised and his eyes glaring, he began to tear up the embankments with the tips of his horns, every now and then passing a little stool and urine.

TEXTS 3–4

यस्य निर्ह्रादितेनांग निष्ठुरेण गवां नृणाम् ।
पतन्त्यकालतो गर्भाः स्रवन्ति स्म भयेन वै ॥३॥
निर्विशन्ति घना यस्य ककुद्यचलशंकया ।
तं तीक्ष्णशृंगमुद्वीक्ष्य गोप्यो गोपाश्च तत्रसुः ॥४॥

yasya nirhrāditenāṅga
niṣṭhureṇa gavāṁ nṛṇām
patanty akālato garbhāḥ
sravanti sma bhayena vai

nirviśanti ghanā yasya
kakudy acala-śaṅkayā
taṁ tīkṣṇa-śṛṅgam udvīkṣya
gopyo gopāś ca tatrasuḥ

yasya—whose; *nirhrāditena*—by the reverberating sound; *aṅga*—my dear King (Parīkṣit); *niṣṭhureṇa*—rough; *gavām*—of cows; *nṛṇām*—of humans; *patanti*—fall; *akālataḥ*—untimely; *garbhāḥ*—the embryos; *sravanti sma*—are miscarried; *bhayena*—out of fear; *vai*—indeed; *nirviśanti*—enter; *ghanāḥ*—clouds; *yasya*—whose; *kakudi*—onto the hump; *acala*—as a mountain; *śaṅkayā*—by the mistaken identification; *tam*—him; *tīkṣṇa*—sharp; *śṛṅgam*—whose horns; *udvīkṣya*—seeing; *gopyaḥ*—the cowherd women; *gopāḥ*—the cowherd men; *ca*—and; *tatrasuḥ*—became frightened.

TRANSLATION

My dear King, clouds hovered about sharp-horned Ariṣṭāsura's hump, mistaking it for a mountain, and when the cowherd men and ladies caught sight of the demon, they were struck with terror. Indeed, the strident reverberation of his roar so frightened the pregnant cows and women that they lost their fetuses in miscarriages.

PURPORT

The Vedic literature categorizes miscarriages as follows: *ā-caturthād bhavet srāvaḥ pātaḥ pañcama-ṣaṣṭhayoḥ/ ata ūrdhvaṁ prasūtiḥ syāt.* "Up to the fourth month a premature delivery is called *srāva,* in the fifth and sixth months it is called *pāta,* and after this it is considered a birth (*prasūti*)."

TEXT 5

पशवो दुद्रुवुर्भीता राजन् सन्त्यज्य गोकुलम् ।
कृष्ण कृष्णेति ते सर्वे गोविन्दं शरणं ययुः ॥५॥

paśavo dudruvur bhītā
rājan santyajya go-kulam
kṛṣṇa kṛṣṇeti te sarve
govindaṁ śaraṇaṁ yayuḥ

paśavaḥ—the domestic animals; *dudruvuḥ*—ran away; *bhītāḥ*—afraid; *rājan*—O King; *santyajya*—abandoning; *go-kulam*—the dairy pasture;

kṛṣṇa kṛṣṇa iti—"Kṛṣṇa, Kṛṣṇa"; *te*—they (the inhabitants of Vṛndāvana); *sarve*—all; *govindam*—to Lord Govinda; *śaraṇam*—for shelter; *yayuḥ*—went.

TRANSLATION

The domestic animals fled the pasture in fear, O King, and all the inhabitants rushed to Lord Govinda for shelter, crying "Kṛṣṇa, Kṛṣṇa!"

TEXT 6

भगवानपि तद्वीक्ष्य गोकुलं भयविद्रुतम् ।
मा भैष्टेति गिराश्वास्य वृषासुरमुपाह्वयत् ॥६॥

bhagavān api tad vīkṣya
go-kulaṁ bhaya-vidrutam
mā bhaiṣṭeti girāśvāsya
vṛṣāsuram upāhvayat

bhagavān—the Supreme Personality of Godhead; *api*—indeed; *tat*—that; *vīkṣya*—seeing; *go-kulam*—the cowherd community; *bhaya*—out of fear; *vidrutam*—made to flee, or distraught; *mā bhaiṣṭa*—"don't be afraid"; *iti*—thus; *girā*—with words; *āśvāsya*—pacifying; *vṛṣa-asuram*—to the bull demon; *upāhvayat*—He called out.

TRANSLATION

When the Supreme Lord saw the cowherd community distraught and fleeing in fear, He calmed them, saying "Don't be afraid." Then He called out to the bull demon as follows.

TEXT 7

गोपालैः पशुभिर्मन्द त्रासितैः किमसत्तम ।
मयि शास्तरि दुष्टानां त्वद्विधानां दुरात्मनाम् ॥७॥

gopālaiḥ paśubhir manda
trāsitaiḥ kim asattama

mayi śāstari duṣṭānāṁ
tvad-vidhānāṁ durātmanām

gopālaiḥ—with the cowherds; *paśubhiḥ*—and with their animals; *manda*—O fool; *trāsitaiḥ*—who are frightened; *kim*—what purpose; *asat-tama*—O most wicked one; *mayi*—when I (am present); *śāstari*—as the punisher; *duṣṭānām*—of the contaminated; *tvat-vidhānām*—like you; *durātmanām*—miscreants.

TRANSLATION

You fool! What do you think you're doing, you wicked rascal, frightening the cowherd community and their animals when I am here just to punish corrupt miscreants like you!

TEXT 8

इत्यास्फोत्याच्युतोऽरिष्टं तलशब्देन कोपयन् ।
सख्युरंसे भुजाभोगं प्रसार्यावस्थितो हरिः ॥८॥

ity āsphotyācyuto 'riṣṭaṁ
tala-śabdena kopayan
sakhyur aṁse bhujābhogaṁ
prasāryāvasthito hariḥ

iti—speaking thus; *āsphotya*—slapping His arms; *acyutaḥ*—the infallible Lord; *ariṣṭam*—Ariṣṭāsura; *tala*—from His palms; *śabdena*—with the sound; *kopayan*—angering; *sakhyuḥ*—of a friend; *aṁse*—over the shoulder; *bhuja*—His arm; *ābhogam*—(which is like) a serpent's body; *prasārya*—throwing; *avasthitaḥ*—was standing; *hariḥ*—Lord Hari.

TRANSLATION

Having spoken these words, the infallible Lord Hari slapped His arms with His palms, further angering Ariṣṭa with the loud sound. The Lord then casually threw His mighty, serpentine arm over the shoulder of a friend and stood facing the demon.

PURPORT

Lord Kṛṣṇa showed His contempt for the ignorant demon.

TEXT 9

सोऽप्येवं कोपितोऽरिष्टः खुरेणावनिमुल्लिखन् ।
उद्यत्पुच्छभ्रमन्मेघः क्रुद्धः कृष्णमुपाद्रवत् ॥९॥

so 'py evaṁ kopito 'riṣṭaḥ
khureṇāvanim ullikhan
udyat-puccha-bhraman-meghaḥ
kruddhaḥ kṛṣṇam upādravat

saḥ—he; *api*—indeed; *evam*—in this way; *kopitaḥ*—angered; *ariṣṭaḥ*—Ariṣṭa; *khureṇa*—with his hoof; *avanim*—the earth; *ullikhan*—scratching; *udyat*—raised; *puccha*—within his tail; *bhraman*—wandering; *meghaḥ*—clouds; *kruddhaḥ*—furious; *kṛṣṇam*—toward Lord Kṛṣṇa; *upādravat*—he charged.

TRANSLATION

Thus provoked, Ariṣṭa pawed the ground with one of his hooves and then, with the clouds hovering around his upraised tail, furiously charged Kṛṣṇa.

TEXT 10

अग्रन्यस्तविषाणाग्रः स्तब्धासृग्लोचनोऽच्युतम् ।
कटाक्षिप्याद्रवत्तूर्णमिन्द्रमुक्तोऽशनिर्यथा ॥१०॥

agra-nyasta-viṣāṇāgraḥ
stabdhāsṛg-locano 'cyutam
kaṭākṣipyādravat tūrṇam
indra-mukto 'śanir yathā

agra—forward; *nyasta*—pointing; *viṣāṇa*—of his horns; *agraḥ*—the front; *stabdha*—glaring; *asṛk*—bloody; *locanaḥ*—his eyes; *acyutam*—at

Lord Kṛṣṇa; *kaṭa-ākṣipya*—looking sideways; *adravat*—he ran; *tūrṇam*—at full speed; *indra-muktaḥ*—released by King Indra; *aśaniḥ*—a thunderbolt; *yathā*—like.

TRANSLATION

Pointing the tips of his horns straight ahead and glaring menacingly at Lord Kṛṣṇa from the corners of his bloodshot eyes, Ariṣṭa rushed toward Him at full speed, like a thunderbolt hurled by Indra.

TEXT 11

गृहीत्वा शृंगयोस्तं वा अष्टादश पदानि सः ।
प्रत्यपोवाह भगवान् गजः प्रतिगजं यथा ॥११॥

gṛhītvā śṛṅgayos taṁ vā
aṣṭādaśa padāni saḥ
pratyapovāha bhagavān
gajaḥ prati-gajaṁ yathā

gṛhītvā—seizing; *śṛṅgayoḥ*—by the horns; *tam*—him; *vai*—indeed; *aṣṭādaśa*—eighteen; *padāni*—steps; *saḥ*—He; *pratyapovāha*—threw back; *bhagavān*—the Supreme Lord; *gajaḥ*—an elephant; *prati-gajam*—a rival elephant; *yathā*—like.

TRANSLATION

The Supreme Lord Kṛṣṇa seized Ariṣṭāsura by the horns and threw him back eighteen steps, just as an elephant might do when fighting a rival elephant.

TEXT 12

सोऽपविद्धो भगवता पुनरुत्थाय सत्वरम् ।
आपतत्स्विन्नसर्वांगो निःश्वसन् क्रोधमूर्च्छितः ॥१२॥

so 'paviddho bhagavatā
punar utthāya satvaram

āpatat svinna-sarvāṅgo
niḥśvasan krodha-mūrcchitaḥ

saḥ—he; *apaviddhaḥ*—thrown back; *bhagavatā*—by the Lord; *punaḥ*—again; *utthāya*—rising; *satvaram*—quickly; *āpatat*—attacked; *svinna*—sweating; *sarva*—all; *aṅgaḥ*—his limbs; *niḥśvasan*—breathing hard; *krodha*—by anger; *mūrcchitaḥ*—stupefied.

TRANSLATION

Thus repulsed by the Supreme Lord, the bull demon got up and, breathing hard and sweating all over his body, again charged Him in a mindless rage.

TEXT 13

तमापतन्तं स निगृह्य शृंगयोः
पदा समाक्रम्य निपात्य भूतले ।
निष्पीडयामास यथार्द्रमम्बरं
कृत्वा विषाणेन जघान सोऽपतत् ॥१३॥

tam āpatantaṁ sa nigṛhya śṛṅgayoḥ
padā samākramya nipātya bhū-tale
niṣpīḍayām āsa yathārdram ambaraṁ
kṛtvā viṣāṇena jaghāna so 'patat

tam—him; *āpatantam*—attacking; *saḥ*—He; *nigṛhya*—seizing; *śṛṅgayoḥ*—by the horns; *padā*—with His foot; *samākramya*—treading; *nipātya*—making him fall; *bhū-tale*—onto the ground; *niṣpīḍayām āsa*—He beat him; *yathā*—like; *ardram*—wet; *ambaram*—a garment; *kṛtvā*—making; *viṣāṇena*—with his horn; *jaghāna*—struck; *saḥ*—he; *apatat*—fell.

TRANSLATION

As Ariṣṭa attacked, Lord Kṛṣṇa seized him by the horns and knocked him to the ground with His foot. The Lord then thrashed him as if he were a wet cloth, and finally He yanked out one of the demon's horns and struck him with it until he lay prostrate.

TEXT 14

असृग् वमन्मूत्रशकृत्समुत्सृजन्
क्षिपंश्च पादाननवस्थितेक्षणः ।
जगाम कृच्छ्रं निरृतेरथ क्षयं
पुष्पैः किरन्तो हरिमीडिरे सुराः ॥१४॥

asṛg vaman mūtra-śakṛt samutsṛjan
kṣipaṁś ca pādān anavasthitekṣaṇaḥ
jagāma kṛcchraṁ nirṛter atha kṣayaṁ
puṣpaiḥ kiranto harim īḍire surāḥ

asṛk—blood; *vaman*—vomiting; *mūtra*—urine; *śakṛt*—and feces; *samutsṛjan*—profusely excreting; *kṣipan*—throwing about; *ca*—and; *pādān*—his legs; *anavasthita*—unsteady; *īkṣaṇaḥ*—his eyes; *jagāma*—he went; *kṛcchram*—with pain; *nirṛteḥ*—of Death; *atha*—then; *kṣayam*—to the abode; *puṣpaiḥ*—flowers; *kirantaḥ*—scattering; *harim*—upon Lord Kṛṣṇa; *īḍire*—worshiped; *surāḥ*—the demigods.

TRANSLATION

Vomiting blood and profusely excreting stool and urine, kicking his legs and rolling his eyes about, Ariṣṭāsura thus went painfully to the abode of Death. The demigods honored Lord Kṛṣṇa by scattering flowers upon Him.

TEXT 15

एवं कुकुद्मिनं हत्वा स्तूयमानः द्विजातिभिः ।
विवेश गोष्ठं सबलो गोपीनां नयनोत्सवः ॥१५॥

evaṁ kukudminaṁ hatvā
stūyamānaḥ dvijātibhiḥ
viveśa goṣṭhaṁ sa-balo
gopīnāṁ nayanotsavaḥ

evam—thus; *kukudminam*—the humped (bull demon); *hatvā*—killing; *stūyamānaḥ*—being praised; *dvijātibhiḥ*—by the *brāhmaṇas; viveśa*—He entered; *goṣṭham*—the cowherd village; *sa-balaḥ*—together with Lord Balarāma; *gopīnām*—of the *gopīs; nayana*—for the eyes; *utsavaḥ*—who is a festival.

TRANSLATION

Having thus killed the bull demon Ariṣṭa, He who is a festival for the *gopīs'* eyes entered the cowherd village with Balarāma.

PURPORT

This verse exemplifies the sublime contrast of spiritual qualities within Śrī Kṛṣṇa. In one four-line verse we simultaneously learn that Lord Kṛṣṇa killed a powerful and wicked demon and that His boyish beauty gave festive pleasure to His young girlfriends. Lord Kṛṣṇa is as hard as a thunderbolt or as soft as a rose, depending on our attitude toward Him. The demon Ariṣṭa wanted to kill Kṛṣṇa and all His friends, so the Lord beat him into a wet rag and killed him. The *gopīs*, however, loved Kṛṣṇa, and thus the Lord boyishly reciprocated their conjugal feelings.

TEXT 16

अरिष्टे निहते दैत्ये कृष्णेनाद्भुतकर्मणा ।
कंसायाथाह भगवान्नारदो देवदर्शनः ॥१६॥

ariṣṭe nihate daitye
kṛṣṇenādbhuta-karmaṇā
kaṁsāyāthāha bhagavān
nārado deva-darśanaḥ

ariṣṭe—Ariṣṭa; *nihate*—having been killed; *daitye*—the demon; *kṛṣṇena*—by Kṛṣṇa; *adbhuta-karmaṇā*—whose activities are wonderful; *kaṁsāya*—to Kaṁsa; *atha*—then; *āha*—spoke; *bhagavān*—the powerful sage; *nāradaḥ*—Nārada; *deva-darśanaḥ*—whose vision is godly.

TRANSLATION

After Ariṣṭāsura had been killed by Kṛṣṇa, who acts wonderfully, Nārada Muni went to speak to King Kaṁsa. That powerful sage of godly vision addressed the King as follows.

PURPORT

The term *deva-darśana* can be understood in many ways, all of which are consistent with the context and purport of this narration. *Deva* means "God," and *darśanaḥ* means "seeing" or "an audience with a great personality." Thus *deva-darśana*, a name for Nārada Muni, indicates that Nārada has attained the perfection of seeing God, that getting Nārada's audience is as good as getting God's (since Nārada is a pure representative of the Lord), and also that Nārada's audience is as good as that of the demigods, who are also known as *devas*. That there are all these meanings of the term *deva-darśanaḥ* reveals something of the richness of the *Śrīmad-Bhāgavatam's* language.

From the *Purāṇas*, Śrīla Viśvanātha Cakravartī Ṭhākura has quoted twenty verses describing a joking conversation between Rādhā and Kṛṣṇa that took place after Kṛṣṇa had killed the demon Ariṣṭa. This conversation, so kindly quoted by the *ācārya*, describes the origin of Rādhā-kuṇḍa and Śyāma-kuṇḍa, Rādhā's and Kṛṣṇa's bathing ponds. The verses are as follows:

māsmān spṛśādya vṛṣabhārdana hanta mugdhā
ghoro 'suro 'yam ayi kṛṣṇa tad apy ayaṁ gauḥ
vṛtro yathā dvija ihāsty ayi niṣkṛtiḥ kiṁ
śudhyed bhavāṁs tri-bhuvana-sthita-tīrtha-kṛcchrāt

"The innocent young *gopīs* said, 'Ah, Kṛṣṇa, don't touch us now, O killer of a bull! Alas, even though Ariṣṭa was a terrible demon, still he was a male cow, so You will have to undergo atonement, just as Lord Indra did after killing Vṛtrāsura. But how can You purify Yourself without going to the trouble of visiting every single holy place in the three worlds?' "

kiṁ paryaṭāmi bhuvanāny adhunaiva sarvā
ānīya tīrtha-vitatīḥ karavāṇi tāsu
snānaṁ vilokayata tāvad idaṁ mukundaḥ
procyaiva tatra kṛtavān bata pārṣṇi-ghātam

"[Kṛṣṇa replied,] 'Why should I have to wander throughout the entire universe? I will at once bring all the countless pilgrimage places here and take My bath in them. Just watch!' With this, Lord Mukunda struck His heel on the ground."

pātālato jalam idaṁ kila bhogavatyā
āyātam atra nikhilā api tīrtha-saṅghāḥ
āgacchateti bhagavad-vacasā ta etya
tatraiva rejur atha kṛṣṇa uvāca gopīḥ

"[Then He said,] 'This is the water of the Bhogavatī River, coming from the Pātāla region. And now, O holy places, all of you please come here!' When the Supreme Lord had spoken these words, all the holy places went there and appeared before Him. Kṛṣṇa then addressed the *gopīs* as follows."

tīrthāni paśyata harer vacasā tavaivaṁ
naiva pratīma iti tā atha tīrtha-varyāḥ
procuḥ kṛtāñjali-puṭā lavaṇābdhir asmi
kṣīrābdhir asmi śṛṇutāmara-dīrghikāsmi

"'See all the holy places!'

"But the *gopīs* replied, 'We don't see them as You describe.'

"Then those best of holy places, joining their palms in supplication, spoke up:

"'I am the salt ocean.'

"'I am the ocean of milk.'

"'I am the Amara-dīrghikā.'"

śoṇo 'pi sindhur aham asmi bhavāmi tāmra-
parṇī ca puṣkaram ahaṁ ca sarasvatī ca
godāvarī ravi-sutā sarayuḥ prayāgo
revāsmi paśyata jalaṁ kuruta pratītim

"'I am the river Śoṇa.'

"'I am the Sindhu.'

"'I am the Tāmraparṇī.'

"'I am the holy place Puṣkara.'

"'I am the river Sarasvatī.'

"'And we are the Godāvarī, Yamunā and Revā rivers and the confluence of rivers at Prayāga. Just see our waters!'"

snātvā tato harir ati-prajagalbha eva
śuddhaḥ saro 'py akaravaṁ sthita-sarva-tīrtham
yuṣmābhir ātma-januṣīha kṛto na dharmaḥ
ko 'pi kṣitāv atha sakhīr nijagāda rādhā

"After purifying Himself by bathing, Lord Hari became quite arrogant and said, 'I have produced a pond containing all the various holy places, whereas you *gopīs* must never have executed any religious duties on this earth for the pleasure of Lord Brahmā.' Then Śrīmatī Rādhārāṇī addressed Her girlfriends as follows."

kāryaṁ mayāpy ati-manohara-kuṇḍam ekaṁ
tasmād yatadhvam iti tad-vacanena tābhiḥ
śrī-kṛṣṇa-kuṇḍa-taṭa-paścima-diśya-mando
gartaḥ kṛto vṛṣabha-daitya-khurair vyaloki

" 'I must create an even more beautiful pond. So go to work!' Having heard these words, the *gopīs* saw that Ariṣṭāsura's hooves had dug a shallow ditch just west of Śrī Kṛṣṇa's pond."

tatrārdra-mṛn-mṛdula-gola-tatīḥ prati-sva-
hastoddhṛtā anati-dūra-gatā vidhāya
divyaṁ saraḥ prakaṭitaṁ ghaṭikā-dvayena
tābhir vilokya sarasaṁ smarate sma kṛṣṇaḥ

"At that nearby spot, all the *gopīs* began digging up lumps of soft mud with their hands, and in this way a divine pond manifested in the short span of an hour. Kṛṣṇa was astonished to see the lake they produced."

proce ca tīrtha-salilaiḥ paripūrayaitan
mat-kuṇḍataḥ sarasijākṣi sahālibhis tvam
rādhā tadā na na na neti jagāda yasmāt
tvat-kuṇḍa-nīram uru-go-vadha-pātakāktam

"He said, 'Go ahead, lotus-eyed one. You and Your companions should fill this pond with water from Mine.'

"But Rādhā replied, 'No, no, no, no! This is impossible, since the water of Your pond is contaminated by Your terrible sin of killing a cow.' "

āhṛtya puṇya-salilaṁ śata-koṭi-kumbhaiḥ
sakhy-arbudena saha mānasa-jāhnavītaḥ
etat saraḥ sva-madhunā paripūrayāmi
tenaiva kīrtim atulāṁ tanavāni loke

"'I will have My countless *gopī* companions bring the pure water of the Mānasa-gaṅgā here in billions of pots. In this way I will fill this lake with My own water and thus make its renown unequaled in the entire world.'"

kṛṣṇeṅgitena sahasaitya samasta-tīrtha-
sakhyas tadīya-saraso dhṛta-divya-mūrtiḥ
tuṣṭāva tatra vṛṣabhānu-sutāṁ praṇamya
bhaktyā kṛtāñjali-puṭaḥ sravad-asra-dhāraḥ

"Lord Kṛṣṇa then gestured to a heavenly personality who was an intimate associate of all the holy places. Suddenly that person rose up out of Kṛṣṇa's pond and bowed down to the daughter of Śrī Vṛṣabhānu [Rādhārāṇi]. Then, with palms joined and tears pouring from his eyes, he began praying to Her in devotion."

devi tvadīya-mahimānam avaiti sarva-
śāstrārtha-vin na ca vidhir na haro na lakṣmīḥ
kintv eka eva puruṣārtha-śiromaṇis tvat-
prasveda-mārjana-paraḥ svayam eva kṛṣṇaḥ

"'O goddess, even Lord Brahmā himself, the knower of all scriptures, cannot understand Your glories, nor can Lord Śiva or Lakṣmī. Only Kṛṣṇa, the supreme goal of all human endeavor, can understand them, and thus He feels obliged to personally make sure that You can wash away Your perspiration when You are fatigued.'"

yaś cāru-yāvaka-rasena bhavat-padābjam
ārajya nūpuram aho nidadhāti nityam
prāpya tvadīya-nayanābja-taṭa-prasādaṁ
svaṁ manyate parama-dhanyatamaṁ prahṛṣyan

tasyājñayaiva sahasā vayam ājagāma
tat-pārṣṇi-ghāta-kṛta-kuṇḍa-vare vasāmaḥ

tvaṁ cet prasīdasi karoṣi kṛpā-kaṭākṣaṁ
tarhy eva tarṣa-viṭapī phalito bhaven naḥ

"'He is always anointing Your lotus feet with nectarean *cāru* and *yāvaka* and decorating them with ankle bells, and He rejoices and feels most fortunate simply by satisfying the tips of the toes of Your lotus feet. On His order we have immediately come here to live in this most excellent pond, which He created by one stroke of His heel. But only if You now feel satisfiied with us and bestow upon us Your merciful glance will the tree of our desire bear fruit.'"

śrutvā stutiṁ nikhila-tīrtha-gaṇasya tuṣṭā
prāha sma tarṣam ayi vedayateti rādhā
yāma tvadīya-sarasīṁ sa-phalā bhavāma
ity eva no vara iti prakaṭaṁ tadocuḥ

"Hearing this prayer spoken by the representative of the full assembly of holy places, Śrī Rādhā was pleased and said, 'So, kindly tell Me your desire.'

"They then told Her plainly, 'Our lives would be successful if we could come to Your pond. That is the benediction we desire.'"

āgacchateti vṛṣabhānu-sutā smitāsyā
provāca kānta-vadanābja-dhṛtākṣi-koṇā
sakhyo 'pi tatra kṛta-sammatayaḥ sukhābdhau
magnā virejur akhilā sthira-jaṅgamāś ca

"Glancing at Her beloved from the corners of Her eyes, the daughter of Vṛṣabhānu replied with a smile, 'Please come.' Her *gopī* companions all agreed with Her decision and became immersed in the ocean of happiness. Indeed, the beauty of all creatures, both mobile and stationary, was enhanced."

prāpya prasādam atha te vṛṣabhānujāyāḥ
śrī-kṛṣṇa-kuṇḍa-gata-tīrtha-varāḥ prasahya
bhittveva bhittim ati-vegata eva rādhā-
kuṇḍaṁ vyadhuḥ sva-salilaiḥ paripūrṇam eva

"Thus gaining the grace of Śrīmatī Rādhārāṇī, the holy rivers and lakes in Śrī Kṛṣṇa-kuṇḍa forcibly broke through its boundary walls and swiftly filled Rādhā-kuṇḍa with their waters."

proce hariḥ priyatame tava kuṇḍam etan
mat-kuṇḍato 'pi mahimādhikam astu loke
atraiva me salila-kelir ihaiva nityaṁ
snānaṁ yathā tvam asi tadvad idaṁ saro me

"Lord Hari then said, 'My dear Rādhā, may this pond of Yours become even more world-renowned than Mine. I will always come here to bathe and to enjoy My water pastimes. Indeed, this lake is as dear to Me as You are.' "

rādhābravīd aham api sva-sakhībhir etya
snāsyāmy ariṣṭa-śata-mardanam astu tasya
yo 'riṣṭa-mardana-sarasy uru-bhaktir atra
snāyād vasen mama sa eva mahā-priyo 'stu

"Rādhā replied, 'I will come to bathe in Your pond as well, even though You may kill hundreds of Ariṣṭa demons here. In the future, anyone who has intense devotion for this lake, which is on the spot where You chastised Ariṣṭāsura, and who bathes or resides here is sure to become very dear to Me.' "

rāsotsavaṁ prakurute sma ca tatra rātrau
kṛṣṇāmbudaḥ kṛta-mahā-rasa-harṣa-varṣaḥ
śrī-rādhikā-pravara-vidyud alaṅkṛta-śrīs
trailokya-madhya-vitatī-kṛta-divya-kīrtiḥ

"That night Lord Kṛṣṇa initiated a *rāsa* dance at Rādhā-kuṇḍa, generating a torrent of the greatest mood of splendorous pleasure. Śrī Kṛṣṇa resembled a cloud, and Śrīmatī Rādhārāṇī a brilliant flash of lightning filling the sky with abundant beauty. In this way Their divine glories permeated the expanses of the three worlds."

As a final note, it should be mentioned that Nārada Muni, being a great sage, understood that the killing of Ariṣṭa more or less concluded the pastimes of Kṛṣṇa in Vṛndāvana. Therefore Nārada, anxious to facilitate the transferal of Kṛṣṇa's pastimes to Mathurā, approached Kaṁsa and addressed him as follows.

TEXT 17

यशोदायाः सुतां कन्यां देवक्याः कृष्णमेव च ।
रामं च रोहिणीपुत्रं वसुदेवेन बिभ्यता ।
न्यस्तौ स्वमित्रे नन्दे वै याभ्यां ते पुरुषा हताः ॥१७॥

yaśodāyāḥ sutāṁ kanyāṁ
devakyāḥ kṛṣṇam eva ca
rāmaṁ ca rohiṇī-putraṁ
vasudevena bibhyatā
nyastau sva-mitre nande vai
yābhyāṁ te puruṣā hatāḥ

yaśodāyāḥ—of Yaśodā; *sutām*—the daughter; *kanyām*—the female child; *devakyāḥ*—of Devakī; *kṛṣṇam*—Kṛṣṇa; *eva ca*—also; *rāmam*—Balarāma; *ca*—and; *rohiṇī-putram*—the son of Rohiṇī; *vasudevena*—by Vasudeva; *bibhyatā*—who was afraid; *nyastau*—placed; *sva-mitre*—with his friend; *nande*—Nanda Mahārāja; *vai*—indeed; *yābhyām*—by which two; *te*—your; *puruṣāḥ*—men; *hatāḥ*—have been killed.

TRANSLATION

[Nārada told Kaṁsa:] Yaśodā's child was actually a daughter, and Kṛṣṇa is the son of Devakī. Also, Rāma is the son of Rohiṇī. Out of fear, Vasudeva entrusted Kṛṣṇa and Balarāma to his friend Nanda Mahārāja, and it is these two boys who have killed your men.

PURPORT

Kaṁsa had been led to believe that Kṛṣṇa was the son of Yaśodā and that Devakī's eighth child had been a daughter. The identity of Devakī's eighth child was extremely important to Kaṁsa because a prophecy had foretold that her eighth child would kill him. Here Nārada informs the King that the eighth child of Devakī was the formidable Kṛṣṇa, thus implying that the prophecy should be taken very seriously. Having received this information, Kaṁsa obviously will now do everything in his power to kill Kṛṣṇa and Balarāma.

TEXT 18

निशम्य तद् भोजपतिः कोपात्प्रचलितेन्द्रियः ।
निशातमसिमादत्त वसुदेवजिघांसया ॥१८॥

niśamya tad bhoja-patiḥ
kopāt pracalitendriyaḥ
niśātam asim ādatta
vasudeva-jighāṁsayā

niśamya—hearing; *tat*—that; *bhoja-patiḥ*—the lord of the Bhoja dynasty (Kaṁsa); *kopāt*—out of anger; *pracalita*—disturbed; *indriyaḥ*—his senses; *niśātam*—sharp; *asim*—a sword; *ādatta*—took up; *vasudeva-jighāṁsayā*—with the desire to kill Vasudeva.

TRANSLATION

Upon hearing this, the master of the Bhojas became furious and lost control of his senses. He picked up a sharp sword to kill Vasudeva.

TEXT 19

निवारितो नारदेन तत्सुतौ मृत्युमात्मनः ।
ज्ञात्वा लोहमयैः पाशैर्बबन्ध सह भार्यया ॥१९॥

nivārito nāradena
tat-sutau mṛtyum ātmanaḥ
jñātvā loha-mayaiḥ pāśair
babandha saha bhāryayā

nivāritaḥ—checked; *nāradena*—by Nārada; *tat-sutau*—his two sons; *mṛtyum*—death; *ātmanaḥ*—his own; *jñātvā*—understanding; *loha-mayaiḥ*—made of iron; *pāśaiḥ*—with shackles; *babandha*—he bound up (Vasudeva); *saha*—together with; *bhāryayā*—his wife.

TRANSLATION

But Nārada restrained Kaṁsa by reminding him that it was the two sons of Vasudeva who would cause his death. Kaṁsa then had Vasudeva and his wife shackled in iron chains.

PURPORT

Kaṁsa realized that there was no use in killing Vasudeva, since it was Vasudeva's sons, Kṛṣṇa and Balarāma, who were to kill him. According to the *ācāryas*, Nārada also advised Kaṁsa that if he killed Vasudeva the two young boys might flee and that it was therefore better not to kill him. Rather, Nārada recommended, Kaṁsa should bring Kṛṣṇa and Balarāma to Kaṁsa's capital city, Mathurā.

Śrīla Viśvanātha Cakravartī points out that Nārada did not act inimically toward the great devotees Vasudeva and Devakī when he revealed this information to Kaṁsa. In fact, as explained in the Eleventh Canto, Vasudeva was grateful to Nārada because he was arranging for Kaṁsa's death at Kṛṣṇa's hands, and further arranging for Kṛṣṇa to come and live in Mathurā, where His loving father could associate with Him.

TEXT 20

प्रतियाते तु देवर्षौ कंस आभाष्य केशिनम् ।
प्रेषयामास हन्येतां भवता रामकेशवौ ॥२०॥

pratiyāte tu devarṣau
kaṁsa ābhāṣya keśinam
preṣayām āsa hanyetāṁ
bhavatā rāma-keśavau

pratiyāte—having left; *tu*—then; *deva-ṛṣau*—the sage among the demigods; *kaṁsaḥ*—King Kaṁsa; *ābhāṣya*—addressing; *keśinam*—the demon Keśī; *preṣayām āsa*—he sent him; *hanyetām*—the two should be killed; *bhavatā*—by you; *rāma-keśavau*—Balarāma and Kṛṣṇa.

TRANSLATION

After Nārada left, King Kaṁsa summoned Keśī and ordered him, "Go kill Rāma and Kṛṣṇa."

PURPORT

Before having Kṛṣṇa and Balarāma brought to Mathurā, Kaṁsa tried sending one more demon to Vṛndāvana.

TEXT 21

ततो मुष्टिकचाणूरशलतोशलकादिकान् ।
अमात्यान् हस्तिपांश्चैव समाहूयाह भोजराट् ॥२१॥

tato muṣṭika-cāṇūra-
śala-tośalakādikān
amātyān hastipāṁś caiva
samāhūyāha bhoja-rāṭ

tataḥ—then; *muṣṭika-cāṇūra-śala-tośalaka-ādikān*—Muṣṭika, Cāṇūra, Śala, Tośala and others; *amātyān*—his ministers; *hasti-pān*—his elephant-keepers; *ca eva*—also; *samāhūya*—calling together; *āha*—spoke; *bhoja-rāṭ*—the King of the Bhojas.

TRANSLATION

The King of the Bhojas next called for his ministers, headed by Muṣṭika, Cāṇūra, Śala and Tośala, and also for his elephant-keepers. The King addressed them as follows.

TEXTS 22–23

भो भो निशम्यतामेतद्वीरचाणूरमुष्टिकौ ।
नन्दव्रजे किलासाते सुतावानकदुन्दुभेः ॥२२॥
रामकृष्णौ ततो मह्यं मृत्युः किल निदर्शितः ।
भवद्भ्यामिह सम्प्राप्तौ हन्येतां मल्ललीलया ॥२३॥

bho bho niśamyatām etad
vīra-cāṇūra-muṣṭikau
nanda-vraje kilāsāte
sutāv ānakadundubheḥ

rāma-kṛṣṇau tato mahyaṁ
mṛtyuḥ kila nidarśitaḥ
bhavadbhyām iha samprāptau
hanyetāṁ malla-līlayā

bhoḥ bhoḥ—my dear (advisers); *niśamyatām*—please listen; *etat*—to this; *vīra*—O heroes; *cāṇūra-muṣṭikau*—Cāṇūra and Muṣṭika; *nanda-vraje*—in the cowherd village of Nanda; *kila*—indeed; *āsāte*—are living; *sutau*—the two sons; *ānakadundubheḥ*—of Vasudeva; *rāma-kṛṣṇau*—Rāma and Kṛṣṇa; *tataḥ*—from Them; *mahyam*—my; *mṛtyuḥ*—death; *kila*—indeed; *nidarśitaḥ*—has been indicated; *bhavadbhyām*—by you two; *iha*—here; *samprāptau*—brought; *hanyetām*—They should be killed; *malla*—of wrestling; *līlayā*—on the pretext of the sport.

TRANSLATION

My dear heroic Cāṇūra and Muṣṭika, please hear this. Rāma and Kṛṣṇa, the sons of Ānakadundubhi [Vasudeva], are living in Nanda's cowherd village. It has been predicted that these two boys will be the cause of my death. When They are brought here, kill Them on the pretext of engaging Them in a wrestling match.

TEXT 24

मञ्चाः क्रियन्तां विविधा मल्लरंगपरिश्रिताः ।
पौरा जानपदाः सर्वे पश्यन्तु स्वैरसंयुगम् ॥२४॥

mañcāḥ kriyantāṁ vividhā
malla-raṅga-pariśritāḥ
paurā jānapadāḥ sarve
paśyantu svaira-saṁyugam

mañcāḥ—stages; *kriyantām*—should be built; *vividhāḥ*—various; *malla-raṅga*—a wrestling ring; *pariśritāḥ*—surrounding; *paurāḥ*—the residents of the city; *jānapadāḥ*—and the residents of the outlying districts; *sarve*—all; *paśyantu*—should see; *svaira*—voluntarily participated in; *saṁ-yugam*—the competition.

TRANSLATION

Erect a wrestling ring with many surrounding viewing stands, and bring all the residents of the city and the outlying districts to see the open competition.

PURPORT

The word *mañcāḥ* refers to platforms constructed with large pillars. Kaṁsa wanted a festive atmosphere so that Kṛṣṇa and Balarāma would not be afraid to come.

TEXT 25

महामात्र त्वया भद्र रंगद्वार्युपनीयताम् ।
द्विपः कुवलयापीडो जहि तेन ममाहितौ ॥२५॥

mahāmātra tvayā bhadra
raṅga-dvāry upanīyatām
dvipaḥ kuvalayāpīḍo
jahi tena mamāhitau

mahā-mātra—O elephant-keeper; *tvayā*—by you; *bhadra*—my good man; *raṅga*—of the arena; *dvāri*—to the doorway; *upanīyatām*—should be brought; *dvipaḥ*—the elephant; *kuvalayāpīḍaḥ*—named Kuvalayāpīḍa; *jahi*—destroy; *tena*—with that (elephant); *mama*—my; *ahitau*—enemies.

TRANSLATION

You, elephant-keeper, my good man, should position the elephant Kuvalayāpīḍa at the entrance to the wrestling arena and have him kill my two enemies.

TEXT 26

आरभ्यतां धनुर्यागश्चतुर्दश्यां यथाविधि ।
विशसन्तु पशून्मेध्यान् भूतराजाय मीढुषे ॥२६॥

ārabhyatāṁ dhanur-yāgaś
caturdaśyāṁ yathā-vidhi
viśasantu paśūn medhyān
bhūta-rājāya mīḍhuṣe

ārabhyatām—should be commenced; *dhanuḥ-yāgaḥ*—the bow sacrifice; *caturdaśyām*—on the fourteenth day of the month; *yathā-vidhi*—in accordance with Vedic injunctions; *viśasantu*—offer in sacrifice; *paśūn*—animals; *medhyān*—which are fit to be offered; *bhūta-rājāya*—to Lord Śiva, the lord of ghostly spirits; *mīḍhuṣe*—the giver of benedictions.

TRANSLATION

Commence the bow sacrifice on the Caturdaśī day in accordance with the relevant Vedic injunctions. In ritual slaughter offer the appropriate kinds of animals to the magnanimous Lord Śiva.

TEXT 27

इत्याज्ञाप्यार्थतन्त्रज्ञ आहूय यदुपुंगवम् ।
गृहीत्वा पाणिना पाणिं ततोऽक्रूरमुवाच ह ॥२७॥

ity ājñāpyārtha-tantra-jña
āhūya yadu-puṅgavam
gṛhītvā pāṇinā pāṇiṁ
tato 'krūram uvāca ha

iti—with these words; *ājñāpya*—ordering; *artha*—of personal interest and advantage; *tantra*—of the doctrine; *jñaḥ*—the knower; *āhūya*—calling for; *yadu-puṅgavam*—the most eminent of the Yadus; *gṛhītvā*—taking; *pāṇinā*—with his own hand; *pāṇim*—his hand; *tataḥ*—then; *akrūram*—to Akrūra; *uvāca ha*—he said.

TRANSLATION

Having thus commanded his ministers, Kaṁsa next called for Akrūra, the most eminent of the Yadus. Kaṁsa knew the art of securing personal advantage, and thus he took Akrūra's hand in his own and spoke to him as follows.

TEXT 28

भो भो दानपते मह्यं क्रियतां मैत्रमादृतः ।
नान्यस्त्वत्तो हिततमो विद्यते भोजवृष्णिषु ॥२८॥

bho bho dāna-pate mahyaṁ
kriyatāṁ maitram ādṛtaḥ
nānyas tvatto hitatamo
vidyate bhoja-vṛṣṇiṣu

bhoḥ bhoḥ—my dear; *dāna*—of charity; *pate*—master; *mahyam*—for me; *kriyatām*—please do; *maitram*—a friendly favor; *ādṛtaḥ*—out of respect; *na*—none; *anyaḥ*—other; *tvattaḥ*—than yourself; *hita-tamaḥ*—who acts most favorably; *vidyate*—exists; *bhoja-vṛṣṇiṣu*—among the Bhojas and Vṛṣṇis.

TRANSLATION

My dear Akrūra, most charitable one, please do me a friendly favor out of respect. Among the Bhojas and Vṛṣṇis, there is no one else as kind to us as you.

TEXT 29

अतस्त्वामाश्रितः सौम्य कार्यगौरवसाधनम् ।
यथेन्द्रो विष्णुमाश्रित्य स्वार्थमध्यगमद्विभुः ॥२९॥

atas tvām āśritaḥ saumya
kārya-gaurava-sādhanam
yathendro viṣṇum āśritya
svārtham adhyagamad vibhuḥ

ataḥ—therefore; *tvām*—on you; *āśritaḥ*—(I am) depending; *saumya*—O gentle one; *kārya*—prescribed duties; *gaurava*—soberly; *sādhanam*—who executes; *yathā*—as similarly; *indraḥ*—Indra; *viṣṇum*—Lord Viṣṇu; *āśritya*—taking shelter of; *sva-artham*—his goals; *adhyagamat*—achieved; *vibhuḥ*—the powerful King of heaven.

TRANSLATION

Gentle Akrūra, you always carry out your duties soberly, and therefore I am depending on you, just as powerful Indra took shelter of Lord Viṣṇu to achieve his goals.

TEXT 30

गच्छ नन्दव्रजं तत्र सुतावानकदुन्दुभेः ।
आसाते ताविहानेन रथेनानय मा चिरम् ॥३०॥

gaccha nanda-vrajaṁ tatra
sutāv ānakadundubheḥ
āsāte tāv ihānena
rathenānaya mā ciram

gaccha—go; *nanda-vrajam*—to the cowherd village of Nanda; *tatra*—there; *sutau*—the two sons; *ānakadundubheḥ*—of Vasudeva; *āsāte*—are living; *tau*—Them; *iha*—here; *anena*—by this; *rathena*—chariot; *ānaya*—bring; *mā ciram*—without delay.

TRANSLATION

Please go to Nanda's village, where the two sons of Ānakadundubhi are living, and without delay bring Them here on this chariot.

PURPORT

Śrīla Viśvanātha Cakravartī gives the following interesting note: "When King Kaṁsa said 'with this chariot,' he pointed with his index finger to a brand-new, attractive chariot. Kaṁsa thought that since Akrūra was innocent by nature, when he saw this fine, new vehicle he would naturally want to drive it and quickly bring the two boys back. But the actual reason Akrūra went on a new chariot was that it would have been clearly inappropriate for the Supreme Personality of Godhead to mount a chariot that had already been enjoyed by the wicked Kaṁsa."

TEXT 31

निसृष्टः किल मे मृत्युर्देवैर्वैकुण्ठसंश्रयैः ।
तावानय समं गोपैर्नन्दाद्यैः साभ्युपायनैः ॥३१॥

nisṛṣṭaḥ kila me mṛtyur
devair vaikuṇṭha-saṁśrayaiḥ
tāv ānaya samaṁ gopair
nandādyaiḥ sābhyupāyanaiḥ

nisṛṣṭaḥ—sent; *kila*—indeed; *me*—my; *mṛtyuḥ*—death; *devaiḥ*—by the demigods; *vaikuṇṭha*—of Lord Viṣṇu; *saṁśrayaiḥ*—who take shelter; *tau*—the two of Them; *ānaya*—bring; *samam*—together with; *gopaiḥ*—the cowherd men; *nanda-ādyaiḥ*—headed by Nanda; *sa*—with; *abhyupāyanaiḥ*—gifts.

TRANSLATION

The demigods, who are under the protection of Viṣṇu, have sent these two boys as my death. Bring Them here, and also have Nanda and the other cowherd men come with gifts of tribute.

TEXT 32

घातयिष्य इहानीतौ कालकल्पेन हस्तिना ।
यदि मुक्तौ ततो मल्लैर्घातये वैद्युतोपमैः ॥३२॥

ghātayiṣya ihānītau
kāla-kalpena hastinā
yadi muktau tato mallair
ghātaye vaidyutopamaiḥ

ghātayiṣye—I shall have Them killed; *iha*—here; *ānītau*—brought; *kāla-kalpena*—like death itself; *hastinā*—by the elephant; *yadi*—if; *muktau*—They go free; *tataḥ*—then; *mallaiḥ*—by wrestlers; *ghātaye*—I will have killed; *vaidyuta*—lightning; *upamaiḥ*—just like.

TRANSLATION

After you bring Kṛṣṇa and Balarāma, I will have Them killed by my elephant, who is as powerful as death itself. And if by chance They escape from him, I will have Them killed by my wrestlers, who are as strong as lightning.

TEXT 33

तयोर्निहतयोस्तप्तान् वसुदेवपुरोगमान् ।
तद्बन्धून्निहनिष्यामि वृष्णिभोजदशार्हकान् ॥३३॥

tayor nihatayos taptān
vasudeva-purogamān
tad-bandhūn nihaniṣyāmi
vṛṣṇi-bhoja-daśārhakān

tayoḥ—the two of Them; *nihatayoḥ*—when They are killed; *taptān*—tormented; *vasudeva-purogamān*—led by Vasudeva; *tad-bandhūn*—Their relatives; *nihaniṣyāmi*—I will kill; *vṛṣṇi-bhoja-daśārhakān*—the Vṛṣṇis, Bhojas and Daśārhas.

TRANSLATION

When these two have been killed, I will kill Vasudeva and all Their lamenting relatives—the Vṛṣṇis, Bhojas and Daśārhas.

PURPORT

Even today there are wicked political leaders throughout the world who make such plans and even carry them out.

TEXT 34

उग्रसेनं च पितरं स्थविरं राज्यकामुकं ।
तद्भ्रातरं देवकं च ये चान्ये विद्विषो मम ॥३४॥

ugrasenaṁ ca pitaraṁ
sthaviraṁ rājya-kāmukaṁ
tad-bhrātaraṁ devakaṁ ca
ye cānye vidviṣo mama

ugrasenam—King Ugrasena; *ca*—and; *pitaram*—my father; *sthaviram*—old; *rājya*—for the kingdom; *kāmukam*—greedy; *tat-bhrātaram*—his brother; *devakam*—Devaka; *ca*—also; *ye*—who; *ca*—and; *anye*—others; *vidviṣaḥ*—enemies; *mama*—my.

TRANSLATION

I will also kill my old father, Ugrasena, who is greedy for my kingdom, and I will kill his brother Devaka and all my other enemies as well.

TEXT 35

ततश्चैषा मही मित्र भवित्री नष्टकण्टका ॥३५॥

tataś caiṣā mahī mitra
bhavitrī naṣṭa-kaṇṭakā

tataḥ—then; *ca*—and; *eṣā*—this; *mahī*—earth; *mitra*—O friend; *bhavitrī*—will be; *naṣṭa*—destroyed; *kaṇṭakā*—her thorns.

TRANSLATION

Then, my friend, this earth will be free of thorns.

TEXT 36

जरासन्धो मम गुरुर्द्विविदो दयितः सखा ।
शम्बरो नरको बाणो मय्येव कृतसौहृदाः ।
तैरहं सुरपक्षीयान् हत्वा भोक्ष्ये महीं नृपान् ॥३६॥

jarāsandho mama gurur
dvivido dayitaḥ sakhā

śambaro narako bāṇo
mayy eva kṛta-sauhṛdāḥ
tair ahaṁ sura-pakṣīyān
hatvā bhokṣye mahīṁ nṛpān

jarāsandhaḥ—Jarāsandha; *mama*—my; *guruḥ*—elder (father-in-law); *dvividaḥ*—Dvivida; *dayitaḥ*—my dear; *sakhā*—friend; *śambaraḥ*—Śambara; *narakaḥ*—Naraka; *bāṇaḥ*—Bāṇa; *mayi*—for me; *eva*—indeed; *kṛta-sauhṛdāḥ*—who have strong friendship; *taiḥ*—with them; *aham*—I; *sura*—of the demigods; *pakṣīyān*—those who are allies; *hatvā*—killing; *bhokṣye*—will enjoy; *mahīm*—the earth; *nṛpān*—the kings.

TRANSLATION

My elder relative Jarāsandha and my dear friend Dvivida are solid well-wishers of mine, as are Śambara, Naraka and Bāṇa. I will use them all to kill off those kings who are allied with the demigods, and then I will rule the earth.

TEXT 37

एतज्ज्ञात्वानय क्षिप्रं रामकृष्णाविहार्भकौ ।
धनुर्मखनिरीक्षार्थं द्रष्टुं यदुपुरश्रियम् ॥३७॥

etaj jñātvānaya kṣipraṁ
rāma-kṛṣṇāv ihārbhakau
dhanur-makha-nirīkṣārthaṁ
draṣṭuṁ yadu-pura-śriyam

etat—this; *jñātvā*—knowing; *ānaya*—bring; *kṣipram*—quickly; *rāma-kṛṣṇau*—Rāma and Kṛṣṇa; *iha*—here; *arbhakau*—the young boys; *dhanuḥ-makha*—the bow sacrifice; *nirīkṣā-artham*—in order to witness; *draṣṭum*—to see; *yadu-pura*—of the capital city of the Yadu dynasty; *śriyam*—the opulence.

TRANSLATION

Now that you understand my intentions, please go at once and bring Kṛṣṇa and Balarāma to watch the bow sacrifice and see the opulence of the Yadus' capital.

TEXT 38

श्रीअक्रूर उवाच
राजन्मनीषितं सध्र्यक् तव स्वावद्यमार्जनम् ।
सिद्ध्यसिद्ध्योः समं कुर्याद्दैवं हि फलसाधनम् ॥३८॥

śrī-akrūra uvāca
rājan manīṣitaṁ sadhryak
tava svāvadya-mārjanam
siddhy-asiddhyoḥ samaṁ kuryād
daivaṁ hi phala-sādhanam

śrī-akrūraḥ uvāca—Śrī Akrūra said; *rājan*—O King; *manīṣitam*—the thinking; *sadhryak*—perfect; *tava*—your; *sva*—your own; *avadya*—misfortune; *mārjanam*—which will wash away; *siddhi-asiddhyoḥ*—in both success and failure; *samam*—equal; *kuryāt*—one should act; *daivam*—destiny; *hi*—after all; *phala*—the fruit, result; *sādhanam*—the cause of achieving.

TRANSLATION

Śrī Akrūra said: O King, you have expertly devised a process to free yourself of misfortune. Still, one should be equal in success and failure, since it is certainly destiny that produces the results of one's work.

TEXT 39

मनोरथान् करोत्युच्चैर्जनो दैवहतानपि ।
युज्यते हर्षशोकाभ्यां तथाप्याज्ञां करोमि ते ॥३९॥

manorathān karoty uccair
jano daiva-hatān api
yujyate harṣa-śokābhyāṁ
tathāpy ājñāṁ karomi te

manaḥ-rathān—his desires; *karoti*—carries out; *uccaiḥ*—fervently; *janaḥ*—the average person; *daiva*—by Providence; *hatān*—thwarted; *api*—even though; *yujyate*—he is confronted; *harṣa-śokābhyām*—by happiness and distress; *tathā api*—nonetheless; *ājñām*—order; *karomi*—I will do; *te*—your.

TRANSLATION

An ordinary person is determined to act on his desires even when fate prevents their fulfillment. Therefore he encounters both happiness and distress. Yet even though such is the case, I will execute your order.

PURPORT

Śrīla Viśvanātha Cakravartī explains that although what Akrūra said was courteous and encouraging, his hidden meaning was far different. What he really meant was this: "Your plan is not fit to execute, yet I will carry it out since you are the King and I am your subject, and in any case, you are about to die."

TEXT 40

श्रीशुक उवाच
एवमादिश्य चाक्रूरं मन्त्रिणश्च विसृज्य सः ।
प्रविवेश गृहं कंसस्तथाक्रूरः स्वमालयम् ॥४०॥

śrī-śuka uvāca
evam ādiśya cākrūraṁ
mantriṇaś ca visṛjya saḥ
praviveśa gṛhaṁ kaṁsas
tathākrūraḥ svam ālayam

śrī-śukaḥ uvāca—Śukadeva Gosvāmī said; *evam*—thus; *ādiśya*—instructing; *ca*—and; *akrūram*—Akrūra; *mantriṇaḥ*—his ministers; *ca*—and; *visṛjya*—dismissing; *saḥ*—he; *praviveśa*—entered; *gṛham*—his quarters; *kaṁsaḥ*—Kaṁsa; *tathā*—also; *akrūraḥ*—Akrūra; *svam*—his own; *ālayam*—residence.

TRANSLATION

Śukadeva Gosvāmī said: Having thus instructed Akrūra, King Kaṁsa dismissed his ministers and retired to his quarters, and Akrūra returned home.

Thus end the purports of the humble servant of His Divine Grace A. C. Bhaktivedanta Swami Prabhupāda to the Tenth Canto, Thirty-sixth Chapter, of the Śrīmad-Bhāgavatam, *entitled "The Slaying of Ariṣṭa, the Bull Demon."*

CHAPTER THIRTY-SEVEN

The Killing of the Demons Keśī and Vyoma

This chapter describes the killing of the horse demon, Keśī; Nārada's glorification of Lord Kṛṣṇa's future pastimes; and Kṛṣṇa's killing of Vyomāsura.

On Kaṁsa's order the Keśī demon assumed the form of a huge horse and went to Vraja. As he approached, his loud neighing terrified all the inhabitants, and they began looking for Śrī Kṛṣṇa. When He saw the demon, Kṛṣṇa came forward and challenged him to come near. Keśī charged Kṛṣṇa and tried to strike Him with his front legs, but the Lord seized them, whirled the demon around several times, and then threw him a distance of one hundred bow-lengths. Keśī remained unconscious for some time. When the demon regained consciousness, he furiously charged Kṛṣṇa again, his mouth agape. The Lord then thrust His left arm into the horse demon's mouth, and as Keśī tried to bite the arm, it felt like a red-hot iron rod. Kṛṣṇa's arm expanded more and more, finally choking the demon, and in extreme agony Keśī gave up his life. Lord Kṛṣṇa then removed His arm. He stood calmly, showing no pride at having killed the demon, as the demigods showered down flowers from the sky and glorified the Lord with prayers.

Soon thereafter Nārada Muni, the great sage among the demigods, approached Kṛṣṇa and prayed to Him in various ways, glorifying the Lord's future pastimes. Then Nārada paid his obeisances and departed.

One day, while tending the cows, Kṛṣṇa, Balarāma and the cowherd boys became engrossed in playing hide-and-go-seek. Some of the boys took the role of sheep, some the role of thieves, and others shepherds. The shepherds would search for the sheep when the thieves stole them. Taking advantage of this game, a demon named Vyoma, sent by Kaṁsa, dressed himself like a cowherd boy and joined the band of "thieves." He abducted a few cowherd boys at a time and threw them into a mountain cave, keeping them there by blocking the entrance with a boulder. Gradually Vyomāsura abducted all but four or five cowherd boys. When Kṛṣṇa saw what the demon was doing, He ran after him, grabbed him and killed him just as one would kill a sacrificial animal.

TEXTS 1–2

श्रीशुक उवाच
केशी तु कंसप्रहितः खुरैर्महीं
महाहयो निर्जरयन्मनोजवः ।
सटावधूताभ्रविमानसंकुलं
कुर्वन्नभो हेषितभीषिताखिलः ॥१॥
तं त्रासयन्तं भगवान् स्वगोकुलं
तद्धेषितैर्वालविघूर्णिताम्बुदम् ।
आत्मानमाजौ मृगयन्तमग्रणीर्
उपाह्वयत्स व्यनदन्मृगेन्द्रवत् ॥२॥

śrī-śuka uvāca
keśī tu kaṁsa-prahitaḥ khurair mahīṁ
mahā-hayo nirjarayan mano-javaḥ
saṭāvadhūtābhra-vimāna-saṅkulaṁ
kurvan nabho heṣita-bhīṣitākhilaḥ

taṁ trāsayantaṁ bhagavān sva-gokulaṁ
tad-dheṣitair vāla-vighūrṇitāmbudam
ātmānam ājau mṛgayantam agra-ṇīr
upāhvayat sa vyanadan mṛgendra-vat

śrī-śukaḥ uvāca—Śrī Śukadeva Gosvāmī said; *keśī*—the demon named Keśī; *tu*—and then; *kaṁsa-prahitaḥ*—sent by Kaṁsa; *khuraiḥ*—with his hooves; *mahīm*—the earth; *mahā-hayaḥ*—a huge horse; *nirjarayan*—ripping apart; *manaḥ*—like that of the mind; *javaḥ*—whose speed; *saṭā*—by the hairs of his mane; *avadhūta*—scattered; *abhra*—with the clouds; *vimāna*—and the airplanes (of the demigods); *saṅkulam*—crowded; *kurvan*—making; *nabhaḥ*—the sky; *heṣita*—by his neighing; *bhīṣita*—frightened; *akhilaḥ*—everyone; *tam*—him; *trāsayantam*—terrifying; *bhagavān*—the Supreme Lord; *sva-gokulam*—His cowherd village; *tat-heṣitaiḥ*—by that neighing; *vāla*—by the hairs of his tail; *vighūrṇita*—shaken; *ambudam*—the clouds; *ātmānam*—Himself; *ājau*—for a fight; *mṛgayantam*—searching after; *agra-nīḥ*—coming forward; *upāhvayat*—called out; *saḥ*—he, Keśī; *vyanadan*—roared; *mṛgendra-vat*—like a lion.

TRANSLATION

Śukadeva Gosvāmī said: The demon Keśī, sent by Kaṁsa, appeared in Vraja as a great horse. Running with the speed of the mind, he tore up the earth with his hooves. The hairs of his mane scattered the clouds and the demigods' airplanes throughout the sky, and he terrified everyone present with his loud neighing.

When the Supreme Personality of Godhead saw how the demon was frightening His village of Gokula by neighing terribly and shaking the clouds with his tail, the Lord came forward to meet him. Keśī was searching for Kṛṣṇa to fight, so when the Lord stood before him and challenged him to approach, the horse responded by roaring like a lion.

TEXT 3

स तं निशाम्याभिमुखो मुखेन खं
पिबन्निवाभ्यद्रवदत्यमर्षण: ।
जघान पद्भ्यामरविन्दलोचनं
दुरासदश्चण्डजवो दुरत्यय: ॥३॥

sa taṁ niśāmyābhimukho mukhena khaṁ
pibann ivābhyadravad aty-amarṣaṇaḥ
jaghāna padbhyām aravinda-locanaṁ
durāsadaś caṇḍa-javo duratyayaḥ

saḥ—he, Keśī; *tam*—Him, Kṛṣṇa; *niśāmya*—seeing; *abhimukhaḥ*—in front of himself; *mukhena*—with his mouth; *kham*—the sky; *piban*—drinking up; *iva*—as if; *abhyadravat*—ran forward; *ati-amarṣaṇaḥ*—very angry; *jaghāna*—he attacked; *padbhyām*—with his two legs; *aravinda-locanam*—the lotus-eyed Lord; *durāsadaḥ*—unapproachable; *caṇḍa*—fierce; *javaḥ*—whose speed; *duratyayaḥ*—unconquerable.

TRANSLATION

Seeing the Lord standing before him, Keśī ran toward Him in extreme rage, his mouth gaping as if to swallow up the sky. Rushing with furious speed, the unconquerable and unapproachable horse demon tried to strike the lotus-eyed Lord with his two front legs.

TEXT 4

तद्वञ्चयित्वा तमधोक्षजो रुषा
प्रगृह्य दोर्भ्यां परिविध्य पादयोः ।
सावज्ञमुत्सृज्य धनुःशतान्तरे
यथोरगं तार्क्ष्यसुतो व्यवस्थितः ॥४॥

tad vañcayitvā tam adhokṣajo ruṣā
pragṛhya dorbhyāṁ parividhya pādayoḥ
sāvajñam utsṛjya dhanuḥ-śatāntare
yathoragaṁ tārkṣya-suto vyavasthitaḥ

tat—that; *vañcayitvā*—avoiding; *tam*—him; *adhokṣajaḥ*—the transcendental Lord; *ruṣā*—angrily; *pragṛhya*—seizing; *dorbhyām*—with His arms; *parividhya*—whirling around; *pādayoḥ*—by the legs; *sa-avajñam*—contemptuously; *utsṛjya*—discarding; *dhanuḥ*—of bow-lengths; *śata*—one hundred; *antare*—to the distance; *yathā*—as; *uragam*—a snake; *tārkṣya*—of Kardama Muni; *sutaḥ*—the son (Garuḍa); *vyavasthitaḥ*—standing.

TRANSLATION

But the transcendental Lord dodged Keśī's blow and then with His arms angrily seized the demon by the legs, whirled him around in the air and contemptuously threw him the distance of one hundred bow-lengths, just as Garuḍa might throw a snake. Lord Kṛṣṇa then stood there.

TEXT 5

सः लब्धसंज्ञः पुनरुत्थितो रुषा
व्यादाय केशी तरसापतद्धरिम् ।
सोऽप्यस्य वक्त्रे भुजमुत्तरं स्मयन्
प्रवेशयामास यथोरगं बिले ॥५॥

saḥ labdha-saṁjñaḥ punar utthito ruṣā
vyādāya keśī tarasāpatad dharim

so 'py asya vaktre bhujam uttaraṁ smayan
praveśayām āsa yathoragaṁ bile

saḥ—he, Keśī; *labdha*—regaining; *saṁjñaḥ*—consciousness; *punaḥ*—again; *utthitaḥ*—rose up; *ruṣā*—in anger; *vyādāya*—opening (his mouth) wide; *keśī*—Keśī; *tarasā*—rapidly; *apatat*—ran; *harim*—toward Kṛṣṇa; *saḥ*—He, Lord Kṛṣṇa; *api*—and; *asya*—his; *vaktre*—in the mouth; *bhujam*—His arm; *uttaram*—left; *smayan*—smiled; *praveśayām āsa*—placed within; *yathā*—as; *uragam*—a snake; *bile*—(enters) within a hole.

TRANSLATION

Upon regaining consciousness Keśī angrily got up, opened his mouth wide and again rushed to attack Lord Kṛṣṇa. But the Lord just smiled and thrust His left arm into the horse's mouth as easily as one would make a snake enter a hole in the ground.

TEXT 6

दन्ता निपेतुर्भगवद्भुजस्पृशस्
ते केशिनस्तप्तमयस्पृशो यथा ।
बाहुश्च तद्देहगतो महात्मनो
यथामयः संववृधे उपेक्षितः ॥६॥

dantā nipetur bhagavad-bhuja-spṛśas
te keśinas tapta-maya-spṛśo yathā
bāhuś ca tad-deha-gato mahātmano
yathāmayaḥ saṁvavṛdhe upekṣitaḥ

dantāḥ—the teeth; *nipetuḥ*—fell out; *bhagavat*—of the Supreme Lord; *bhuja*—the arm; *spṛśaḥ*—touching; *te*—they; *keśinaḥ*—of Keśī; *tapta-maya*—red-hot (iron); *spṛśaḥ*—touching; *yathā*—as; *bāhuḥ*—the arm; *ca*—and; *tat*—his, Keśī's; *deha*—body; *gataḥ*—having entered; *mahā-ātmanaḥ*—of the Supreme Soul; *yathā*—like; *āmayaḥ*—a diseased condition (particularly, distension of the stomach); *saṁvavṛdhe*—increased greatly in size; *upekṣitaḥ*—neglected.

TRANSLATION

Keśī's teeth immediately fell out when they touched the Supreme Lord's arm, which to the demon felt as hot as molten iron. Within Keśī's body the Supreme Personality's arm then expanded greatly, like a diseased stomach swelling because of neglect.

PURPORT

Śrīla Viśvanātha Cakravartī points out that although Lord Kṛṣṇa's arm is more tender and cooling than a blue lotus, to Keśī it felt extremely hot, as if made of lightning bolts.

TEXT 7

समेधमानेन स कृष्णबाहुना
निरुद्धवायुश्चरणांश्च विक्षिपन् ।
प्रस्विन्नगात्रः परिवृत्तलोचनः
पपात लण्डं विसृजन् क्षितौ व्यसुः ॥७॥

samedhamānena sa kṛṣṇa-bāhunā
niruddha-vāyuś caraṇāṁś ca vikṣipan
prasvinna-gātraḥ parivṛtta-locanaḥ
papāta laṇḍaṁ visṛjan kṣitau vyasuḥ

samedhamānena—expanding; *saḥ*—he; *kṛṣṇa-bāhunā*—by Lord Kṛṣṇa's arm; *niruddha*—stopped; *vāyuḥ*—his breathing; *caraṇān*—his legs; *ca*—and; *vikṣipan*—throwing about; *prasvinna*—perspiring; *gātraḥ*—his body; *parivṛtta*—rolling; *locanaḥ*—his eyes; *papāta*—he fell down; *laṇḍam*—feces; *visṛjan*—excreting; *kṣitau*—onto the ground; *vyasuḥ*—lifeless.

TRANSLATION

As Lord Kṛṣṇa's expanding arm completely blocked Keśī's breathing, his legs kicked convulsively, his body became covered with sweat, and his eyes rolled around. The demon then passed stool and fell on the ground, dead.

TEXT 8

तद्देहतः कर्कटिकाफलोपमाद्
व्यसोरपाकृष्य भुजं महाभुजः ।
अविस्मितोऽयत्नहतारिकः सुरैः
प्रसूनवर्षैर्वर्षद्भिरीडितः ॥८॥

tad-dehataḥ karkaṭikā-phalopamād
vyasor apākṛṣya bhujaṁ mahā-bhujaḥ
avismito 'yatna-hatārikaḥ suraiḥ
prasūna-varṣair varṣadbhir īḍitaḥ

tat-dehataḥ—from Keśī's body; *karkaṭikā-phala*—a *karkaṭikā* fruit; *upamāt*—which resembled; *vyasoḥ*—from which the vital airs had departed; *apākṛṣya*—withdrawing; *bhujam*—His arm; *mahā-bhujaḥ*—the mighty-armed Lord; *avismitaḥ*—without undue pride; *ayatna*—without effort; *hata*—having killed; *arikaḥ*—His enemy; *suraiḥ*—by the demigods; *prasūna*—of flowers; *varṣaiḥ*—with downpours; *varṣadbhiḥ*—who were raining upon Him; *īḍitaḥ*—worshiped.

TRANSLATION

The mighty-armed Kṛṣṇa withdrew His arm from Keśī's body, which now appeared like a long *karkaṭikā* fruit. Without the least display of pride at having so effortlessly killed His enemy, the Lord accepted the demigods' worship in the form of flowers rained down from above.

TEXT 9

देवर्षिरुपसंगम्य भागवतप्रवरो नृप ।
कृष्णमक्लिष्टकर्माणं रहस्येतदभाषत ॥९॥

devarṣir upasaṅgamya
bhāgavata-pravaro nṛpa
kṛṣṇam akliṣṭa-karmāṇaṁ
rahasy etad abhāṣata

deva-ṛṣiḥ—the sage among the demigods (Nārada Muni); *upasaṅgamya*—approaching; *bhāgavata*—of devotees of the Lord; *pravaraḥ*—the most exalted; *nṛpa*—O King (Parīkṣit); *kṛṣṇam*—Lord Kṛṣṇa; *akliṣṭa*—without trouble; *karmāṇam*—whose activities; *rahasi*—in privacy; *etat*—this; *abhāṣata*—said.

TRANSLATION

My dear King, thereafter Lord Kṛṣṇa was approached in a solitary place by the great sage among the demigods, Nārada Muni. That most exalted devotee spoke as follows to the Lord, who effortlessly performs His pastimes.

PURPORT

After speaking with Kaṁsa, Nārada went to see Lord Kṛṣṇa. The Lord's Vṛndāvana pastimes were nearly completed, and Nārada wanted to see those He would enact in Mathurā.

TEXTS 10–11

कृष्ण कृष्णाप्रमेयात्मन् योगेश जगदीश्वर ।
वासुदेवाखिलावास सात्वतां प्रवर प्रभो ॥१०॥
त्वमात्मा सर्वभूतानामेको ज्योतिरिवैधसाम् ।
गूढो गुहाशयः साक्षी महापुरुष ईश्वरः ॥११॥

kṛṣṇa kṛṣṇāprameyātman
yogeśa jagad-īśvara
vāsudevākhilāvāsa
sātvatāṁ pravara prabho

tvam ātmā sarva-bhūtānām
eko jyotir ivaidhasām
gūḍho guhā-śayaḥ sākṣī
mahā-puruṣa īśvaraḥ

kṛṣṇa kṛṣṇa—O Kṛṣṇa, Kṛṣṇa; *aprameya-ātman*—O immeasurable one; *yoga-īśa*—O source of all mystic power; *jagat-īśvara*—O Lord of the universe; *vāsudeva*—O son of Vasudeva; *akhila-āvāsa*—O shelter of all beings; *sātvatām*—of the Yadu dynasty; *pravara*—O You who are the best; *prabho*—O master; *tvam*—You; *ātmā*—the Supreme Soul; *sarva*—of all; *bhūtānām*—created beings; *ekaḥ*—alone; *jyotiḥ*—fire; *iva*—like; *edhasām*—in kindling wood; *gūḍhaḥ*—hidden; *guhā*—within the cave of the heart; *śayaḥ*—sitting; *sākṣī*—the witness; *mahā-puruṣaḥ*—the Supreme Personality of Godhead; *īśvaraḥ*—the supreme controller.

TRANSLATION

O Kṛṣṇa, Kṛṣṇa, unlimited Lord, source of all mystic power, Lord of the universe! O Vāsudeva, shelter of all beings and best of the Yadus! O master, You are the Supreme Soul of all created beings, sitting unseen within the cave of the heart like the fire dormant within kindling wood. You are the witness within everyone, the Supreme Personality and the ultimate controlling Deity.

TEXT 12

आत्मनात्माश्रयः पूर्वं मायया ससृजे गुणान् ।
तैरिदं सत्यसंकल्पः सृजस्यत्स्यवसीश्वरः ॥१२॥

ātmanātmāśrayaḥ pūrvaṁ
māyayā sasṛje guṇān
tair idaṁ satya-saṅkalpaḥ
sṛjasy atsy avasīśvaraḥ

ātmanā—by Your personal potency; *ātma*—of the spirit soul; *āśrayaḥ*—the shelter; *pūrvam*—first; *māyayā*—by Your creative energy; *sasṛje*—You produced; *guṇān*—the basic modes of material nature; *taiḥ*—through these; *idam*—this (universe); *satya*—always realized in fact; *saṅkalpaḥ*—whose desires; *sṛjasi*—You create; *atsi*—withdraw; *avasi*—and maintain; *īśvaraḥ*—the controller.

TRANSLATION

You are the shelter of all souls, and being the supreme controller, You fulfill Your desires simply by Your will. By Your

personal creative potency You manifested in the beginning the primal modes of material nature, and through their agency You create, maintain and then destroy this universe.

TEXT 13

स त्वं भूधरभूतानां दैत्यप्रमथरक्षसाम् ।
अवतीर्णो विनाशाय साधूनां रक्षणाय च ॥१३॥

sa tvaṁ bhūdhara-bhūtānāṁ
daitya-pramatha-rakṣasām
avatīrṇo vināśāya
sādhūnāṁ rakṣaṇāya ca

saḥ—He; *tvam*—Yourself; *bhū-dhara*—as kings; *bhūtānām*—who are appearing; *daitya-pramatha-rakṣasām*—of various kinds of demons; *avatīrṇaḥ*—You have descended; *vināśāya*—for the destruction; *sādhūnām*—of saintly persons; *rakṣaṇāya*—for the protection; *ca*—and.

TRANSLATION

You, that very same creator, have now descended on the earth to annihilate the Daitya, Pramatha and Rākṣasa demons who are posing as kings, and also to protect the godly.

TEXT 14

दिष्ट्या ते निहतो दैत्यो लीलयायं हयाकृतिः ।
यस्य हेषितसन्त्रस्तास्त्यजन्त्यनिमिषा दिवम् ॥१४॥

diṣṭyā te nihato daityo
līlayāyaṁ hayākṛtiḥ
yasya heṣita-santrastās
tyajanty animiṣā divam

diṣṭyā—by (our) good fortune; *te*—by You; *nihataḥ*—killed; *daityaḥ*—demon; *līlayā*—as a game; *ayam*—this; *haya-ākṛtiḥ*—having the form of a horse; *yasya*—whose; *heṣita*—by the neighing; *santrastāḥ*—terrified; *tyajanti*—abandon; *animiṣāḥ*—the demigods; *divam*—heaven.

TRANSLATION

The horse demon was so terrifying that his neighing frightened the demigods into leaving their heavenly kingdom. But by our good fortune You have enjoyed the sport of killing him.

TEXTS 15–20

चाणूरं मुष्टिकं चैव मल्लानन्यांश्च हस्तिनम् ।
कंसं च निहतं द्रक्ष्ये परश्वोऽहनि ते विभो ॥१५॥
तस्यानु शंखयवनमुराणां नरकस्य च ।
पारिजातापहरणमिन्द्रस्य च पराजयम् ॥१६॥
उद्वाहं वीरकन्यानां वीर्यशुल्कादिलक्षणम् ।
नृगस्य मोक्षणं शापाद् द्वारकायां जगत्पते ॥१७॥
स्यमन्तकस्य च मणेरादानं सह भार्यया ।
मृतपुत्रप्रदानं च ब्राह्मणस्य स्वधामतः ॥१८॥
पौण्ड्रकस्य वधं पश्चात्काशिपुर्याश्च दीपनम् ।
दन्तवक्रस्य निधनं चैद्यस्य च महाक्रतौ ॥१९॥
यानि चान्यानि वीर्याणि द्वारकामावसन् भवान् ।
कर्ता द्रक्ष्याम्यहं तानि गेयानि कविभिर्भुवि ॥२०॥

cāṇūraṁ muṣṭikaṁ caiva
mallān anyāṁś ca hastinam
kaṁsaṁ ca nihataṁ drakṣye
paraśvo 'hani te vibho

tasyānu śaṅkha-yavana-
murāṇāṁ narakasya ca
pārijātāpaharaṇam
indrasya ca parājayam

udvāhaṁ vīra-kanyānāṁ
vīrya-śulkādi-lakṣaṇam
nṛgasya mokṣaṇaṁ śāpād
dvārakāyāṁ jagat-pate

syamantakasya ca maṇer
ādānaṁ saha bhāryayā
mṛta-putra-pradānaṁ ca
brāhmaṇasya sva-dhāmataḥ

pauṇḍrakasya vadhaṁ paścāt
kāśi-puryāś ca dīpanam
dantavakrasya nidhanaṁ
caidyasya ca mahā-kratau

yāni cānyāni vīryāṇi
dvārakām āvasan bhavān
kartā drakṣyāmy ahaṁ tāni
geyāni kavibhir bhuvi

cāṇūram—Cāṇūra; *muṣṭikam*—Muṣṭika; *ca*—and; *eva*—also; *mallān*—the wrestlers; *anyān*—others; *ca*—and; *hastinam*—the elephant (Kuvalayāpīḍa); *kaṁsam*—King Kaṁsa; *ca*—and; *nihatam*—killed; *drakṣye*—I will see; *para-śvaḥ*—the day after tomorrow; *ahani*—on that day; *te*—by You; *vibho*—O almighty Lord; *tasya anu*—after that; *śaṅkha-yavana-murāṇām*—of the demons Śaṅkha (Pañcajana), Kālayavana and Mura; *narakasya*—of Narakāsura; *ca*—as well; *pārijāta*—of the heavenly *pārijāta* flower; *apaharaṇam*—the stealing; *indrasya*—of Lord Indra; *ca*—and; *parājayam*—the defeat; *udvāham*—the marriage; *vīra*—of heroic kings; *kanyānām*—of the daughters; *vīrya*—by Your valor; *śulka*—as the payment for the brides; *ādi*—and so forth; *lakṣaṇam*—characterized; *nṛgasya*—of King Nṛga; *mokṣaṇam*—the deliverance; *śāpāt*—from his curse; *dvārakāyām*—in the city of Dvārakā; *jagat-pate*—O master of the universe; *syamantakasya*—named Syamantaka; *ca*—and; *maṇeḥ*—of the jewel; *ādānam*—the taking; *saha*—together with; *bhāryayā*—a wife (Jāmbavatī); *mṛta*—dead; *putra*—of the son; *pradānam*—the presenting; *ca*—and; *brāhmaṇasya*—of a *brāhmaṇa; sva-dhāmataḥ*—from Your own domain (i.e., from the abode of Death); *pauṇḍrakasya*—of Pauṇḍraka;

vadham—the killing; *paścāt*—after; *kāśi-puryāḥ*—of the city of Kāśī (Benares); *ca*—and; *dīpanam*—the burning; *dantavakrasya*—of Dantavakra; *nidhanam*—the demise; *caidyasya*—of Caidya (Śiśupāla); *ca*—and; *mahā-kratau*—during the great sacrificial performance (the Rājasūya-yajña of Mahārāja Yudhiṣṭhira); *yāni*—which; *ca*—and; *anyāni*—other; *vīryāṇi*—great feats; *dvārakām*—in Dvārakā; *āvasan*—dwelling; *bhavān*—You; *kartā*—are going to perform; *drakṣyāmi*—will see; *aham*—I; *tāni*—them; *geyāni*—to be sung about; *kavibhiḥ*—by poets; *bhuvi*—on this earth.

TRANSLATION

In just two days, O almighty Lord, I will see the deaths of Cāṇūra, Muṣṭika and other wrestlers, along with those of the elephant Kuvalayāpīḍa and King Kaṁsa—all by Your hand. Then I will see You kill Kālayavana, Mura, Naraka and the conch demon, and I will also see You steal the *pārijāta* flower and defeat Indra. I will then see You marry many daughters of heroic kings after paying for them with Your valor. Then, O Lord of the universe, in Dvārakā You will deliver King Nṛga from a curse and take for Yourself the Syamantaka jewel, together with another wife. You will bring back a *brāhmaṇa's* dead son from the abode of Your servant Yamarāja, and thereafter You will kill Pauṇḍraka, burn down the city of Kāśī and annihilate Dantavakra and the King of Cedi during the great Rājasūya sacrifice. I shall see all these heroic pastimes, along with many others You will perform during Your residence in Dvārakā. These pastimes are glorified on this earth in the songs of transcendental poets.

TEXT 21

अथ ते कालरूपस्य क्षपयिष्णोरमुष्य वै ।
अक्षौहिणीनां निधनं द्रक्ष्याम्यर्जुनसारथेः ॥२१॥

atha te kāla-rūpasya
kṣapayiṣṇor amuṣya vai
akṣauhiṇīnāṁ nidhanaṁ
drakṣyāmy arjuna-sāratheḥ

atha—then; *te*—by You; *kāla-rūpasya*—who are assuming the form of time; *kṣapayiṣṇoḥ*—who is intending to effect the destruction; *amuṣya*—of (the burden of) this world; *vai*—indeed; *akṣauhiṇīnām*—of entire armies; *nidhanam*—the destruction; *drakṣyāmi*—I will see; *arjuna-sāratheḥ*—by the chariot driver of Arjuna.

TRANSLATION

Subsequently I will see You appear as time personified, serving as Arjuna's chariot driver and destroying entire armies of soldiers to rid the earth of her burden.

TEXT 22

विशुद्धविज्ञानघनं स्वसंस्थया
समाप्तसर्वार्थममोघवाञ्छितम् ।
स्वतेजसा नित्यनिवृत्तमाया-
गुणप्रवाहं भगवन्तमीमहि ॥२२॥

viśuddha-vijñāna-ghanaṁ sva-saṁsthayā
samāpta-sarvārtham amogha-vāñchitam
sva-tejasā nitya-nivṛtta-māyā-
guṇa-pravāhaṁ bhagavantam īmahi

viśuddha—perfectly pure; *vijñāna*—spiritual awareness; *ghanam*—full of; *sva-saṁsthayā*—in His original identity; *samāpta*—already fulfilled; *sarva*—in all; *artham*—purposes; *amogha*—never frustrated; *vāñchitam*—whose desires; *sva-tejasā*—by His own potency; *nitya*—eternally; *nivṛtta*—desisting; *māyā*—of the illusory, material energy; *guṇa*—of the manifest modes; *pravāham*—from the flowing interaction; *bhagavantam*—the Supreme Personality of Godhead; *īmahi*—let us approach.

TRANSLATION

Let us approach You, the Supreme Personality of Godhead, for shelter. You are full of perfectly pure spiritual awareness and are always situated in Your original identity. Since Your will is never thwarted, You have already achieved all possible desirable things,

and by the power of Your spiritual energy You remain eternally aloof from the flow of the qualities of illusion.

TEXT 23

त्वामीश्वरं स्वाश्रयमात्ममायया
विनिर्मिताशेषविशेषकल्पनम् ।
क्रीडार्थमद्यात्तमनुष्यविग्रहं
नतोऽस्मि धुर्यं यदुवृष्णिसात्वताम् ॥२३॥

tvāṁ īśvaraṁ svāśrayam ātma-māyayā
vinirmitāśeṣa-viśeṣa-kalpanam
krīḍārtham adyātta-manuṣya-vigrahaṁ
nato 'smi dhuryaṁ yadu-vṛṣṇi-sātvatām

tvām—to You; *īśvaram*—the supreme controller; *sva-āśrayam*—self-contained; *ātma*—Your own; *māyayā*—by the creative potency; *vinirmita*—constructed; *aśeṣa*—unlimited; *viśeṣa*—particular; *kalpanam*—arrangements; *krīḍā*—of playing; *artham*—for the sake; *adya*—now; *ātta*—taken on; *manuṣya*—among humans; *vigraham*—battle; *nataḥ*—bowed down; *asmi*—I am; *dhuryam*—to the greatest; *yadu-vṛṣṇi-sātvatām*—of the Yadu, Vṛṣṇi and Sātvata dynasties.

TRANSLATION

I bow down to You, the supreme controller, who are dependent only on Yourself. By Your potency You have constructed the unlimited particular arrangements of this universe. Now you have appeared as the greatest hero among the Yadus, Vṛṣṇis and Sātvatas and have chosen to participate in human warfare.

TEXT 24

श्रीशुक उवाच
एवं यदुपतिं कृष्णं भागवतप्रवरो मुनिः ।
प्रणिपत्याभ्यनुज्ञातो ययौ तद्दर्शनोत्सवः ॥२४॥

śrī-śuka uvāca
evaṁ yadu-patiṁ kṛṣṇaṁ
bhāgavata-pravaro muniḥ
praṇipatyābhyanujñāto
yayau tad-darśanotsavaḥ

śrī-śukaḥ uvāca—Śukadeva Gosvāmī said; *evam*—thus; *yadu-patim*—to the chief of the Yadus; *kṛṣṇam*—Lord Kṛṣṇa; *bhāgavata*—of devotees; *pravaraḥ*—most eminent; *muniḥ*—the sage Nārada; *praṇipatya*—respectfully bowing down; *abhyanujñātaḥ*—given leave; *yayau*—went; *tat*—Him, Kṛṣṇa; *darśana*—by having seen; *utsavaḥ*—experiencing great joy.

TRANSLATION

Śukadeva Gosvāmī said: Having thus addressed Lord Kṛṣṇa, the chief of the Yadu dynasty, Nārada bowed down and offered Him obeisances. Then that great sage and most eminent devotee took his leave from the Lord and went away, feeling great joy at having directly seen Him.

TEXT 25

भगवानपि गोविन्दो हत्वा केशिनमाहवे ।
पशूनपालयत्पालैः प्रीतैर्व्रजसुखावहः ॥२५॥

bhagavān api govindo
hatvā keśinam āhave
paśūn apālayat pālaiḥ
prītair vraja-sukhāvahaḥ

bhagavān—the Supreme Lord; *api*—and; *govindaḥ*—Govinda; *hatvā*—having killed; *keśinam*—the demon Keśī; *āhave*—in battle; *paśūn*—the animals; *apālayat*—He tended; *pālaiḥ*—together with the cowherd boys; *prītaiḥ*—who were pleased; *vraja*—to the inhabitants of Vṛndāvana; *sukha*—happiness; *āvahaḥ*—bringing.

TRANSLATION

After killing the demon Keśī in battle, the Supreme Personality of Godhead continued to tend the cows and other animals in the

company of His joyful cowherd boyfriends. Thus He brought happiness to all the residents of Vṛndāvana.

TEXT 26

एकदा ते पशून् पालाश्चारयन्तोऽद्रिसानुषु ।
चक्रुर्निलायनक्रीडाश्चोरपालापदेशतः ॥२६॥

ekadā te paśūn pālāś
cārayanto 'dri-sānuṣu
cakrur nilāyana-krīḍāś
cora-pālāpadeśataḥ

ekadā—one day; *te*—they; *paśūn*—the animals; *pālāḥ*—the cowherd boys; *cārayantaḥ*—grazing; *adri*—of a mountain; *sānuṣu*—on the sides; *cakruḥ*—they enacted; *nilāyana*—of "stealing and hiding"; *krīḍāḥ*—games; *cora*—of thieves; *pāla*—and protectors; *apadeśataḥ*—playing the roles.

TRANSLATION

One day the cowherd boys, while grazing their animals on the mountain slopes, played the game of stealing and hiding, acting out the roles of rival thieves and herders.

TEXT 27

तत्रासन् कतिचिच्चोराः पालाश्च कतिचिन्नृप ।
मेषायिताश्च तत्रैके विजह्रुरकुतोभयाः ॥२७॥

tatrāsan katicic corāḥ
pālāś ca katicin nṛpa
meṣāyitāś ca tatraike
vijahrur akuto-bhayāḥ

tatra—in that; *āsan*—were; *katicit*—some; *corāḥ*—thieves; *pālāḥ*—herders; *ca*—and; *katicit*—some; *nṛpa*—O King (Parīkṣit); *meṣāyitāḥ*—acting as the sheep; *ca*—and; *tatra*—therein; *eke*—some of them; *vijahruḥ*—they played; *akutaḥ-bhayāḥ*—without any fear.

TRANSLATION

In that game, O King, some acted as thieves, others as shepherds and others as sheep. They played their game happily, without fear of danger.

TEXT 28

मयपुत्रो महामायो व्योमो गोपालवेषधृक् ।
मेषायितानपोवाह प्रायश्चोरायितो बहून् ॥२८॥

maya-putro mahā-māyo
vyomo gopāla-veṣa-dhṛk
meṣāyitān apovāha
prāyaś corāyito bahūn

maya-putraḥ—a son of the demon Maya; *mahā-māyaḥ*—a powerful magician; *vyomaḥ*—named Vyoma; *gopāla*—of a cowherd boy; *veṣa*—the disguise; *dhṛk*—assuming; *meṣāyitān*—those who were acting as sheep; *apovāha*—he took away; *prāyaḥ*—almost all; *corāyitaḥ*—pretending to be playing as a thief; *bahūn*—many.

TRANSLATION

A powerful magician named Vyoma, son of the demon Maya, then appeared on the scene in the guise of a cowherd boy. Pretending to join the game as a thief, he proceeded to steal most of the cowherd boys who were acting as sheep.

TEXT 29

गिरिदर्यां विनिक्षिप्य नीतं नीतं महासुरः ।
शिलया पिदधे द्वारं चतुःपञ्चावशेषिताः ॥२९॥

giri-daryāṁ vinikṣipya
nītaṁ nītaṁ mahāsuraḥ
śilayā pidadhe dvāraṁ
catuḥ-pañcāvaśeṣitāḥ

giri—of a mountain; *daryām*—in a cave; *vinikṣipya*—throwing; *nītam nītam*—gradually bringing them; *mahā-asuraḥ*—the great demon; *śilayā*—with a stone; *pidadhe*—he blocked; *dvāram*—the entrance; *catuḥ-pañca*—four or five; *avaśeṣitāḥ*—remained.

TRANSLATION

Gradually the great demon abducted more and more of the cowherd boys and cast them into a mountain cave, which he sealed shut with a boulder. Finally only four or five boys acting as sheep remained in the game.

TEXT 30

तस्य तत्कर्म विज्ञाय कृष्णः शरणदः सताम् ।
गोपान्नयन्तं जग्राह वृकं हरिरिवौजसा ॥३०॥

tasya tat karma vijñāya
kṛṣṇaḥ śaraṇa-daḥ satām
gopān nayantaṁ jagrāha
vṛkaṁ harir ivaujasā

tasya—of him, Vyomāsura; *tat*—that; *karma*—activity; *vijñāya*—fully understanding; *kṛṣṇaḥ*—Lord Kṛṣṇa; *śaraṇa*—of shelter; *daḥ*—the giver; *satām*—to saintly devotees; *gopān*—cowherd boys; *nayantam*—who was leading; *jagrāha*—He seized; *vṛkam*—a wolf; *hariḥ*—a lion; *iva*—just as; *ojasā*—forcefully.

TRANSLATION

Lord Kṛṣṇa, who shelters all saintly devotees, understood perfectly well what Vyomāsura was doing. Just as a lion grabs a wolf, Kṛṣṇa forcefully seized the demon as he was taking away more cowherd boys.

TEXT 31

स निजं रूपमास्थाय गिरीन्द्रसदृशं बली ।
इच्छन् विमोक्तुमात्मानं नाशक्नोद् ग्रहणातुरः ॥३१॥

sa nijaṁ rūpam āsthāya
girīndra-sadṛśaṁ balī
icchan vimoktum ātmānaṁ
nāśaknod grahaṇāturaḥ

saḥ—he, the demon; *nijam*—his original; *rūpam*—form; *āsthāya*—assuming; *giri-indra*—a kingly mountain; *sadṛśam*—just like; *balī*—powerful; *icchan*—wanting; *vimoktum*—to free; *ātmānam*—himself; *na aśaknot*—he was not able; *grahaṇa*—by being forcibly held; *āturaḥ*—debilitated.

TRANSLATION

The demon changed into his original form, as big and powerful as a great mountain. But try as he might to free himself, he could not do so, having lost his strength from being held in the Lord's tight grip.

TEXT 32

तं निगृह्याच्युतो दोर्भ्यां पातयित्वा महीतले ।
पश्यतां दिवि देवानां पशुमारममारयत् ॥३२॥

taṁ nigṛhyācyuto dorbhyāṁ
pātayitvā mahī-tale
paśyatāṁ divi devānāṁ
paśu-māram amārayat

tam—him; *nigṛhya*—holding fast; *acyutaḥ*—Lord Kṛṣṇa; *dorbhyām*—with His arms; *pātayitvā*—making him fall; *mahī-tale*—onto the ground; *paśyatām*—while they were watching; *divi*—in the heavenly planets; *devānām*—the demigods; *paśu-māram*—as a sacrificial animal is slaughtered; *amārayat*—He killed him.

TRANSLATION

Lord Acyuta clutched Vyomāsura between His arms and threw him to the ground. Then, while the demigods in heaven looked on, Kṛṣṇa killed him in the same way that one kills a sacrificial animal.

PURPORT

The *ācāryas* inform us that sacrificial animals were killed by means of strangulation.

TEXT 33

गुहापिधानं निर्भिद्य गोपान्निःसार्य कृच्छ्रतः ।
स्तूयमानः सुरैर्गोपैः प्रविवेश स्वगोकुलम् ॥३३॥

guhā-pidhānaṁ nirbhidya
gopān niḥsārya kṛcchrataḥ
stūyamānaḥ surair gopaiḥ
praviveśa sva-gokulam

guhā—of the cave; *pidhānam*—the blockage; *nirbhidya*—breaking; *gopān*—the cowherd boys; *niḥsārya*—leading out; *kṛcchrataḥ*—from the dangerous place; *stūyamānaḥ*—being praised; *suraiḥ*—by the demigods; *gopaiḥ*—and by the cowherd boys; *praviveśa*—he entered; *sva*—His own; *gokulam*—cowherd village.

TRANSLATION

Kṛṣṇa then smashed the boulder blocking the cave's entrance and led the trapped cowherd boys to safety. Thereafter, as the demigods and cowherd boys sang His glories, He returned to His cowherd village, Gokula.

Thus end the purports of the humble servant of His Divine Grace A. C. Bhaktivedanta Swami Prabhupāda to the Tenth Canto, Thirty-seventh Chapter, of the Śrīmad-Bhāgavatam, *entitled "The Killing of the Demons Keśī and Vyoma."*

CHAPTER THIRTY-EIGHT

Akrūra's Arrival in Vṛndāvana

This chapter describes Akrūra's trip from Mathurā to Vṛndāvana, his meditation on Kṛṣṇa and Balarāma along the way and the honor the two Lords showed Akrūra upon his arrival.

Early in the morning on the day after Kaṁsa had ordered him to bring Kṛṣṇa and Balarāma to Mathurā, Akrūra prepared his chariot and set off for Gokula. As he traveled, he thought as follows: "I am about to attain the great good fortune of seeing Śrī Kṛṣṇa's lotus feet, which are worshiped by Brahmā, Rudra and the other demigods. Although Kaṁsa is an enemy of the Supreme Lord and His devotees, still, it is by Kaṁsa's grace that I will get this great boon of seeing the Lord. When I first catch sight of His lotus feet, all my sinful reactions will be destroyed at once. I will descend from my chariot and fall at the feet of Kṛṣṇa and Balarāma, and even though I have been sent by Kaṁsa, the omniscient Śrī Kṛṣṇa will certainly harbor no animosity toward me." As Akrūra thus thought to himself, he arrived in Gokula at sunset. Alighting from his chariot in the cowherd pasture, he began rolling about in the dust in great ecstasy.

Then Akrūra continued on to Vraja. When he saw Kṛṣṇa and Balarāma he fell at Their lotus feet, and both the Lords embraced him. Afterward They brought him to Their residence, inquired from him about the comfort of his trip and honored him in various ways—offering him water for washing his feet, *arghya*, a seat and so forth. They relieved him of his fatigue by massaging his feet and served him a delicious banquet. Mahārāja Nanda also honored Akrūra with many sweet words.

TEXT 1

श्रीशुक उवाच

अक्रूरोऽपि च तां रात्रिं मधुपुर्यां महामतिः ।
उषित्वा रथमास्थाय प्रययौ नन्दगोकुलम् ॥१॥

śrī-śuka uvāca
akrūro 'pi ca tāṁ rātriṁ
madhu-puryāṁ mahā-matiḥ
uṣitvā ratham āsthāya
prayayau nanda-gokulam

śrī-śukaḥ uvāca—Śukadeva Gosvāmī said; *akrūraḥ*—Akrūra; *api ca*—and; *tām*—that; *rātrim*—night; *madhu-puryām*—in the city of Mathurā; *mahā-matiḥ*—high-minded; *uṣitvā*—remaining; *ratham*—his chariot; *āsthāya*—mounting; *prayayau*—he set off; *nanda-gokulam*—for the cowherd village of Nanda Mahārāja.

TRANSLATION

Śukadeva Gosvāmī said: After passing the night in the city of Mathurā, the high-minded Akrūra mounted his chariot and set off for the cowherd village of Nanda Mahārāja.

PURPORT

King Kaṁsa ordered Akrūra to go to Vṛndāvana on the Ekādaśī of the dark fortnight of the Vedic month of Phālguna. After spending the night in Mathurā, Akrūra left early the next day. That morning Nārada offered his prayers to Kṛṣṇa in Vṛndāvana, and in the afternoon the demon Vyoma was killed there. At dusk Akrūra entered the Lord's village.

TEXT 2

गच्छन् पथि महाभागो भगवत्यम्बुजेक्षणे ।
भक्तिं परामुपगत एवमेतदचिन्तयत् ॥२॥

gacchan pathi mahā-bhāgo
bhagavaty ambujekṣaṇe
bhaktiṁ parām upagata
evam etad acintayat

gacchan—traveling; *pathi*—along the road; *mahā-bhāgaḥ*—the greatly fortunate; *bhagavati*—for the Supreme Personality of Godhead; *ambuja-īkṣaṇe*—the lotus-eyed Lord; *bhaktim*—devotion; *parām*—exceptional; *upagataḥ*—he experienced; *evam*—thus; *etat*—this (as follows); *acintayat*—he thought.

TRANSLATION

As he traveled on the road, the great soul Akrūra felt tremendous devotion for the lotus-eyed Personality of Godhead, and thus he began to consider as follows.

TEXT 3

किं मयाचरितं भद्रं किं तप्तं परमं तपः ।
किं वाथाप्यर्हते दत्तं यद्द्रक्ष्याम्यद्य केशवम् ॥३॥

kiṁ mayācaritaṁ bhadraṁ
kiṁ taptaṁ paramaṁ tapaḥ
kiṁ vāthāpy arhate dattaṁ
yad drakṣyāmy adya keśavam

kim—what; *mayā*—by me; *ācaritam*—has been performed; *bhadram*—good works; *kim*—what; *taptam*—suffered; *paramam*—severe; *tapaḥ*—austerity; *kim*—what; *vā*—or else; *atha api*—otherwise; *arhate*—worship performed; *dattam*—charity given; *yat*—by which; *drakṣyāmi*—I am going to see; *adya*—today; *keśavam*—Lord Kṛṣṇa.

TRANSLATION

What pious deeds have I done, what severe austerities undergone, what worship performed or charity given so that today I will see Lord Keśava?

TEXT 4

ममैतद्दुर्लभं मन्य उत्तमःश्लोकदर्शनम् ।
विषयात्मनो यथा ब्रह्मकीर्तनं शूद्रजन्मनः ॥४॥

mamaitad durlabhaṁ manya
uttamaḥ-śloka-darśanam
viṣayātmano yathā brahma-
kīrtanaṁ śūdra-janmanaḥ

mama—my; *etat*—this; *durlabham*—difficult to achieve; *manye*—I consider; *uttamaḥ-śloka*—of the Supreme Lord, who is praised in the best poetry; *darśanam*—the audience; *viṣaya-ātmanaḥ*—for one who is absorbed in sense gratification; *yathā*—just as; *brahma*—of the *Vedas; kīrtanam*—chanting; *śūdra*—as a low-class man; *janmanaḥ*—by one who has taken his birth.

TRANSLATION

Since I am a materialistic person absorbed simply in sense gratification, I think it is as difficult for me to have gotten this opportunity to see Lord Uttamaḥśloka as it would be for one born a *śūdra* to be allowed to recite the Vedic *mantras*.

TEXT 5

मैवं ममाधमस्यापि स्यादेवाच्युतदर्शनम् ।
ह्रियमाणः कालनद्या क्वचित्तरति कश्चन ॥५॥

maivaṁ mamādhamasyāpi
syād evācyuta-darśanam
hriyamāṇaḥ kāla-nadyā
kvacit tarati kaścana

mā evam—I should not speak like this; *mama*—for me; *adhamasya*—who am most fallen; *api*—even; *syāt*—it may come about; *eva*—certainly; *acyuta*—of the infallible Lord; *darśanam*—the sight; *hriyamāṇaḥ*—being pulled along; *kāla*—of time; *nadyā*—by the river; *kvacit*—sometimes; *tarati*—crosses to the shore; *kaścana*—someone.

TRANSLATION

But enough of such talk! After all, even a fallen soul like me can have the chance to behold the infallible Supreme Lord, for one of the conditioned souls being swept along in the river of time may sometimes reach the shore.

TEXT 6

ममाद्यामंगलं नष्टं फलवांश्चैव मे भवः ।
यन्नमस्ये भगवतो योगिध्येयाङ्घ्रिपंकजम् ॥६॥

mamādyāmaṅgalaṁ naṣṭaṁ
phalavāṁś caiva me bhavaḥ
yan namasye bhagavato
yogi-dhyeyāṅghri-paṅkajam

mama—my; *adya*—today; *amaṅgalam*—inauspicious sinful reactions; *naṣṭam*—eradicated; *phala-vān*—fruitful; *ca*—and; *eva*—indeed; *me*—my; *bhavaḥ*—birth; *yat*—since; *namasye*—I am going to offer obeisances; *bhagavataḥ*—of the Supreme Lord; *yogi-dhyeya*—meditated upon by *yogīs; aṅghri*—to the feet; *paṅkajam*—lotuslike.

TRANSLATION

Today all my sinful reactions have been eradicated and my birth has become worthwhile, since I will offer my obeisances to the Supreme Lord's lotus feet, which mystic *yogīs* meditate upon.

TEXT 7

कंसो बताद्याकृत मेऽत्यनुग्रहं
द्रक्ष्येऽङ्घ्रिपद्मं प्रहितोऽमुना हरेः ।
कृतावतारस्य दुरत्ययं तमः
पूर्वेऽतरन् यन्नखमण्डलत्विषा ॥७॥

kaṁso batādyākṛta me 'ty-anugrahaṁ
drakṣye 'ṅghri-padmaṁ prahito 'munā hareḥ
kṛtāvatārasya duratyayaṁ tamaḥ
pūrve 'taran yan-nakha-maṇḍala-tviṣā

kaṁsaḥ—King Kaṁsa; *bata*—indeed; *adya*—today; *akṛta*—has done; *me*—toward me; *ati-anugraham*—an act of extreme kindness; *drakṣye*—I will see; *aṅghri-padmam*—the lotus feet; *prahitaḥ*—sent; *amunā*—by him; *hareḥ*—of the Supreme Personality of Godhead; *kṛta*—who has enacted; *avatārasya*—His descent to this world; *duratyayam*—insurmountable; *tamaḥ*—the darkness of material existence; *pūrve*—persons in the past; *ataran*—transcended; *yat*—whose; *nakha-maṇḍala*—of the orb of the toenails; *tviṣā*—by the effulgence.

TRANSLATION

Indeed, today King Kaṁsa has shown me extreme mercy by sending me to see the lotus feet of Lord Hari, who has now appeared in this world. Simply by the effulgence of His toenails, many souls in the past have transcended the insurmountable darkness of material existence and achieved liberation.

PURPORT

Akrūra noted how ironic it was that the envious, demoniac Kaṁsa had given him an extraordinary blessing by sending him to see the Supreme Lord Kṛṣṇa.

TEXT 8

यदर्चितं ब्रह्मभवादिभिः सुरैः
श्रिया च देव्या मुनिभिः ससात्वतैः ।
गोचारणायानुचरैश्चरद्वने
यद् गोपिकानां कुचकुंकुमांकितम् ॥८॥

yad arcitaṁ brahma-bhavādibhiḥ suraiḥ
śriyā ca devyā munibhiḥ sa-sātvataiḥ
go-cāraṇāyānucaraiś carad vane
yad gopikānāṁ kuca-kuṅkumāṅkitam

yat—which (lotus feet); *arcitam*—worshiped; *brahma-bhava*—by Brahmā and Śiva; *ādibhiḥ*—and other; *suraiḥ*—demigods; *śriyā*—by Śrī; *ca*—also; *devyā*—the goddess of fortune; *munibhiḥ*—by the sages; *sa-sātvataiḥ*—along with the devotees; *go*—the cows; *cāraṇāya*—for tending; *anucaraiḥ*—together with His companions; *carat*—moving about; *vane*—in the forest; *yat*—which; *gopikānām*—of the cowherd girls; *kuca*—from the breasts; *kuṅkuma*—by the red *kuṅkuma* powder; *aṅkitam*—marked.

TRANSLATION

Those lotus feet are worshiped by Brahmā, Śiva and all the other demigods, by the goddess of fortune, and also by the great sages and Vaiṣṇavas. Upon those lotus feet the Lord walks about

the forest while herding the cows with His companions, and those feet are smeared with the *kuṅkuma* from the *gopīs'* breasts.

TEXT 9

द्रक्ष्यामि नूनं सुकपोलनासिकं
स्मितावलोकारुणकञ्जलोचनम् ।
मुखं मुकुन्दस्य गुडालकावृतं
प्रदक्षिणं मे प्रचरन्ति वै मृगाः ॥९॥

drakṣyāmi nūnaṁ su-kapola-nāsikaṁ
smitāvalokāruṇa-kañja-locanam
mukhaṁ mukundasya guḍālakāvṛtaṁ
pradakṣiṇaṁ me pracaranti vai mṛgāḥ

drakṣyāmi—I am going to see; *nūnam*—for certain; *su*—beautiful; *kapola*—whose cheeks; *nāsikam*—and nose; *smita*—smiling; *avaloka*—with glances; *aruṇa*—reddish; *kañja*—lotuslike; *locanam*—the eyes; *mukham*—the face; *mukundasya*—of Lord Kṛṣṇa; *guḍa*—twisting; *alaka*—with hair; *āvṛtam*—framed; *pradakṣiṇam*—clockwise circumambulation; *me*—of me; *pracaranti*—are performing; *vai*—indeed; *mṛgāḥ*—the deer.

TRANSLATION

Surely I shall see the face of Lord Mukunda, since the deer are now walking past me on my right. That face, framed by His curly hair, is beautified by His attractive cheeks and nose, His smiling glances and His reddish lotus eyes.

PURPORT

Akrūra saw an auspicious omen—the passing of the deer on his right—and thus felt sure he would see the Supreme Lord Kṛṣṇa.

TEXT 10

अप्यद्य विष्णोर्मनुजत्वमीयुषो
भारावताराय भुवो निजेच्छया ।

लावण्यधाम्नो भवितोपलम्भनं
मह्यं न न स्यात्फलमञ्जसा दृशः ॥१०॥

apy adya viṣṇor manujatvam īyuṣo
bhārāvatārāya bhuvo nijecchayā
lāvaṇya-dhāmno bhavitopalambhanaṁ
mahyaṁ na na syāt phalam añjasā dṛśaḥ

api—furthermore; *adya*—today; *viṣṇoḥ*—of the Supreme Lord Viṣṇu; *manujatvam*—the form of a human being; *īyuṣaḥ*—who has assumed; *bhāra*—the burden; *avatārāya*—for diminishing; *bhuvaḥ*—of the earth; *nija*—by His own; *icchayā*—desire; *lāvaṇya*—of beauty; *dhāmnaḥ*—of the abode; *bhavitā*—there will be; *upalambhanam*—the perceiving; *mahyam*—for me; *na*—it is not the case; *na syāt*—that it will not happen; *phalam*—the fruit; *añjasā*—directly; *dṛśaḥ*—of sight.

TRANSLATION

I am going to see the Supreme Lord Viṣṇu, the reservoir of all beauty, who by His own sweet will has now assumed a humanlike form to relieve the earth of her burden. Thus there is no denying that my eyes will achieve the perfection of their existence.

TEXT 11

य ईक्षिताहंरहितोऽप्यसत्सतोः
स्वतेजसापास्ततमोभिदाभ्रमः ।
स्वमाययात्मन् रचितैस्तदीक्षया
प्राणाक्षधीभिः सदनेष्वभीयते ॥११॥

ya īkṣitāhaṁ-rahito 'py asat-satoḥ
sva-tejasāpāsta-tamo-bhidā-bhramaḥ
sva-māyayātman racitais tad-īkṣayā
prāṇākṣa-dhībhiḥ sadaneṣv abhīyate

yaḥ—who; *īkṣitā*—the witness; *aham*—false ego; *rahitaḥ*—devoid of; *api*—nevertheless; *asat-satoḥ*—of material products and causes; *sva-tejasā*—by His personal potency; *apāsta*—having dispelled; *tamaḥ*—the darkness of ignorance; *bhidā*—the idea of being separate; *bhramaḥ*—and bewilderment; *sva-māyayā*—by His material creative energy; *ātman*—within Himself; *racitaiḥ*—by those who are produced (the living entities); *tat-īkṣayā*—by His glancing upon that Māyā; *prāṇa*—by the vital airs; *akṣa*—the senses; *dhībhiḥ*—and intelligence; *sadaneṣu*—within the bodies of the living beings; *abhīyate*—His presence is surmised.

TRANSLATION

He is the witness of material cause and effect, yet He is always free from false identification with them. By His internal potency He dispels the darkness of separation and confusion. The individual souls in this world, who are manifested here when He glances upon His material creative energy, indirectly perceive Him in the activities of their life airs, senses and intelligence.

PURPORT

In this verse Akrūra establishes the all-powerful position of the Supreme Lord, whom he is about to see in Vṛndāvana. The false concept of separation from the Lord is described in the Eleventh Canto of the *Bhāgavatam* (11.2.37): *bhayaṁ dvitīyābhiniveśataḥ syād īśād apetasya viparyayo 'smṛtiḥ.* Although all existence emanates from the Absolute Truth, Kṛṣṇa, we imagine a "second thing," this material world, to be entirely separate from the Lord's existence. With this mentality, we try to exploit that "second thing" for our sense gratification. Thus the psychological underpinning of material life is the illusion that this world is somehow separate from God and therefore meant for our enjoyment.

It is ironic that the impersonal philosophers, in their radical renunciation of this world, claim it to be utterly false and totally separate from the Absolute. Unfortunately, this artificial attempt to divest this world of its divine nature, or, in other words, its relation to God, does not lead people to utterly reject it but rather to try to enjoy it. While it is true that this world is temporary and thus in one sense illusory, the mechanism of illusion is a spiritual potency of the Supreme Lord. Realizing this, we should immediately desist from any attempt to exploit this world; rather, we should recognize it as God's energy. We will actually give up our material desires only when we understand that this world belongs to God and is therefore not meant for our selfish gratification.

The word *abhīyate* here refers to a process of surmising the presence of the Lord through meditative introspection. This process is also described in the Second Canto of the *Bhāgavatam* (2.2.35),

bhagavān sarva-bhūteṣu
lakṣitaḥ svātmanā hariḥ
dṛśyair buddhy-ādibhir draṣṭā
lakṣaṇair anumāpakaiḥ

"The Personality of Godhead, Lord Śrī Kṛṣṇa, is in every living being along with the individual soul. And this fact is perceived and hypothesized in our acts of seeing and taking help from the intelligence."

Akrūra states that the Lord is free of the egoistic pride afflicting ordinary, embodied souls. Yet the Lord appears to be embodied like everyone else, and therefore someone might object to the statement that He is free of egoism. Śrīla Viśvanātha Cakravartī comments on this puzzle as follows: "How can we distinguish between being free of false ego and being afflicted by it? 'If a living entity is situated in a body,' [argues the objector,] 'he will encounter the unhappiness and confusion that occur within it, just as a person living in a house, whether he be attached to it or not, cannot avoid experiencing the darkness, warmth and cold that occur within it.' This objection is answered as follows: By His internal potency the Lord dispels the darkness of ignorance along with the separateness and bewilderment it produces."

TEXT 12

यस्याखिलामीवहभिः सुमंगलैः
वाचो विमिश्रा गुणकर्मजन्मभिः ।
प्राणन्ति शुम्भन्ति पुनन्ति वै जगत्
यास्तद्विरक्ताः शवशोभना मताः ॥१२॥

yasyākhilāmīva-habhiḥ su-maṅgalaiḥ
vāco vimiśrā guṇa-karma-janmabhiḥ
prāṇanti śumbhanti punanti vai jagat
yās tad-viraktāḥ śava-śobhanā matāḥ

yasya—of whom; *akhila*—all; *amīva*—sins; *habhiḥ*—which destroy; *su-maṅgalaiḥ*—most auspicious; *vācaḥ*—words; *vimiśrāḥ*—joined; *guṇa*—

with the qualities; *karma*—activities; *janmabhiḥ*—and incarnations; *prāṇanti*—they give life; *śumbhanti*—make beautiful; *punanti*—and purify; *vai*—indeed; *jagat*—the entire universe; *yāḥ*—which (words); *tat*—of these; *viraktāḥ*—devoid; *śava*—of a corpse; *śobhanāḥ*—(like) the decorating; *matāḥ*—considered.

TRANSLATION

All sins are destroyed and all good fortune is created by the Supreme Lord's qualities, activities and appearances, and words that describe them animate, beautify and purify the world. On the other hand, words bereft of His glories are like the decorations on a corpse.

PURPORT

Śrīla Śrīdhara Svāmī brings up the following possible objection: How can one who is devoid of ordinary ego, who is fully self-satisfied, engage in pastimes? The answer is given here. Lord Kṛṣṇa acts on the pure, spiritual platform for the pleasure of His loving devotees, not for any kind of mundane gratification.

TEXT 13

स चावतीर्णः किल सात्वतान्वये
स्वसेतुपालामरवर्यशर्मकृत् ।
यशो वितन्वन् व्रज आस्त ईश्वरो
गायन्ति देवा यदशेषमंगलम् ॥१३॥

sa cāvatīrṇaḥ kila sātvatānvaye
sva-setu-pālāmara-varya-śarma-kṛt
yaśo vitanvan vraja āsta īśvaro
gāyanti devā yad aśeṣa-maṅgalam

saḥ—He; *ca*—and; *avatīrṇaḥ*—having descended; *kila*—indeed; *sātvata*—of the Sātvatas; *anvaye*—in the dynasty; *sva*—His own; *setu*—codes of religion; *pāla*—who maintain; *amara-varya*—of the chief demigods; *śarma*—delight; *kṛt*—creating; *yaśaḥ*—His fame; *vitanvan*—spreading;

vraje—in Vraja; *āste*—is present; *īśvaraḥ*—the Supreme Lord; *gāyanti*—sing; *devāḥ*—the demigods; *yat*—of which (fame); *aśeṣa-maṅgalam*—all-auspicious.

TRANSLATION

That same Supreme Lord has descended into the dynasty of the Sātvatas to delight the exalted demigods, who maintain the principles of religion He has created. Residing in Vṛndāvana, He spreads His fame, which the demigods glorify in song and which brings auspiciousness to all.

TEXT 14

तं त्वद्य नूनं महतां गतिं गुरुं
त्रैलोक्यकान्तं दृशिमन्महोत्सवम् ।
रूपं दधानं श्रिय ईप्सितास्पदं
द्रक्ष्ये ममासन्नुषसः सुदर्शनाः ॥१४॥

taṁ tv adya nūnaṁ mahatāṁ gatiṁ guruṁ
trailokya-kāntaṁ dṛśiman-mahotsavam
rūpaṁ dadhānaṁ śriya īpsitāspadaṁ
drakṣye mamāsann uṣasaḥ su-darśanāḥ

tam—Him; *tu*—yet; *adya*—today; *nūnam*—certainly; *mahatām*—of great souls; *gatim*—the destination; *gurum*—and the spiritual master; *trai-lokya*—of all the three worlds; *kāntam*—the real beauty; *dṛśi-mat*—for all who have eyes; *mahā-utsavam*—a great festivity; *rūpam*—His personal form; *dadhānam*—exhibiting; *śriyaḥ*—of the goddess of fortune; *īpsita*—the desired; *āspadam*—place of shelter; *drakṣye*—I shall see; *mama*—my; *āsan*—have become; *uṣasaḥ*—the dawns; *su-darśanāḥ*—auspicious to see.

TRANSLATION

Today I shall certainly see Him, the goal and spiritual master of the great souls. Seeing Him brings jubilation to all who have eyes, for He is the true beauty of the universe. Indeed, His personal

form is the shelter desired by the goddess of fortune. Now all the dawns of my life have become auspicious.

TEXT 15

अथावरूढः सपदीशयो रथात्
प्रधानपुंसोश्चरणं स्वलब्धये ।
धिया धृतं योगिभिरप्यहं ध्रुवं
नमस्य आभ्यां च सखीन् वनौकसः ॥१५॥

athāvarūḍhaḥ sapadīśayo rathāt
pradhāna-puṁsoś caraṇaṁ sva-labdhaye
dhiyā dhṛtaṁ yogibhir apy ahaṁ dhruvaṁ
namasya ābhyāṁ ca sakhīn vanaukasaḥ

atha—then; *avarūḍhaḥ*—getting down; *sapadi*—at once; *īśayoḥ*—of the two Lords; *rathāt*—from my chariot; *pradhāna-puṁsoḥ*—of the Supreme Personalities; *caraṇam*—to the feet; *sva-labdhaye*—for the sake of self-realization; *dhiyā*—with their intelligence; *dhṛtam*—held on to; *yogibhiḥ*—by mystic *yogīs; api*—even; *aham*—I; *dhruvam*—surely; *namasye*—will bow down; *ābhyām*—with Them; *ca*—also; *sakhīn*—to the friends; *vana-okasaḥ*—to the residents of the forest.

TRANSLATION

Then I will at once alight from my chariot and bow down to the lotus feet of Kṛṣṇa and Balarāma, the Supreme Personalities of Godhead. Theirs are the same feet that great mystic *yogīs* striving for self-realization bear within their minds. I will also offer my obeisances to the Lords' cowherd boyfriends and to all the other residents of Vṛndāvana.

TEXT 16

अप्यङ्घ्रिमूले पतितस्य मे विभुः
शिरस्यधास्यन्निजहस्तपंकजम् ।
दत्ताभयं कालभुजांगरंहसा
प्रोद्वेजितानां शरणैषिणां नृणाम् ॥१६॥

apy aṅghri-mūle patitasya me vibhuḥ
śirasy adhāsyan nija-hasta-paṅkajam
dattābhayaṁ kāla-bhujāṅga-raṁhasā
prodvejitānāṁ śaraṇaiṣiṇāṁ nṛṇām

api—furthermore; *aṅghri*—of His feet; *mūle*—at the base; *patitasya*—who have fallen; *me*—of me; *vibhuḥ*—the almighty Lord; *śirasi*—upon the head; *adhāsyat*—will place; *nija*—His own; *hasta*—hand; *paṅkajam*—lotuslike; *datta*—which grants; *abhayam*—fearlessness; *kāla*—time; *bhuja-aṅga*—of the serpent; *raṁhasā*—by the swift force; *prodvejitānām*—who are greatly disturbed; *śaraṇa*—shelter; *eṣiṇām*—searching for; *nṛṇām*—to persons.

TRANSLATION

And when I have fallen at His feet, the almighty Lord will place His lotus hand upon my head. For those who seek shelter in Him because they are greatly disturbed by the powerful serpent of time, that hand removes all fear.

TEXT 17

समर्हणं यत्र निधाय कौशिकस्
तथा बलिश्चाप जगत्त्रयेन्द्रताम् ।
यद्वा विहारे व्रजयोषितां श्रमं
स्पर्शेन सौगन्धिकगन्ध्यपानुदत् ॥१७॥

samarhaṇaṁ yatra nidhāya kauśikas
tathā baliś cāpa jagat-trayendratām
yad vā vihāre vraja-yoṣitāṁ śramaṁ
sparśena saugandhika-gandhy apānudat

samarhaṇam—the respectful offering; *yatra*—into which; *nidhāya*—by placing; *kauśikaḥ*—Purandara; *tathā*—as well as; *baliḥ*—Bali Mahārāja; *ca*—also; *āpa*—attained; *jagat*—of the worlds; *traya*—three; *indratām*—rulership (as Indra, the King of heaven); *yat*—which (lotus hand of the Lord); *vā*—and; *vihāre*—during the pastimes (of the *rāsa* dance); *vraja-yoṣitām*—of the ladies of Vraja; *śramam*—the fatigue; *sparśena*—by their contact; *saugandhika*—like an aromatic flower; *gandhi*—fragrant; *apā-nudat*—wiped away.

TRANSLATION

By offering charity to that lotus hand, Purandara and Bali earned the status of Indra, King of heaven, and during the pleasure pastimes of the *rāsa* dance, when the Lord wiped away the *gopīs'* perspiration and removed their fatigue, the touch of their faces made that hand as fragrant as a sweet flower.

PURPORT

The *Purāṇas* call the lotus found in the Mānasa-sarovara Lake a *saugandhika*. Lord Kṛṣṇa's lotus hand acquired the fragrance of this flower by coming in contact with the beautiful faces of the *gopīs*. This specific incident, which occurred during the *rāsa-līlā*, is described in the Thirty-third Chapter of the Tenth Canto.

TEXT 18

न मय्युपैष्यत्यरिबुद्धिमच्युतः
कंसस्य दूतः प्रहितोऽपि विश्वदृक् ।
योऽन्तर्बहिश्चेतस एतदीहितं
क्षेत्रज्ञ ईक्षत्यमलेन चक्षुषा ॥१८॥

na mayy upaiṣyaty ari-buddhim acyutaḥ
kaṁsasya dūtaḥ prahito 'pi viśva-dṛk
yo 'ntar bahiś cetasa etad īhitaṁ
kṣetra-jña īkṣaty amalena cakṣuṣā

na—not; *mayi*—toward me; *upaiṣyati*—will He develop; *ari*—of being an enemy; *buddhim*—the attitude; *acyutaḥ*—the infallible Lord; *kaṁsasya*—of Kaṁsa; *dūtaḥ*—a messenger; *prahitaḥ*—sent; *api*—although; *viśva*—of everything; *dṛk*—the witness; *yaḥ*—who; *antaḥ*—inside; *bahiḥ*—and outside; *cetasaḥ*—of the heart; *etat*—this; *īhitam*—whatever is done; *kṣetra*—of the field (of the material body); *jñaḥ*—the knower; *īkṣati*—He sees; *amalena*—with perfect; *cakṣuṣā*—vision.

TRANSLATION

The infallible Lord will not consider me an enemy, even though Kaṁsa has sent me here as his messenger. After all, the omniscient Lord is the actual knower of the field of this material body, and with His perfect vision He witnesses, both externally and internally, all the endeavors of the conditioned soul's heart.

PURPORT

Being omniscient, Lord Kṛṣṇa knew that Akrūra was only externally a friend of Kaṁsa. Internally he was an eternal devotee of Lord Kṛṣṇa.

TEXT 19

अप्यङ्‌घ्रिमूलेऽवहितं कृताञ्जलिं
मामीक्षिता सस्मितमार्द्रया दृशा ।
सपद्यपध्वस्तसमस्तकिल्बिषो
वोढा मुदं वीतविशंक ऊर्जिताम् ॥१९॥

apy aṅghri-mūle 'vahitaṁ kṛtāñjaliṁ
mām īkṣitā sa-smitam ārdrayā dṛśā
sapady apadhvasta-samasta-kilbiṣo
voḍhā mudaṁ vīta-viśaṅka ūrjitām

api—and; *aṅghri*—of His feet; *mūle*—at the base; *avahitam*—fixed; *kṛta-añjalim*—with joined palms; *mām*—me; *īkṣitā*—will look upon; *sa-smitam*—smiling; *ārdrayā*—with an affectionate; *dṛśā*—glance; *sapadi*—immediately; *apadhvasta*—eradicated; *samasta*—all; *kilbiṣaḥ*—contamination; *voḍhā*—I will achieve; *mudam*—happiness; *vīta*—freed; *viśaṅkaḥ*—from doubt; *ūrjitām*—intense.

TRANSLATION

Thus He will cast His smiling, affectionate glance upon me as I remain fixed with joined palms, fallen in obeisances at His feet. Then all my contamination will at once be dispelled, and I will give up all doubts and feel the most intense bliss.

TEXT 20

सुहृत्तमं ज्ञातिमनन्यदैवतं
दोर्भ्यां बृहद्भ्यां परिरप्स्यतेऽथ माम् ।
आत्मा हि तीर्थीक्रियते तदैव मे
बन्धश्च कर्मात्मक उच्छ्वसित्यतः ॥२०॥

suhṛttamaṁ jñātim ananya-daivataṁ
dorbhyāṁ bṛhadbhyāṁ parirapsyate 'tha mām
ātmā hi tīrthī-kriyate tadaiva me
bandhaś ca karmātmaka ucchvasity ataḥ

suhṛt-tamam—the best of friends; *jñātim*—a family member; *ananya*—exclusive; *daivatam*—(having Him) as my object of worship; *dorbhyām*—with His two arms; *bṛhadbhyām*—large; *parirapsyate*—He will embrace; *atha*—thereupon; *mām*—me; *ātmā*—the body; *hi*—indeed; *tīrthī*—sanctified; *kriyate*—will become; *tadā eva*—exactly then; *me*—my; *bandhaḥ*—the bondage; *ca*—and; *karma-ātmakaḥ*—due to fruitive activity; *ucchvasiti*—will become slackened; *ataḥ*—as a result of this.

TRANSLATION

Recognizing me as an intimate friend and relative, Kṛṣṇa will embrace me with His mighty arms, instantly sanctifying my body and diminishing to nil all my material bondage, which is due to fruitive activities.

TEXT 21

लब्ध्वांगसंगं प्रणतं कृताञ्जलिं
मां वक्ष्यतेऽक्रूर ततेत्युरुश्रवाः ।
तदा वयं जन्मभृतो महीयसा
नैवादृतो यो धिगमुष्य जन्म तत् ॥२१॥

labdhvāṅga-saṅgaṁ praṇataṁ kṛtāñjaliṁ
māṁ vakṣyate 'krūra tatety uruśravāḥ

tadā vayaṁ janma-bhṛto mahīyasā
naivādṛto yo dhig amuṣya janma tat

labdhvā—having achieved; *aṅga-saṅgam*—physical contact; *praṇatam*—who am standing with head bowed; *kṛta-añjalim*—with palms joined together in supplication; *mām*—to me; *vakṣyate*—He will speak; *akrūra*—O Akrūra; *tata*—My dear relative; *iti*—in such words; *uru-śravāḥ*—Lord Kṛṣṇa, whose fame is vast; *tadā*—then; *vayam*—we; *janma-bhṛtaḥ*—our birth becoming successful; *mahīyasā*—by the greatest of all persons; *na*—not; *eva*—indeed; *ādṛtaḥ*—honored; *yaḥ*—who; *dhik*—to be pitied; *amuṣya*—his; *janma*—birth; *tat*—that.

TRANSLATION

Having been embraced by the all-famous Lord Kṛṣṇa, I will humbly stand before Him with bowed head and joined palms, and He will address me, "My dear Akrūra." At that very moment my life's purpose will be fulfilled. Indeed, the life of anyone whom the Supreme Personality fails to recognize is simply pitiable.

TEXT 22

न तस्य कश्चिद्दयितः सुहृत्तमो
न चाप्रियो द्वेष्य उपेक्ष्य एव वा ।
तथापि भक्तान् भजते यथा तथा
सुरद्रुमो यद्वदुपाश्रितोऽर्थदः ॥२२॥

na tasya kaścid dayitaḥ suhṛttamo
na cāpriyo dveṣya upekṣya eva vā
tathāpi bhaktān bhajate yathā tathā
sura-drumo yadvad upāśrito 'rtha-daḥ

na tasya—He does not have; *kaścit*—any; *dayitaḥ*—favorite; *suhṛt-tamaḥ*—best friend; *na ca*—nor; *apriyaḥ*—unfavored; *dveṣyaḥ*—hated; *upekṣyaḥ*—neglected; *eva*—indeed; *vā*—or; *tathā api*—still; *bhaktān*—with His devotees; *bhajate*—He reciprocates; *yathā*—as they are; *tathā*—accordingly; *sura-drumaḥ*—a heavenly desire tree; *yadvat*—just as; *upāśritaḥ*—taken shelter of; *artha*—desired benefits; *daḥ*—giving.

TRANSLATION

The Supreme Lord has no favorite and no dearmost friend, nor does He consider anyone undesirable, despicable or fit to be neglected. All the same, He lovingly reciprocates with His devotees in whatever manner they worship Him, just as the trees of heaven fulfill the desires of whoever approaches them.

PURPORT

The Lord says something similar in the *Bhagavad-gītā* (9.29):

samo 'haṁ sarva-bhūteṣu
na me dveṣyo 'sti na priyaḥ
ye bhajanti tu māṁ bhaktyā
mayi te teṣu cāpy aham

"I envy no one, nor am I partial to anyone. I am equal to all. But whoever renders service unto Me in devotion is a friend and is in Me, and I am also a friend to him."

Similarly, Lord Caitanya was as hard as a thunderbolt for those who envied Him, and as soft as a rose for those who understood His divine mission.

TEXT 23

किं चाग्रजो मावनतं यदूत्तमः
स्मयन् परिष्वज्य गृहीतमञ्जलौ ।
गृहं प्रवेष्याप्तसमस्तसत्कृतं
सम्प्रक्ष्यते कंसकृतं स्वबन्धुषु ॥२३॥

kiṁ cāgrajo māvanataṁ yadūttamaḥ
smayan pariṣvajya gṛhītam añjalau
gṛhaṁ praveṣyāpta-samasta-satkṛtaṁ
samprakṣyate kaṁsa-kṛtaṁ sva-bandhuṣu

kim ca—furthermore; *agra-jaḥ*—His elder brother (Lord Balarāma); *mā*—me; *avanatam*—who am standing with head bowed; *yadu-uttamaḥ*—the most exalted of the Yadus; *smayan*—smiling; *pariṣvajya*—embracing; *gṛhītam*—taken hold of; *añjalau*—by my joined palms; *gṛham*—His house; *praveṣya*—bringing into; *āpta*—who will have received; *samasta*—all; *sat-kṛtam*—signs of respect; *samprakṣyate*—He will inquire; *kaṁsa*—by Kaṁsa; *kṛtam*—what has been done; *sva-bandhuṣu*—to His family members.

TRANSLATION

And then Lord Kṛṣṇa's elder brother, the foremost of the Yadus, will grasp my joined hands while I am still standing with my head bowed, and after embracing me He will take me to His house. There He will honor me with all items of ritual welcome and inquire from me about how Kaṁsa has been treating His family members.

TEXT 24

श्रीशुक उवाच
इति सञ्चिन्तयन् कृष्णं श्वफल्कतनयोऽध्वनि ।
रथेन गोकुलं प्राप्तः सूर्यश्चास्तगिरिं नृप ॥२४॥

śrī-śuka uvāca
iti sañcintayan kṛṣṇaṁ
śvaphalka-tanayo 'dhvani
rathena gokulaṁ prāptaḥ
sūryaś cāsta-giriṁ nṛpa

śrī-śukaḥ uvāca—Śukadeva Gosvāmī said; *iti*—thus; *sañcintayan*—thinking deeply; *kṛṣṇam*—about Lord Kṛṣṇa; *śvaphalka-tanayaḥ*—Akrūra, the son of Śvaphalka; *adhvani*—on the road; *rathena*—by his chariot; *gokulam*—the village of Gokula; *prāptaḥ*—reached; *sūryaḥ*—the sun; *ca*—and; *asta-girim*—the mountain behind which the sun sets; *nṛpa*—O King (Parīkṣit).

TRANSLATION

Śukadeva Gosvāmī continued: My dear King, while the son of Śvaphalka, traveling on the road, thus meditated deeply on Śrī Kṛṣṇa, he reached Gokula as the sun was beginning to set.

PURPORT

Śrīla Śrīdhara Svāmī comments that although Akrūra did not even notice the road, being deeply absorbed in meditation on Lord Kṛṣṇa, he still reached Gokula on his chariot.

TEXT 25

पदानि तस्याखिललोकपाल-
किरीटजुष्टामलपादरेणोः ।
ददर्श गोष्ठे क्षितिकौतुकानि
विलक्षितान्यब्जयवांकुशाद्यैः ॥२५॥

padāni tasyākhila-loka-pāla-
kirīṭa-juṣṭāmala-pāda-reṇoḥ
dadarśa goṣṭhe kṣiti-kautukāni
vilakṣitāny abja-yavāṅkuśādyaiḥ

padāni—the footprints; *tasya*—of Him; *akhila*—all; *loka*—of the planets; *pāla*—by the superintendents; *kirīṭa*—upon their crowns; *juṣṭa*—placed; *amala*—pure; *pāda*—of His feet; *reṇoḥ*—the dust; *dadarśa*—he (Akrūra) saw; *goṣṭhe*—in the cow pasture; *kṣiti*—the earth; *kautukāni*—wonderfully decorating; *vilakṣitāni*—distinguishable; *abja*—by the lotus; *yava*—barleycorn; *aṅkuśa*—elephant goad; *ādyaiḥ*—and so on.

TRANSLATION

In the cowherd pasture Akrūra saw the footprints of those feet whose pure dust the rulers of all the planets in the universe hold on their crowns. Those footprints of the Lord, distinguished by such marks as the lotus, barleycorn and elephant goad, made the ground wonderfully beautiful.

TEXT 26

तद्दर्शनाह्लादविवृद्धसम्भमः
प्रेम्णोर्ध्वरोमाश्रुकलाकुलेक्षणः ।

रथादवस्कन्द्य स तेष्वचेष्टत
प्रभोरमून्यङ्घ्रिरजांस्यहो इति ॥२६॥

tad-darśanāhlāda-vivṛddha-sambhramaḥ
premṇordhva-romāśru-kalākulekṣaṇaḥ
rathād avaskandya sa teṣv aceṣṭata
prabhor amūny aṅghri-rajāṁsy aho iti

tat—of Lord Kṛṣṇa's footprints; *darśana*—from the sight; *āhlāda*—by the ecstasy; *vivṛddha*—greatly increased; *sambhramaḥ*—whose agitation; *premṇā*—out of pure love; *ūrdhva*—standing erect; *roma*—whose bodily hairs; *aśru-kalā*—with teardrops; *ākula*—filled; *īkṣaṇaḥ*—whose eyes; *rathāt*—from the chariot; *avaskandya*—getting down; *saḥ*—he, Akrūra; *teṣu*—among those (footprints); *aceṣṭata*—rolled about; *prabhoḥ*—of my master; *amūni*—these; *aṅghri*—from the feet; *rajāṁsi*—particles of dust; *aho*—ah; *iti*—with these words.

TRANSLATION

Increasingly agitated by ecstasy at seeing the Lord's footprints, his bodily hairs standing on end because of his pure love, and his eyes filled with tears, Akrūra jumped down from his chariot and began rolling about among those footprints, exclaiming, "Ah, this is the dust from my master's feet!"

TEXT 27

देहंभृतामियानर्थो हित्वा दम्भं भियं शुचम् ।
सन्देशाद्यो हरेर्लिंगदर्शनश्रवणादिभिः ॥२७॥

dehaṁ-bhṛtām iyān artho
hitvā dambhaṁ bhiyaṁ śucam
sandeśād yo harer liṅga-
darśana-śravaṇādibhiḥ

deham-bhṛtām—of embodied beings; *iyān*—this much; *arthaḥ*—the goal of life; *hitvā*—giving up; *dambham*—pride; *bhiyam*—fear; *śucam*—and sorrow; *sandeśāt*—beginning from his being ordered (by Kaṁsa);

yaḥ—which; *hareḥ*—of Lord Kṛṣṇa; *liṅga*—the signs; *darśana*—with the seeing; *śravaṇa*—hearing about; *ādibhiḥ*—and so on.

TRANSLATION

The very goal of life for all embodied beings is this ecstasy, which Akrūra experienced when, upon receiving Kaṁsa's order, he put aside all pride, fear and lamentation and absorbed himself in seeing, hearing and describing the things that reminded him of Lord Kṛṣṇa.

PURPORT

Śrīla Viśvanātha Cakravartī explains that Akrūra gave up fear by openly showing his love and reverence for Kṛṣṇa, even though he or his family might have been punished by the angry Kaṁsa. Akrūra gave up his pride in being an aristocratic member of society and worshiped the cowherd residents of the simple village of Vṛndāvana. And he gave up lamenting for his house, wife and family, which were in danger from King Kaṁsa. Giving up all these things, he rolled in the dust of the lotus feet of God.

TEXTS 28–33

ददर्श कृष्णं रामं च व्रजे गोदोहनं गतौ ।
पीतनीलाम्बरधरौ शरदम्बुरुहेक्षणौ ॥२८॥
किशोरौ श्यामलश्वेतौ श्रीनिकेतौ बृहद्भुजौ ।
सुमुखौ सुन्दरवरौ बलद्विरदविक्रमौ ॥२९॥
ध्वजवज्रांकुशाम्भोजैश्चिह्नितैरङ्घ्रिभिर्व्रजम् ।
शोभयन्तौ महात्मानौ सानुक्रोशस्मितेक्षणौ ॥३०॥
उदाररुचिरक्रीडौ स्रग्विणौ वनमालिनौ ।
पुण्यगन्धानुलिप्तांगौ स्नातौ विरजवाससौ ॥३१॥
प्रधानपुरुषावाद्यौ जगद्धेतू जगत्पती ।
अवतीर्णौ जगत्यर्थे स्वांशेन बलकेशवौ ॥३२॥
दिशो वितिमिरा राजन् कुर्वाणौ प्रभया स्वया ।
यथा मारकतः शैलो रौप्यश्च कनकाचितौ ॥३३॥

dadarśa kṛṣṇaṁ rāmaṁ ca
vraje go-dohanaṁ gatau
pīta-nīlāmbara-dharau
śarad-amburuhekṣaṇau

kiśorau śyāmala-śvetau
śrī-niketau bṛhad-bhujau
su-mukhau sundara-varau
bala-dvirada-vikramau

dhvaja-vajrāṅkuśāmbhojaiś
cihnitair aṅghribhir vrajam
śobhayantau mahātmānau
sānukrośa-smitekṣaṇau

udāra-rucira-krīḍau
sragviṇau vana-mālinau
puṇya-gandhānuliptāṅgau
snātau viraja-vāsasau

pradhāna-puruṣāv ādyau
jagad-dhetū jagat-patī
avatīrṇau jagaty-arthe
svāṁśena bala-keśavau

diśo vitimirā rājan
kurvāṇau prabhayā svayā
yathā mārakataḥ śailo
raupyaś ca kanakācitau

dadarśa—he saw; *kṛṣṇam rāmam ca*—Lord Kṛṣṇa and Lord Balarāma; *vraje*—in the village of Vraja; *go*—the cows; *dohanam*—to the place of milking; *gatau*—gone; *pīta-nīla*—yellow and blue; *ambara*—clothes; *dharau*—wearing; *śarat*—of the autumn season; *amburuha*—like lotuses; *īkṣaṇau*—whose eyes; *kiśorau*—the two youths; *śyāmala-śvetau*—dark-blue and white; *śrī-niketau*—the shelters of the goddess of fortune; *bṛhat*—mighty; *bhujau*—whose arms; *su-mukhau*—with attractive faces; *sundara-varau*—the most beautiful; *bala*—young; *dvirada*—like an elephant; *vikramau*—whose walking; *dhvaja*—by the flag; *vajra*—lightning bolt; *aṅkuśa*—elephant goad; *ambhojaiḥ*—and lotus; *cihnitaiḥ*—marked; *aṅghribhiḥ*—with Their feet; *vrajam*—the cow pasture; *śobhayantau*—beautifying; *mahā-ātmānau*—great souls; *sa-anukrośa*—compassionate; *smita*—and smiling; *īkṣaṇau*—whose glances; *udāra*—magnanimous; *rucira*—and attractive; *krīḍau*—whose pastimes; *srak-vinau*—wearing jeweled necklaces; *vana-mālinau*—and wearing flower garlands; *puṇya*—auspicious; *gandha*—with fragrant substances; *anulipta*—anointed; *aṅgau*—whose limbs; *snātau*—freshly bathed; *viraja*—spotless; *vāsasau*—whose garments; *pradhāna*—the most exalted; *puruṣau*—two persons; *ādyau*—primeval; *jagat-dhetū*—the causes of the universe; *jagat-patī*—the masters of the universe; *avatīrṇau*—having descended; *jagati-arthe*—for the benefit of the universe; *sva-aṁśena*—in Their distinct forms; *bala-keśavau*—Balarāma and Keśava; *diśaḥ*—all the directions; *vitimirāḥ*—free from darkness; *rājan*—O King; *kurvāṇau*—making; *prabhayā*—with the effulgence; *svayā*—Their own; *yathā*—as; *mārakataḥ*—made of emerald; *śailaḥ*—a mountain; *raupyaḥ*—one made of silver; *ca*—and; *kanaka*—with gold; *acitau*—both decorated.

TRANSLATION

Akrūra then saw Kṛṣṇa and Balarāma in the village of Vraja, going to milk the cows. Kṛṣṇa wore yellow garments, Balarāma blue, and Their eyes resembled autumnal lotuses. One of those two mighty-armed youths, the shelters of the goddess of fortune, had a dark-blue complexion, and the other's was white. With Their fine-featured faces They were the most beautiful of all persons. As they walked with the gait of young elephants, glancing about with compassionate smiles, those two exalted personalities beautified the cow pasture with the impressions of Their feet, which bore the marks of the flag, lightning bolt, elephant goad and lotus. The two Lords, whose pastimes are most magnanimous and attractive, were ornamented with jeweled necklaces and flower garlands, anointed with auspicious, fragrant substances, freshly bathed, and dressed in spotless raiment. They were the primeval Supreme Personalities, the masters and original causes of the universes, who had for the welfare of the earth now descended in Their distinct forms of Keśava and Balarāma. O King Parīkṣit, They resembled two gold-bedecked mountains, one of emerald and the other of silver, as with Their effulgence They dispelled the sky's darkness in all directions.

TEXT 34

रथात्तूर्णमवप्लुत्य सोऽक्रूरः स्नेहविह्वलः ।
पपात चरणोपान्ते दण्डवद् रामकृष्णयोः ॥३४॥

rathāt tūrṇam avaplutya
so 'krūraḥ sneha-vihvalaḥ
papāta caraṇopānte
daṇḍa-vad rāma-kṛṣṇayoḥ

rathāt—from his chariot; *tūrṇam*—quickly; *avaplutya*—climbing down; *saḥ*—he; *akrūraḥ*—Akrūra; *sneha*—by affection; *vihvalaḥ*—overcome; *papāta*—fell; *caraṇa-upānte*—next to the feet; *daṇḍa-vat*—flat like a rod; *rāma-kṛṣṇayoḥ*—of Balarāma and Kṛṣṇa.

TRANSLATION

Akrūra, overwhelmed with affection, quickly jumped down from his chariot and fell at the feet of Kṛṣṇa and Balarāma like a rod.

TEXT 35

भगवद्दर्शनाह्लादबाष्पपर्याकुलेक्षणः ।
पुलकाचितांग औत्कण्ठयात्स्वाख्याने नाशकन्नृप ॥३५॥

bhagavad-darśanāhlāda-
bāṣpa-paryākulekṣaṇaḥ
pulakācitāṅga autkaṇṭhyāt
svākhyāne nāśakan nṛpa

bhagavat—the Supreme Personality of Godhead; *darśana*—because of seeing; *āhlāda*—due to the joy; *bāṣpa*—with tears; *paryākula*—overflowing; *īkṣaṇaḥ*—whose eyes; *pulaka*—with eruptions; *ācita*—marked; *aṅgaḥ*—whose limbs; *autkaṇṭhyāt*—from eagerness; *sva-ākhyāne*—to announce himself; *na aśakat*—he was not able; *nṛpa*—O King.

TRANSLATION

The joy of seeing the Supreme Lord flooded Akrūra's eyes with tears and decorated his limbs with eruptions of ecstasy. He felt such eagerness that he could not speak to present himself, O King.

TEXT 36

भगवांस्तमभिप्रेत्य रथांगांकितपाणिना ।
परिरेभेऽभ्युपाकृष्य प्रीतः प्रणतवत्सलः ॥३६॥

bhagavāṁs tam abhipretya
rathāṅgāṅkita-pāṇinā
parirebhe 'bhyupākṛṣya
prītaḥ praṇata-vatsalaḥ

bhagavān—the Supreme Lord; *tam*—him, Akrūra; *abhipretya*—recognizing; *ratha-aṅga*—with a chariot wheel; *aṅkita*—marked; *pāṇinā*—by His hand; *parirebhe*—He embraced; *abhyupākṛṣya*—pulling near; *prītaḥ*—pleased; *praṇata*—to those who are surrendered; *vatsalaḥ*—who is benignly disposed.

TRANSLATION

Recognizing Akrūra, Lord Kṛṣṇa drew him close with His hand, which bears the sign of the chariot wheel, and then embraced him. Kṛṣṇa felt pleased, for He is always benignly disposed toward His surrendered devotees.

PURPORT

According to the *ācāryas*, by extending His hand, marked with the chariot wheel, or *cakra*, Lord Kṛṣṇa indicated His ability to kill Kaṁsa.

TEXTS 37–38

संकर्षणश्च प्रणतमुपगुह्य महामनाः ।
गृहीत्वा पाणिना पाणी अनयत्सानुजो गृहम् ॥३७॥

पृष्ट्वाथ स्वागतं तस्मै निवेद्य च वरासनम् ।
प्रक्षाल्य विधिवत्पादौ मधुपर्कार्हणमाहरत् ॥३८॥

saṅkarṣaṇaś ca praṇatam
upaguhya mahā-manāḥ
gṛhītvā pāṇinā pāṇī
anayat sānujo gṛham

pṛṣṭvātha sv-āgataṁ tasmai
nivedya ca varāsanam
prakṣālya vidhi-vat pādau
madhu-parkārhaṇam āharat

saṅkarṣaṇaḥ—Lord Balarāma; *ca*—and; *praṇatam*—who was standing with his head bowed; *upaguhya*—embracing; *mahā-manāḥ*—magnanimous; *gṛhītvā*—taking hold of; *pāṇinā*—with His hand; *pāṇī*—his two hands; *anayat*—He took; *sa-anujaḥ*—with His younger brother (Lord Kṛṣṇa); *gṛham*—to His residence; *pṛṣṭvā*—inquiring; *atha*—then; *su-āgatam*—about the comfort of his trip; *tasmai*—to him; *nivedya*—offering; *ca*—and; *vara*—excellent; *āsanam*—a seat; *prakṣālya*—washing; *vidhi-vat*—in accordance with scriptural injunctions; *pādau*—his feet; *madhu-parka*—honey mixed with milk; *arhaṇam*—as a respectful offering; *āharat*—He brought.

TRANSLATION

As Akrūra stood with his head bowed, Lord Saṅkarṣaṇa [Balarāma] grasped his joined hands, and then He took him to His house in the company of Lord Kṛṣṇa. After inquiring from Akrūra whether his trip had been comfortable, Balarāma offered him a first-class seat, bathed his feet in accordance with the injunctions of scripture and respectfully served him milk with honey.

TEXT 39

निवेद्य गां चातिथये संवाह्य श्रान्तमादृतः ।
अन्नं बहुगुणं मेध्यं श्रद्धयोपाहरद्विभुः ॥३९॥

nivedya gāṁ cātithaye
saṁvāhya śrāntam ādṛtaḥ
annaṁ bahu-guṇaṁ medhyaṁ
śraddhayopāharad vibhuḥ

nivedya—presenting in charity; *gām*—a cow; *ca*—and; *atithaye*—to the guest; *saṁvāhya*—massaging; *śrāntam*—who was tired; *ādṛtaḥ*—with great respect; *annam*—cooked food; *bahu-guṇam*—of various tastes; *medhyam*—suitable for offering; *śraddhayā*—faithfully; *upāharat*—offered; *vibhuḥ*—the almighty Lord.

TRANSLATION

The almighty Lord Balarāma presented Akrūra with the gift of a cow, massaged his feet to relieve him of fatigue and then with great respect and faith fed him suitably prepared food of various fine tastes.

PURPORT

According to Śrīla Viśvanātha Cakravartī, Akrūra went to Kṛṣṇa's and Balarāma's house on the twelfth lunar day, on which one should not break a fast at night. However, Akrūra dispensed with this formality because he was eager to receive food in the Lord's house.

TEXT 40

तस्मै भुक्तवते प्रीत्या रामः परमधर्मवित् ।
मुखवासैर्गन्धमाल्यैः परां प्रीतिं व्यधात्पुनः ॥४०॥

tasmai bhuktavate prītyā
rāmaḥ parama-dharma-vit
mukha-vāsair gandha-mālyaiḥ
parāṁ prītiṁ vyadhāt punaḥ

tasmai—to him; *bhuktavate*—who had finished eating; *prītyā*—affectionately; *rāmaḥ*—Lord Balarāma; *parama*—the supreme; *dharma-vit*—knower of religious principles; *mukha-vāsaiḥ*—with aromatic herbs for sweetening the mouth; *gandha*—with perfume; *mālyaiḥ*—and flower garlands; *parām*—the highest; *prītim*—satisfaction; *vyadhāt*—arranged; *punaḥ*—further.

TRANSLATION

When Akrūra had eaten to his satisfaction, Lord Balarāma, the supreme knower of religious duties, offered him aromatic herbs for sweetening his mouth, along with fragrances and flower garlands. Thus Akrūra once again enjoyed the highest pleasure.

TEXT 41

पप्रच्छ सत्कृतं नन्दः कथं स्थ निरनुग्रहे ।
कंसे जीवति दाशार्ह सौनपाला इवावयः ॥४१॥

papraccha sat-kṛtaṁ nandaḥ
kathaṁ stha niranugrahe
kaṁse jīvati dāśārha
sauna-pālā ivāvayaḥ

papraccha—asked; *sat-kṛtam*—who had been honored; *nandaḥ*—Nanda Mahārāja; *katham*—how; *stha*—you are living; *niranugrahe*—the merciless; *kaṁse*—Kaṁsa; *jīvati*—while he is alive; *dāśārha*—O descendant of Daśārha; *sauna*—an animal slaughterer; *pālāḥ*—whose keeper; *iva*—just like; *avayaḥ*—sheep.

TRANSLATION

Nanda Mahārāja asked Akrūra: O descendant of Daśārha, how are all of you maintaining yourselves while that merciless Kaṁsa remains alive? You are just like sheep under the care of a butcher.

TEXT 42

योऽवधीत्स्वस्वसुस्तोकान् क्रोशन्त्या असुतृप् खलः ।
किं नु स्वित्तत्प्रजानां वः कुशलं विमृशामहे ॥४२॥

yo 'vadhīt sva-svasus tokān
krośantyā asu-tṛp khalaḥ
kiṁ nu svit tat-prajānāṁ vaḥ
kuśalaṁ vimṛśāmahe

yaḥ—who; *avadhīt*—killed; *sva*—of his own; *svasuḥ*—sister; *tokān*—the babies; *krośantyāḥ*—who was crying; *asu-tṛp*—self-indulgent; *khalaḥ*—cruel; *kim nu*—what then; *svit*—indeed; *tat*—his; *prajānām*—of the subjects; *vaḥ*—you; *kuśalam*—well-being; *vimṛśāmahe*—we should conjecture.

TRANSLATION

That cruel, self-serving Kaṁsa murdered the infants of his own sister in her presence, even as she cried in anguish. So why should we even ask about the well-being of you, his subjects?

TEXT 43

इत्थं सूनृतया वाचा नन्देन सुसभाजितः ।
अक्रूरः परिपृष्टेन जहावध्वपरिश्रमम् ॥४३॥

itthaṁ sūnṛtayā vācā
nandena su-sabhājitaḥ
akrūraḥ paripṛṣṭena
jahāv adhva-pariśramam

ittham—thus; *sū-nṛtayā*—very true and pleasing; *vācā*—with words; *nandena*—by Nanda Mahārāja; *su*—well; *sabhājitaḥ*—honored; *akrūraḥ*—Akrūra; *paripṛṣṭena*—by the inquiry; *jahau*—put aside; *adhva*—of the road; *pariśramam*—his fatigue.

TRANSLATION

Honored by Nanda Mahārāja with these true and pleasing words of inquiry, Akrūra forgot the fatigue of his journey.

Thus end the purports of the humble servant of His Divine Grace A. C. Bhaktivedanta Swami Prabhupāda to the Tenth Canto, Thirty-eighth Chapter, of the Śrīmad-Bhāgavatam, *entitled "Akrūra's Arrival in Vṛndāvana."*

CHAPTER THIRTY-NINE

Akrūra's Vision

This chapter describes how Akrūra informed Lord Kṛṣṇa and Lord Balarāma of Kaṁsa's plans and his activities in Mathurā; what the *gopīs* cried out in distress when Kṛṣṇa left for Mathurā; and also the vision of Lord Viṣṇu's abode that Akrūra saw within the water of the Yamunā.

When Kṛṣṇa and Balarāma offered Akrūra great respect and comfortably seated him on a couch, he felt that all the desires he had reflected on while traveling to Vṛndāvana were now fulfilled. After the evening meal, Kṛṣṇa asked Akrūra whether his trip had been peaceful and whether he was well. The Lord also inquired about how Kaṁsa was behaving toward their family members, and finally He asked why Akrūra had come.

Akrūra described how Kaṁsa had been persecuting the Yādavas, what Nārada had told Kaṁsa and how Kaṁsa had been treating Vasudeva cruelly. Akrūra also spoke of Kaṁsa's desire to bring Kṛṣṇa and Balarāma to Mathurā to kill Them on the pretext of Their seeing the bow sacrifice and engaging in a wrestling match. Kṛṣṇa and Balarāma laughed out loud when They heard this. They went to Their father, Nanda, and informed him of Kaṁsa's orders. Nanda then issued an order to all the residents of Vraja that they should collect various offerings for the King and prepare to go to Mathurā.

The young *gopīs* were extremely upset to hear that Kṛṣṇa and Balarāma would be going to Mathurā. They lost all external awareness and began to remember Kṛṣṇa's pastimes. Condemning the creator for separating them from Him, they began to lament. They said that Akrūra did not deserve his name (*a,* "not"; *krūra,* "cruel"), since he was so cruel to be taking away their dearmost Kṛṣṇa. "It must be that fate is against us," they lamented, "because otherwise the elders of Vraja would have forbidden Kṛṣṇa to leave. So let us forget our shyness and try to stop Lord Mādhava from going." With these words the young cowherd girls began to chant Kṛṣṇa's names and cry.

But even as they wept, Akrūra began taking Kṛṣṇa and Balarāma to Mathurā in his chariot. The cowherd men of Gokula followed behind on their wagons, and the young *gopīs* also walked behind for some distance, but then they became placated by Kṛṣṇa's glances and gestures and pacified by a message from Him that said "I will return." With their minds completely absorbed in Kṛṣṇa, the cowherd girls stood as still as figures in a painting until they could no longer see the chariot's flag or the dust cloud being raised on the road. Then, chanting Kṛṣṇa's glories all the while, they despondently returned to their homes.

Akrūra halted the chariot at the bank of the Yamunā so Kṛṣṇa and Balarāma could perform a ritual of purification and drink some water. After the two Lords had gotten back into the chariot, Akrūra took Their permission to bathe in the Yamunā. As he recited Vedic *mantras,* he was startled to see the two Lords standing in the water. Akrūra came out of the river and returned to the chariot—where he saw the Lords still sitting. Then he returned to the water to find out if the two figures he had seen there were real or not.

What Akrūra saw in the water was four-armed Lord Vāsudeva. His complexion was dark blue like a fresh raincloud, He wore yellow garments and He lay on the lap of thousand-hooded Ananta Śeṣa. Lord Vāsudeva was receiving the prayers of perfected beings, celestial serpents and demons, and He was encircled by His personal attendants. Serving Him were His many potencies, such as Śrī, Puṣṭi and Ilā, while Brahmā and other demigods sang His praises. Akrūra rejoiced at this vision and, joining his palms in supplication, began to pray to the Supreme Lord in a voice choked with emotion.

TEXT 1

श्रीशुक उवाच

सुखोपविष्टः पर्यंके रामकृष्णोरुमानितः ।
लेभे मनोरथान् सर्वान् पथि यान् स चकार ह ॥१॥

śrī-śuka uvāca
sukhopaviṣṭaḥ paryaṅke
rāma-kṛṣṇoru-mānitaḥ
lebhe manorathān sarvān
pathi yān sa cakāra ha

śrī-śukaḥ uvāca—Śukadeva Gosvāmī said; *sukha*—comfortably; *upaviṣṭaḥ*—seated; *paryaṅke*—on a couch; *rāma-kṛṣṇa*—by Lord Balarāma and Lord Kṛṣṇa; *uru*—very much; *mānitaḥ*—honored; *lebhe*—he attained; *manaḥ-rathān*—his desires; *sarvān*—all; *pathi*—on the road; *yān*—which; *saḥ*—he; *cakāra ha*—had manifested.

TRANSLATION

Śukadeva Gosvāmī said: Having been honored so much by Lord Balarāma and Lord Kṛṣṇa, Akrūra, seated comfortably on a couch, felt that all the desires he had contemplated on the road were now fulfilled.

TEXT 2

किमलभ्यं भगवति प्रसन्ने श्रीनिकेतने ।
तथापि तत्परा राजन्न हि वाञ्छन्ति किञ्चन ॥२॥

kim alabhyaṁ bhagavati
prasanne śrī-niketane
tathāpi tat-parā rājan
na hi vāñchanti kiñcana

kim—what; *alabhyam*—is unattainable; *bhagavati*—the Supreme Lord; *prasanne*—being satisfied; *śrī*—of the goddess of fortune; *niketane*—the resting place; *tathā api*—nevertheless; *tat-parāḥ*—those who are devoted to Him; *rājan*—O King (Parīkṣit); *na*—do not; *hi*—indeed; *vāñchanti*—desire; *kiñcana*—anything.

TRANSLATION

My dear King, what is unattainable for one who has satisfied the Supreme Personality of Godhead, the shelter of the goddess of fortune? Even so, those who are dedicated to His devotional service never want anything from Him.

TEXT 3

सायन्तनाशनं कृत्वा भगवान् देवकीसुतः ।
सुहृत्सु वृत्तं कंसस्य पप्रच्छान्यच्चिकीर्षितम् ॥३॥

sāyantanāśanaṁ kṛtvā
bhagavān devakī-sutaḥ
suhṛtsu vṛttaṁ kaṁsasya
papracchānyac cikīrṣitam

sāyantana—of the evening; *aśanam*—the dining; *kṛtvā*—having done; *bhagavān*—the Supreme Lord; *devakī-sutaḥ*—the son of Devakī; *suhṛtsu*—toward His well-wishing relatives and friends; *vṛttam*—about the behavior; *kaṁsasya*—of Kaṁsa; *papraccha*—He inquired; *anyat*—other; *cikīrṣitam*—intentions.

TRANSLATION

After the evening meal, Lord Kṛṣṇa, the son of Devakī, asked Akrūra how Kaṁsa was treating their dear relatives and friends and what the King was planning to do.

TEXT 4

श्रीभगवानुवाच
तात सौम्यागतः कच्चित्स्वागतं भद्रमस्तु वः ।
अपि स्वज्ञातिबन्धूनामनमीवमनामयम् ॥४॥

śrī-bhagavān uvāca
tāta saumyāgataḥ kaccit
sv-āgataṁ bhadram astu vaḥ
api sva-jñāti-bandhūnām
anamīvam anāmayam

śrī-bhagavān uvāca—the Supreme Personality of Godhead said; *tāta*—O uncle; *saumya*—O gentle one; *āgataḥ*—arrived; *kaccit*—whether; *su-āgatam*—welcome; *bhadram*—all good; *astu*—may there be; *vaḥ*—for you; *api*—whether; *sva*—for your well-wishing friends; *jñāti*—intimate relatives; *bandhūnām*—and other family members; *anamīvam*—freedom from unhappiness; *anāmayam*—freedom from disease.

TRANSLATION

The Supreme Lord said: My dear, gentle Uncle Akrūra, was your trip here comfortable? May all good fortune be yours. Are

our well-wishing friends and our relatives, both close and distant, happy and in good health?

TEXT 5

किं नु नः कुशलं पृच्छे एधमाने कुलामये ।
कंसे मातुलनाम्नांग स्वानां नस्तत्प्रजासु च ॥५॥

kiṁ nu naḥ kuśalaṁ pṛcche
edhamāne kulāmaye
kaṁse mātula-nāmnāṅga
svānāṁ nas tat-prajāsu ca

kim—what; *nu*—rather; *naḥ*—our; *kuśalam*—about the well-being; *pṛcche*—I should inquire; *edhamāne*—when he is prospering; *kula*—of our family; *āmaye*—the disease; *kaṁse*—King Kaṁsa; *mātula-nāmnā*—by the name "maternal uncle"; *aṅga*—my dear; *svānām*—of the relatives; *naḥ*—our; *tat*—his; *prajāsu*—of the citizens; *ca*—and.

TRANSLATION

But, my dear Akrūra, as long as King Kaṁsa—that disease of our family who goes by the name "maternal uncle"—is still prospering, why should I even bother to ask about the well-being of our family members and his other subjects?

TEXT 6

अहो अस्मदभूद् भूरि पित्रोर्वृजिनमार्ययोः ।
यद्धेतोः पुत्रमरणं यद्धेतोर्बन्धनं तयोः ॥६॥

aho asmad abhūd bhūri
pitror vṛjinam āryayoḥ
yad-dhetoḥ putra-maraṇaṁ
yad-dhetor bandhanaṁ tayoḥ

aho—ah; *asmat*—because of Me; *abhūt*—there was; *bhūri*—great; *pitroḥ*—for My parents; *vṛjinam*—suffering; *āryayoḥ*—for the offenseless ones; *yat-hetoḥ*—because of whom; *putra*—of their sons; *maraṇam*—the death; *yat-hetoḥ*—because of whom; *bandhanam*—bondage; *tayoḥ*—their.

TRANSLATION

Just see how much suffering I have caused My offenseless parents! Because of Me their sons were killed and they themselves imprisoned.

PURPORT

Because Kaṁsa had heard a prophecy that the eighth son of Devakī would kill him, he tried to kill all her children. For the same reason, he imprisoned her and her husband, Vasudeva.

TEXT 7

दिष्टयाद्य दर्शनं स्वानां मह्यं वः सौम्य काङ्क्षितम् ।
सञ्जातं वर्ण्यतां तात तवागमनकारणम् ॥७॥

diṣṭyādya darśanaṁ svānāṁ
mahyaṁ vaḥ saumya kāṅkṣitam
sañjātaṁ varṇyatāṁ tāta
tavāgamana-kāraṇam

diṣṭyā—by good fortune; *adya*—today; *darśanam*—the sight; *svānām*—of My close relative; *mahyam*—for Me; *vaḥ*—yourself; *saumya*—O gentle one; *kāṅkṣitam*—desired; *sañjātam*—has come about; *varṇyatām*—please explain; *tāta*—O uncle; *tava*—your; *āgamana*—for the coming; *kāraṇam*—the reason.

TRANSLATION

By good fortune We have today fulfilled Our desire to see you, Our dear relative. O gentle uncle, please tell Us why you have come.

TEXT 8

श्रीशुक उवाच
पृष्टो भगवता सर्वं वर्णयामास माधवः ।
वैरानुबन्धं यदुषु वसुदेववधोद्यमम् ॥८॥

śrī-śuka uvāca
pṛṣṭo bhagavatā sarvaṁ
varṇayām āsa mādhavaḥ
vairānubandhaṁ yaduṣu
vasudeva-vadhodyamam

śrī-śukaḥ uvāca—Śukadeva Gosvāmī said; *pṛṣṭaḥ*—requested; *bhagavatā*—by the Supreme Lord; *sarvam*—everything; *varṇayām āsa*—described; *mādhavaḥ*—Akrūra, descendant of Madhu; *vaira-anubandham*—the inimical attitude; *yaduṣu*—toward the Yadus; *vasudeva*—Vasudeva; *vadha*—to murder; *udyamam*—the attempt.

TRANSLATION

Śukadeva Gosvāmī said: In response to the Supreme Lord's request, Akrūra, the descendant of Madhu, described the whole situation, including King Kaṁsa's enmity toward the Yadus and his attempt to murder Vasudeva.

TEXT 9

यत्सन्देशो यदर्थं वा दूतः सम्प्रेषितः स्वयम् ।
यदुक्तं नारदेनास्य स्वजन्मानकदुन्दुभेः ॥९॥

yat-sandeśo yad-arthaṁ vā
dūtaḥ sampreṣitaḥ svayam
yad uktaṁ nāradenāsya
sva-janmānakadundubheḥ

yat—having which; *sandeśaḥ*—message; *yat*—which; *artham*—purpose; *vā*—and; *dūtaḥ*—as a messenger; *sampreṣitaḥ*—sent; *svayam*—himself (Akrūra); *yat*—what; *uktam*—was spoken; *nāradena*—by Nārada;

asya—to him (Kaṁsa); *sva*—His (Kṛṣṇa's); *janma*—birth; *ānaka-dundubheḥ*—from Vasudeva.

TRANSLATION

Akrūra relayed the message he had been sent to deliver. He also described Kaṁsa's real intentions and how Nārada had informed Kaṁsa that Kṛṣṇa had been born as the son of Vasudeva.

TEXT 10

श्रुत्वाक्रूरवचः कृष्णो बलश्च परवीरहा ।
प्रहस्य नन्दं पितरं राज्ञा दिष्टं विजज्ञतुः ॥१०॥

śrutvākrūra-vacaḥ kṛṣṇo
balaś ca para-vīra-hā
prahasya nandaṁ pitaraṁ
rājñā diṣṭaṁ vijajñatuḥ

śrutvā—hearing; *akrūra-vacaḥ*—Akrūra's words; *kṛṣṇaḥ*—Lord Kṛṣṇa; *balaḥ*—Lord Balarāma; *ca*—and; *para-vīra*—of opposing heroes; *hā*—the destroyer; *prahasya*—laughing; *nandam*—to Nanda Mahārāja; *pitaram*—Their father; *rājñā*—by the King; *diṣṭam*—the order given; *vijajñatuḥ*—They informed.

TRANSLATION

Lord Kṛṣṇa and Lord Balarāma, the vanquisher of heroic opponents, laughed when They heard Akrūra's words. The Lords then informed Their father, Nanda Mahārāja, of King Kaṁsa's orders.

TEXTS 11–12

गोपान् समादिशत्सोऽपि गृह्यतां सर्वगोरसः ।
उपायनानि गृह्णीध्वं युज्यन्तां शकटानि च ॥११॥
यास्यामः श्वो मधुपुरीं दास्यामो नृपते रसान् ।
द्रक्ष्यामः सुमहत्पर्व यान्ति जानपदाः किल ।
एवमाघोषयत्क्षत्रा नन्दगोपः स्वगोकुले ॥१२॥

gopān samādiśat so 'pi
gṛhyatāṁ sarva-go-rasaḥ
upāyanāni gṛhṇīdhvaṁ
yujyantāṁ śakaṭāni ca

yāsyāmaḥ śvo madhu-purīṁ
dāsyāmo nṛpate rasān
drakṣyāmaḥ su-mahat parva
yānti jānapadāḥ kila
evam āghoṣayat kṣatrā
nanda-gopaḥ sva-gokule

gopān—the cowherd men; *samādiśat*—ordered; *saḥ*—he (Nanda Mahārāja); *api*—also; *gṛhyatām*—have collected; *sarva*—all; *go-rasaḥ*—the milk products; *upāyanāni*—excellent gifts; *gṛhṇīdhvam*—take; *yujyantām*—yoke; *śakaṭāni*—the wagons; *ca*—and; *yāsyāmaḥ*—we shall go; *śvaḥ*—tomorrow; *madhu-purīm*—to Mathurā; *dāsyāmaḥ*—we shall give; *nṛpateḥ*—to the King; *rasān*—our milk products; *drakṣyāmaḥ*—we shall see; *su-mahat*—a very great; *parva*—festival; *yānti*—are going; *jānapadāḥ*—the residents of all the outlying districts; *kila*—indeed; *evam*—thus; *āghoṣayat*—he had announced; *kṣatrā*—by the village constable; *nanda-gopaḥ*—Nanda Mahārāja; *sva-gokule*—to the people of his Gokula.

TRANSLATION

Nanda Mahārāja then issued orders to the cowherd men by having the village constable make the following announcement throughout Nanda's domain of Vraja: "Go collect all the available milk products. Bring valuable gifts and yoke your wagons. Tomorrow we shall go to Mathurā, present our milk products to the King and see a very great festival. The residents of all the outlying districts are also going."

PURPORT

Nanda wanted to bring ghee and other milk products as taxes for the King.

TEXT 13

गोप्यस्तास्तदुपश्रुत्य बभूवुर्व्यथिता भृशम् ।
रामकृष्णौ पुरीं नेतुमक्रूरं व्रजमागतम् ॥१३॥

gopyas tās tad upaśrutya
babhūvur vyathitā bhṛśam
rāma-kṛṣṇau purīṁ netum
akrūraṁ vrajam āgatam

gopyaḥ—the cowherd girls; *tāḥ*—they; *tat*—then; *upaśrutya*—hearing; *babhūvuḥ*—became; *vyathitāḥ*—distressed; *bhṛśam*—extremely; *rāma-kṛṣṇau*—Balarāma and Kṛṣṇa; *purīm*—to the city; *netum*—to take; *akrūram*—Akrūra; *vrajam*—to Vṛndāvana; *āgatam*—come.

TRANSLATION

When the young *gopīs* heard that Akrūra had come to Vraja to take Kṛṣṇa and Balarāma to the city, they became extremely distressed.

TEXT 14

काश्चित्तत्कृतहृत्तापश्वासम्लानमुखश्रियः ।
स्रंसद्दुकूलवलयकेशग्रन्थ्यश्च काश्चन ॥१४॥

kāścit tat-kṛta-hṛt-tāpa-
śvāsa-mlāna-mukha-śriyaḥ
sraṁsad-dukūla-valaya-
keśa-granthyaś ca kāścana

kāścit—some of them; *tat*—by that (hearing); *kṛta*—created; *hṛt*—in their hearts; *tāpa*—from the torment; *śvāsa*—by the sighing; *mlāna*—made pale; *mukha*—of their faces; *śriyaḥ*—the luster; *sraṁsat*—loosening; *dukūla*—their dresses; *valaya*—bracelets; *keśa*—in their hair; *granthyaḥ*—the knots; *ca*—and; *kāścana*—others.

TRANSLATION

Some *gopīs* felt so pained at heart that their faces turned pale from their heavy breathing. Others were so anguished that their dresses, bracelets and braids became loose.

TEXT 15

अन्याश्च तदनुध्याननिवृत्ताशेषवृत्तयः ।
नाभ्यजानन्निमं लोकमात्मलोकं गता इव ॥१५॥

anyāś ca tad-anudhyāna-
nivṛttāśeṣa-vṛttayaḥ
nābhyajānann imaṁ lokam
ātma-lokaṁ gatā iva

anyāḥ—others; *ca*—and; *tat*—on Him; *anudhyāna*—by fixed meditation; *nivṛtta*—ceased; *aśeṣa*—all; *vṛttayaḥ*—their sensory functions; *na abhyajānan*—they were unaware; *imam*—of this; *lokam*—world; *ātma*—of self-realization; *lokam*—the realm; *gatāḥ*—those who have attained; *iva*—just as.

TRANSLATION

Other *gopīs* entirely stopped their sensory activities and became fixed in meditation on Kṛṣṇa. They lost all awareness of the external world, just like those who attain the platform of self-realization.

PURPORT

The *gopīs* were in fact already on the platform of self-realization. The *Caitanya-caritāmṛta* (*Madhya* 20.108) states, *jīvera svarūpa haya kṛṣṇera nitya-dāsa:* "The self, or individual soul, is an eternal servant of Kṛṣṇa." Thus because they were rendering the most intense loving service to the Lord, the *gopīs* were situated at the highest stage of self-realization.

TEXT 16

स्मरन्त्यश्चापराः शौरेरनुरागस्मितेरिताः ।
हृदिस्पृशश्चित्रपदा गिरः सम्मुमुहुः स्त्रियः ॥१६॥

smarantyaś cāparāḥ śaurer
anurāga-smiteritāḥ

hṛdi-spṛśaś citra-padā
giraḥ sammumuhuḥ striyaḥ

smarantyaḥ—remembering; *ca*—and; *aparāḥ*—others; *śaureḥ*—of Kṛṣṇa; *anurāga*—affectionate; *smita*—by His smile; *īritāḥ*—sent; *hṛdi*—the heart; *spṛśaḥ*—touching; *citra*—wonderful; *padāḥ*—with phrases; *giraḥ*—the speech; *sammumuhuḥ*—fainted; *striyaḥ*—women.

TRANSLATION

And still other young women fainted simply by remembering the words of Lord Śauri [Kṛṣṇa]. These words, decorated with wonderful phrases and expressed with affectionate smiles, would deeply touch the young girls' hearts.

TEXTS 17–18

गतिं सुललितां चेष्टां स्निग्धहासावलोकनम् ।
शोकापहानि नर्माणि प्रोद्दामचरितानि च ॥१७॥
चिन्तयन्त्यो मुकुन्दस्य भीता विरहकातराः ।
समेताः सङ्घशः प्रोचुरश्रुमुख्योऽच्युताशयाः ॥१८॥

gatiṁ su-lalitāṁ ceṣṭāṁ
snigdha-hāsāvalokanam
śokāpahāni narmāṇi
proddāma-caritāni ca

cintayantyo mukundasya
bhītā viraha-kātarāḥ
sametāḥ saṅghaśaḥ procur
aśru-mukhyo 'cyutāśayāḥ

gatim—the movements; *su-lalitām*—very charming; *ceṣṭām*—the activities; *snigdha*—affectionate; *hāsa*—smiling; *avalokanam*—the glances; *śoka*—unhappiness; *apahāni*—which remove; *narmāṇi*—the joking words; *proddāma*—mighty; *caritāni*—the deeds; *ca*—and; *cintayantyaḥ*—thinking about; *mukundasya*—of Lord Kṛṣṇa; *bhītāḥ*—afraid; *viraha*—because of separation; *kātarāḥ*—greatly distressed; *sametāḥ*—

joining together; *saṅghaśaḥ*—in groups; *procuḥ*—they spoke; *aśru*—with tears; *mukhyaḥ*—their faces; *acyuta-āśayāḥ*—their minds absorbed in Lord Acyuta.

TRANSLATION

The *gopīs* were frightened at the prospect of even the briefest separation from Lord Mukunda, so now, as they remembered His graceful gait, His pastimes, His affectionate, smiling glances, His heroic deeds and His joking words, which would relieve their distress, they were beside themselves with anxiety at the thought of the great separation about to come. They gathered in groups and spoke to one another, their faces covered with tears and their minds fully absorbed in Acyuta.

TEXT 19

श्रीगोप्य ऊचुः
अहो विधातस्तव न क्वचिद्दया
संयोज्य मैत्र्या प्रणयेन देहिनः ।
तांश्चाकृतार्थान् वियुनङ्क्ष्यपार्थकं
विक्रीडितं तेऽर्भकचेष्टितं यथा ॥१९॥

śrī-gopya ūcuḥ
aho vidhātas tava na kvacid dayā
saṁyojya maitryā praṇayena dehinaḥ
tāṁś cākṛtārthān viyunaṅkṣy apārthakaṁ
vikrīḍitaṁ te 'rbhaka-ceṣṭitaṁ yathā

śrī-gopyaḥ ūcuḥ—the *gopīs* said; *aho*—O; *vidhātaḥ*—Providence; *tava*—your; *na*—there is not; *kvacit*—anywhere; *dayā*—mercy; *saṁyojya*—bringing together; *maitryā*—with friendship; *praṇayena*—and with love; *dehinaḥ*—embodied living beings; *tān*—them; *ca*—and; *akṛta*—unfulfilled; *arthān*—their aims; *viyunaṅkṣi*—you separate; *apārthakam*—uselessly; *vikrīḍitam*—play; *te*—your; *arbhaka*—of a child; *ceṣṭitam*—the activity; *yathā*—as.

TRANSLATION

The *gopīs* said: O Providence, you have no mercy! You bring embodied creatures together in friendship and love and then senselessly separate them before they fulfill their desires. This whimsical play of yours is like a child's game.

TEXT 20

यस्त्वं प्रदर्श्यासितकुन्तलावृतं
मुकुन्दवक्त्रं सुकपोलमुन्नसम् ।
शोकापनोदस्मितलेशसुन्दरं
करोषि पारोक्ष्यमसाधु ते कृतम् ॥२०॥

yas tvaṁ pradarśyāsita-kuntalāvṛtaṁ
mukunda-vaktraṁ su-kapolam un-nasam
śokāpanoda-smita-leśa-sundaraṁ
karoṣi pārokṣyam asādhu te kṛtam

yaḥ—who; *tvam*—you; *pradarśya*—showing; *asita*—black; *kuntala*—by locks; *āvṛtam*—framed; *mukunda*—of Kṛṣṇa; *vaktram*—the face; *su-kapolam*—with fine cheeks; *ut-nasam*—and raised nose; *śoka*—misery; *apanoda*—eradicating; *smita*—with His smile; *leśa*—slight; *sundaram*—beautiful; *karoṣi*—you make; *pārokṣyam*—invisible; *asādhu*—not good; *te*—by you; *kṛtam*—done.

TRANSLATION

Having shown us Mukunda's face, framed by dark locks and beautified by His fine cheeks, raised nose and gentle smiles, which eradicate all misery, you are now making that face invisible. This behavior of yours is not at all good.

TEXT 21

क्रूरस्त्वमक्रूरसमाख्यया स्म नश्
चक्षुर्हि दत्तं हरसे बताज्ञवत् ।
येनैकदेशेऽखिलसर्गसौष्ठवं
त्वदीयमद्राक्ष्म वयं मधुद्विषः ॥२१॥

krūras tvam akrūra-samākhyayā sma naś
cakṣur hi dattaṁ harase batājña-vat
yenaika-deśe 'khila-sarga-sauṣṭhavaṁ
tvadīyam adrākṣma vayaṁ madhu-dviṣaḥ

krūraḥ—cruel; *tvam*—you (are); *akrūra-samākhyayā*—by the name Akrūra (which means "not cruel"); *sma*—certainly; *naḥ*—our; *cakṣuḥ*—eyes; *hi*—indeed; *dattam*—given; *harase*—you are taking; *bata*—alas; *ajña*—a fool; *vat*—just like; *yena*—with which (eyes); *eka*—in one; *deśe*—place; *akhila*—of all; *sarga*—the creation; *sauṣṭhavam*—the perfection; *tvadīyam*—your; *adrākṣma*—have seen; *vayam*—we; *madhu-dviṣaḥ*—of Lord Kṛṣṇa, enemy of the demon Madhu.

TRANSLATION

O Providence, though you come here with the name Akrūra, you are indeed cruel, for like a fool you are taking away what you once gave us—those eyes with which we have seen, even in one feature of Lord Madhudviṣa's form, the perfection of your entire creation.

PURPORT

The *gopīs* did not care to see anything but Kṛṣṇa; therefore if Kṛṣṇa left Vṛndāvana, their eyes would have no function. Thus Kṛṣṇa's departure was blinding these poor girls, and in their distress they berated Akrūra, whose name means "not cruel," as cruel indeed.

TEXT 22

न नन्दसूनुः क्षणभंगसौहृदः
समीक्षते नः स्वकृतातुरा बत ।
विहाय गेहान् स्वजनान् सुतान् पतींस्
तद्दास्यमद्धोपगता नवप्रियः ॥२२॥

na nanda-sūnuḥ kṣaṇa-bhaṅga-sauhṛdaḥ
samīkṣate naḥ sva-kṛtāturā bata
vihāya gehān sva-janān sutān patīṁs
tad-dāsyam addhopagatā nava-priyaḥ

na—does not; *nanda-sūnuḥ*—the son of Nanda Mahārāja; *kṣaṇa*—in a moment; *bhaṅga*—the breaking; *sauhṛdaḥ*—of whose friendship; *samīkṣate*—look upon; *naḥ*—us; *sva*—by Him; *kṛta*—made; *āturāḥ*—under His control; *bata*—alas; *vihāya*—giving up; *gehān*—our homes; *sva-janān*—relatives; *sutān*—children; *patīn*—husbands; *tat*—to Him; *dāsyam*—servitude; *addhā*—directly; *upagatāḥ*—who have taken up; *nava*—ever new; *priyaḥ*—whose lovers.

TRANSLATION

Alas, Nanda's son, who breaks loving friendships in a second, will not even look directly at us. Forcibly brought under His control, we abandoned our homes, relatives, children and husbands just to serve Him, but He is always looking for new lovers.

TEXT 23

सुखं प्रभाता रजनीयमाशिषः
सत्या बभूवुः पुरयोषितां ध्रुवम् ।
याः संप्रविष्टस्य मुखं व्रजस्पतेः
पास्यन्त्यपांगोत्कलितस्मितासवम् ॥२३॥

sukhaṁ prabhātā rajanīyam āśiṣaḥ
satyā babhūvuḥ pura-yoṣitāṁ dhruvam
yāḥ sampraviṣṭasya mukhaṁ vrajas-pateḥ
pāsyanty apāṅgotkalita-smitāsavam

sukham—happy; *prabhātā*—its dawn; *rajanī*—the night; *iyam*—this; *āśiṣaḥ*—the hopes; *satyāḥ*—true; *babhūvuḥ*—have become; *pura*—of the city; *yoṣitām*—of the women; *dhruvam*—certainly; *yāḥ*—who; *sampraviṣṭasya*—of Him who has entered (Mathurā); *mukham*—the face; *vrajaḥ-pateḥ*—of the master of Vraja; *pāsyanti*—they will drink; *apāṅga*—upon the corners of His eyes; *utkalita*—expanded; *smita*—a smile; *āsavam*—nectar.

TRANSLATION

The dawn following this night will certainly be auspicious for the women of Mathurā. All their hopes will now be fulfilled, for as

the Lord of Vraja enters their city, they will be able to drink from His face the nectar of the smile emanating from the corners of His eyes.

TEXT 24

तासां मुकुन्दो मधुमञ्जुभाषितैर्
गृहीतचित्तः परवान्मनस्व्यपि ।
कथं पुनर्नः प्रतियास्यतेऽबला
ग्राम्याः सलज्जस्मितविभ्रमैर्भ्रमन् ॥२४॥

tāsāṁ mukundo madhu-mañju-bhāṣitair
gṛhīta-cittaḥ para-vān manasvy api
kathaṁ punar naḥ pratiyāsyate 'balā
grāmyāḥ salajja-smita-vibhramair bhraman

tāsām—their; *mukundaḥ*—Kṛṣṇa; *madhu*—like honey; *mañju*—sweet; *bhāṣitaiḥ*—by the words; *gṛhīta*—seized; *cittaḥ*—whose mind; *para-vān*—subservient; *manasvī*—intelligent; *api*—although; *katham*—how; *punaḥ*—again; *naḥ*—to us; *pratiyāsyate*—will He return; *abalāḥ*—O girls; *grāmyāḥ*—who are rustic; *sa-lajja*—shyly; *smita*—smiling; *vibhramaiḥ*—by their enchantments; *bhraman*—becoming bewildered.

TRANSLATION

O *gopīs*, although our Mukunda is intelligent and very obedient to His parents, once He has fallen under the spell of the honey-sweet words of the women of Mathurā and been enchanted by their alluring, shy smiles, how will He ever return to us unsophisticated village girls?

TEXT 25

अद्य ध्रुवं तत्र दृशो भविष्यते
दाशार्हभोजान्धकवृष्णिसात्वताम् ।
महोत्सवः श्रीरमणं गुणास्पदं
द्रक्ष्यन्ति ये चाध्वनि देवकीसुतम् ॥२५॥

adya dhruvaṁ tatra dṛśo bhaviṣyate
dāśārha-bhojāndhaka-vṛṣṇi-sātvatām
mahotsavaḥ śrī-ramaṇaṁ guṇāspadaṁ
drakṣyanti ye cādhvani devakī-sutam

adya—today; *dhruvam*—certainly; *tatra*—there; *dṛśaḥ*—for the eyes; *bhaviṣyate*—there will be; *dāśārha-bhoja-andhaka-vṛṣṇi-sātvatām*—of the members of the Dāśārha, Bhoja, Andhaka, Vṛṣṇi and Sātvata clans; *mahā-utsavaḥ*—a great festivity; *śrī*—of the goddess of fortune; *ramaṇam*—the darling; *guṇa*—of all transcendental qualities; *āspadam*—the reservoir; *drakṣyanti*—they will see; *ye*—those who; *ca*—also; *adhvani*—on the road; *devakī-sutam*—Kṛṣṇa, the son of Devakī.

TRANSLATION

When the Dāśārhas, Bhojas, Andhakas, Vṛṣṇis and Sātvatas see the son of Devakī in Mathurā, they will certainly enjoy a great festival for their eyes, as will all those who see Him traveling along the road to the city. After all, He is the darling of the goddess of fortune and the reservoir of all transcendental qualities.

TEXT 26

मैतद्विधस्याकरुणस्य नाम भूद्
अक्रूर इत्येतदतीव दारुणः ।
योऽसावनाश्वास्य सुदुःखितं जनं
प्रियात्प्रियं नेष्यति पारमध्वनः ॥२६॥

maitad-vidhasyākaruṇasya nāma bhūd
akrūra ity etad atīva dāruṇaḥ
yo 'sāv anāśvāsya su-duḥkhitaṁ janaṁ
priyāt priyaṁ neṣyati pāram adhvanaḥ

mā—should not; *etat-vidhasya*—of such; *akaruṇasya*—an unkind person; *nāma*—the name; *bhūt*—be; *akrūraḥ iti*—"Akrūra"; *etat*—this; *atīva*—extremely; *dāruṇaḥ*—cruel; *yaḥ*—who; *asau*—he; *anāśvāsya*—not consoling; *su-duḥkhitam*—who are very miserable; *janam*—people; *priyāt*—than the most dear; *priyam*—dear (Kṛṣṇa); *neṣyati*—will take; *pāram adhvanaḥ*—beyond our sight.

TRANSLATION

He who is doing this merciless deed should not be called Akrūra. He is so extremely cruel that without even trying to console the sorrowful residents of Vraja, he is taking away Kṛṣṇa, who is more dear to us than life itself.

TEXT 27

अनार्द्रधीरेष समास्थितो रथं
तमन्वमी च त्वरयन्ति दुर्मदाः ।
गोपा अनोभिः स्थविरैरुपेक्षितं
दैवं च नोऽद्य प्रतिकूलमीहते ॥२७॥

anārdra-dhīr eṣa samāsthito ratham
tam anv amī ca tvarayanti durmadāḥ
gopā anobhiḥ sthavirair upekṣitaṁ
daivaṁ ca no 'dya pratikūlam īhate

anārdra-dhīḥ—hard-hearted; *eṣaḥ*—this (Kṛṣṇa); *samāsthitaḥ*—having mounted; *ratham*—the chariot; *tam*—Him; *anu*—following; *amī*—these; *ca*—and; *tvarayanti*—hurry; *durmadāḥ*—befooled; *gopāḥ*—cowherds; *anobhiḥ*—in their bullock carts; *sthaviraiḥ*—by the elders; *upekṣitam*—disregarded; *daivam*—fate; *ca*—and; *naḥ*—with us; *adya*—today; *pratikūlam*—unfavorably; *īhate*—is acting.

TRANSLATION

Hard-hearted Kṛṣṇa has already mounted the chariot, and now the foolish cowherds are hurrying after Him in their bullock carts. Even the elders are saying nothing to stop Him. Today fate is working against us.

PURPORT

Śrīla Śrīdhara Svāmī reveals what the *gopīs* thought: "These foolish cowherd men and elders are not even trying to stop Kṛṣṇa. Don't they realize they are committing suicide? They are helping Kṛṣṇa go to Mathurā, but they will have to come back to Vṛndāvana and will certainly die in His absence. The whole world has become nonsensical."

TEXT 28

निवारयामः समुपेत्य माधवं
किं नोऽकरिष्यन् कुलवृद्धबान्धवाः ।
मुकुन्दसंगान्निमिषार्धदुस्त्यजाद्
दैवेन विध्वंसितदीनचेतसाम् ॥२८॥

nivārayāmaḥ samupetya mādhavaṁ
kiṁ no 'kariṣyan kula-vṛddha-bāndhavāḥ
mukunda-saṅgān nimiṣārdha-dustyajād
daivena vidhvaṁsita-dīna-cetasām

nivārayāmaḥ—let us stop; *samupetya*—going up to Him; *mādhavam*—Kṛṣṇa; *kim*—what; *naḥ*—to us; *akariṣyan*—will do; *kula*—of the family; *vṛddha*—the elders; *bāndhavāḥ*—and our relatives; *mukunda-saṅgāt*—from the association of Lord Mukunda; *nimiṣa*—of the wink of an eye; *ardha*—for one half; *dustyajāt*—which is impossible to give up; *daivena*—by fate; *vidhvaṁsita*—separated; *dīna*—wretched; *cetasām*—whose hearts.

TRANSLATION

Let us directly approach Mādhava and stop Him from going. What can our family elders and other relatives do to us? Now that fate is separating us from Mukunda, our hearts are already wretched, for we cannot bear to give up His association even for a fraction of a second.

PURPORT

Śrīla Viśvanātha Cakravartī describes what the *gopīs* thought: "Let us go right up to Kṛṣṇa and pull at His clothes and hands and insist that He get down from His chariot and stay here with us. We will tell Him, 'Don't bring upon Yourself the sinful reaction for murdering so many women!' "

"But if we do that," said other *gopīs*, "our relatives and the village elders will discover our secret love for Kṛṣṇa and abandon us."

"But what can they do to us?"

"Yes, our lives are already wretched now that Kṛṣṇa is leaving. We have nothing to lose."

"That's right. We will remain in the Vṛndāvana forest just like presiding goddesses, and then we can fulfill our true desire—to stay with Kṛṣṇa in the forest."

"Yes, and even if the elders and our relatives punish us by beating us or locking us up, we can still live happily with the knowledge that Kṛṣṇa is residing in our village. Some of our girlfriends who are not imprisoned will cleverly find a way to bring us the remnants of Kṛṣṇa's food, and then we can remain alive. But if Kṛṣṇa is not stopped, we will certainly die."

TEXT 29

यस्यानुरागललितस्मितवल्गुमन्त्र-
लीलावलोकपरिरम्भणरासगोष्ठाम् ।
नीताः स्म नः क्षणमिव क्षणदा विना तं
गोप्यः कथं न्वतितरेम तमो दुरन्तम् ॥२९॥

yasyānurāga-lalita-smita-valgu-mantra-
līlāvaloka-parirambhaṇa-rāsa-goṣṭhām
nītāḥ sma naḥ kṣaṇam iva kṣaṇadā vinā taṁ
gopyaḥ kathaṁ nv atitarema tamo durantam

yasya—whose; *anurāga*—with loving affection; *lalita*—charming; *smita*—(where there were) smiles; *valgu*—attractive; *mantra*—intimate discussions; *līlā*—playful; *avaloka*—glances; *parirambhaṇa*—and embraces; *rāsa*—of the *rāsa* dance; *goṣṭhām*—to the assembly; *nītāḥ sma*—who were brought; *naḥ*—for us; *kṣaṇam*—a moment; *iva*—like; *kṣaṇadāḥ*—the nights; *vinā*—without; *tam*—Him; *gopyaḥ*—O *gopīs; katham*—how; *nu*—indeed; *atitarema*—will we cross over; *tamaḥ*—the darkness; *durantam*—insurmountable.

TRANSLATION

When He brought us to the assembly of the *rāsa* dance, where we enjoyed His affectionate and charming smiles, His delightful secret talks, His playful glances and His embraces, we passed many nights as if they were a single moment. O *gopīs*, how can we possibly cross over the insurmountable darkness of His absence?

PURPORT

For the *gopīs,* a long time in Kṛṣṇa's association passed like a moment, and a single moment in His absence seemed like a very long time.

TEXT 30

योऽह्नः क्षये व्रजमनन्तसखः परीतो
गोपैर्विशन् खुररजश्छुरितालकस्रक् ।
वेणुं क्वणन् स्मितकटाक्षनिरीक्षणेन
चित्तं क्षिणोत्यमुमृते नु कथं भवेम ॥३०॥

yo 'hnaḥ kṣaye vrajam ananta-sakhaḥ parīto
gopair viśan khura-rajaś-churitālaka-srak
veṇuṁ kvaṇan smita-kaṭākṣa-nirīkṣaṇena
cittaṁ kṣiṇoty amum ṛte nu kathaṁ bhavema

yaḥ—who; *ahnaḥ*—of the day; *kṣaye*—at the demise; *vrajam*—the village of Vraja; *ananta*—of Ananta, Lord Balarāma; *sakhaḥ*—the friend, Kṛṣṇa; *parītaḥ*—accompanied on all sides; *gopaiḥ*—by the cowherd boys; *viśan*—entering; *khura*—of the hoofprints (of the cows); *rajaḥ*—with the dust; *churita*—smeared; *alaka*—the locks of His hair; *srak*—and His garlands; *veṇum*—His flute; *kvaṇan*—playing; *smita*—smiling; *kaṭa-akṣa*—from the corners of His eyes; *nirīkṣaṇena*—with glances; *cittam*—our minds; *kṣiṇoti*—He destroys; *amum*—Him; *ṛte*—without; *nu*—indeed; *katham*—how; *bhavema*—we can exist.

TRANSLATION

How can we exist without Ananta's friend Kṛṣṇa, who in the evening would return to Vraja in the company of the cowherd boys, His hair and garland powdered with the dust raised by the cows' hooves? As He played His flute, He would captivate our minds with His smiling sidelong glances.

TEXT 31

श्रीशुक उवाच
एवं ब्रुवाणा विरहातुरा भृशं
व्रजस्त्रियः कृष्णविषक्तमानसाः ।
विसृज्य लज्जां रुरुदुः स्म सुस्वरं
गोविन्द दामोदर माधवेति ॥३१॥

śrī-śuka uvāca
evaṁ bruvāṇā virahāturā bhṛśaṁ
vraja-striyaḥ kṛṣṇa-viṣakta-mānasāḥ
visṛjya lajjāṁ ruruduḥ sma su-svaraṁ
govinda dāmodara mādhaveti

śrī-śukaḥ uvāca—Śukadeva Gosvāmī said; *evam*—thus; *bruvāṇāḥ*—speaking; *viraha*—by feelings of separation; *āturāḥ*—distraught; *bhṛśam*—thoroughly; *vraja-striyaḥ*—the ladies of Vraja; *kṛṣṇa*—to Kṛṣṇa; *viṣakta*—attached; *mānasāḥ*—their minds; *visṛjya*—abandoning; *lajjām*—shame; *ruruduḥ sma*—they cried; *su-svaram*—loudly; *govinda dāmodara mādhava iti*—O Govinda, O Dāmodara, O Mādhava.

TRANSLATION

Śukadeva Gosvāmī said: After speaking these words, the ladies of Vraja, who were so attached to Kṛṣṇa, felt extremely agitated by their imminent separation from Him. They forgot all shame and loudly cried out, "O Govinda! O Dāmodara! O Mādhava!"

PURPORT

For a long time the *gopīs* had carefully hidden their conjugal love for Kṛṣṇa. But now that Kṛṣṇa was leaving, the *gopīs* were so distressed that they could no longer hide their feelings.

TEXT 32

स्त्रीणामेवं रुदन्तीनामुदिते सवितर्यथ ।
अक्रूरश्चोदयामास कृतमैत्रादिको रथम् ॥३२॥

strīṇām evaṁ rudantīnām
udite savitary atha
akrūraś codayām āsa
kṛta-maitrādiko ratham

strīṇām—the women; *evam*—in this manner; *rudantīnām*—while they were crying; *udite*—rising; *savitari*—the sun; *atha*—then; *akrūraḥ*—Akrūra; *codayām āsa*—started; *kṛta*—having performed; *maitra-ādikaḥ*—his morning worship and other regular duties; *ratham*—the chariot.

TRANSLATION

But even as the *gopīs* cried out in this way, Akrūra, having at sunrise performed His morning worship and other duties, began to drive the chariot.

PURPORT

According to some Vaiṣṇava authorities, Akrūra offended the *gopīs* by not consoling them when he took Kṛṣṇa to Mathurā, and because of this offense Akrūra was later forced to leave Dvārakā and be separated from Kṛṣṇa during the episode of the Syamantaka jewel. At that time Akrūra had to take up an ignoble residence in Vārāṇasī.

Apparently, mother Yaśodā and the other residents of Vṛndāvana were not crying like the *gopīs*, for they sincerely believed Kṛṣṇa would be coming back within a few days.

TEXT 33

गोपास्तमन्वसज्जन्त नन्दाद्याः शकटैस्ततः ।
आदायोपायनं भूरि कुम्भान् गोरससम्भृतान् ॥३३॥

gopās tam anvasajjanta
nandādyāḥ śakaṭais tataḥ
ādāyopāyanaṁ bhūri
kumbhān go-rasa-sambhṛtān

gopāḥ—the cowherd men; *tam*—Him; *anvasajjanta*—followed; *nanda-ādyāḥ*—headed by Nanda; *śakaṭaiḥ*—in their wagons; *tataḥ*—then;

ādāya—having taken; *upāyanam*—offerings; *bhūri*—abundant; *kumbhān*—clay pots; *go-rasa*—with milk products; *sambhṛtān*—filled.

TRANSLATION

Led by Nanda Mahārāja, the cowherd men followed behind Lord Kṛṣṇa in their wagons. The men brought along many offerings for the King, including clay pots filled with ghee and other milk products.

TEXT 34

गोप्यश्च दयितं कृष्णमनुव्रज्यानुरञ्जिताः ।
प्रत्यादेशं भगवतः काङ्क्षन्त्यश्चावतस्थिरे ॥३४॥

gopyaś ca dayitaṁ kṛṣṇam
anuvrajyānurañjitāḥ
pratyādeśaṁ bhagavataḥ
kāṅkṣantyaś cāvatasthire

gopyaḥ—the *gopīs;* *ca*—and; *dayitam*—their beloved; *kṛṣṇam*—Kṛṣṇa; *anuvrajya*—following; *anurañjitāḥ*—pleased; *pratyādeśam*—some instruction in reply; *bhagavataḥ*—from the Lord; *kāṅkṣantyaḥ*—hoping for; *ca*—and; *avatasthire*—they stood.

TRANSLATION

[With His glances] Lord Kṛṣṇa somewhat pacified the *gopīs*, and they also followed behind for some time. Then, hoping He would give them some instruction, they stood still.

TEXT 35

तास्तथा तप्यतीर्वीक्ष्य स्वप्रस्थाने यदूत्तमः ।
सान्त्वयामास सप्रेमैरायास्य इति दौत्यकैः ॥३५॥

tās tathā tapyatīr vīkṣya
sva-prasthāne yadūttamaḥ
sāntvayām āsa sa-premair
āyāsya iti dautyakaiḥ

tāḥ—them (the *gopīs*); *tathā*—thus; *tapyatīḥ*—lamenting; *vīkṣya*—seeing; *sva-prasthāne*—as He was leaving; *yadu-uttamaḥ*—the greatest of the Yadus; *sāntvayām āsa*—He consoled them; *sa-premaiḥ*—full of love; *āyāsye iti*—"I will return"; *dautyakaiḥ*—with words sent through a messenger.

TRANSLATION

As He departed, that best of the Yadus saw how the *gopīs* were lamenting, and thus He consoled them by sending a messenger with this loving promise: "I will return."

TEXT 36

यावदालक्ष्यते केतुर्यावद् रेणू रथस्य च ।
अनुप्रस्थापितात्मानो लेख्यानीवोपलक्षिताः ॥३६॥

yāvad ālakṣyate ketur
yāvad reṇū rathasya ca
anuprasthāpitātmāno
lekhyānīvopalakṣitāḥ

yāvat—as long as; *ālakṣyate*—was visible; *ketuḥ*—the flag; *yāvat*—as long as; *reṇuḥ*—the dust; *rathasya*—of the chariot; *ca*—and; *anuprasthāpita*—sending after; *ātmānaḥ*—their minds; *lekhyāni*—painted figures; *iva*—like; *upalakṣitāḥ*—they appeared.

TRANSLATION

Sending their minds after Kṛṣṇa, the *gopīs* stood as motionless as figures in a painting. They remained there as long as the flag atop the chariot was visible, and even until they could no longer see the dust raised by the chariot wheels.

TEXT 37

ता निराशा निववृतुर्गोविन्दविनिवर्तने ।
विशोका अहनी निन्युर्गायन्त्यः प्रियचेष्टितम् ॥३७॥

tā nirāśā nivavṛtur
govinda-vinivartane
viśokā ahanī ninyur
gāyantyaḥ priya-ceṣṭitam

tāḥ—they; *nirāśāḥ*—without hope; *nivavṛtuḥ*—turned back; *govinda-vinivartane*—of Govinda's returning; *viśokāḥ*—extremely sorrowful; *ahanī*—the days and nights; *ninyuḥ*—they spent; *gāyantyaḥ*—chanting; *priya*—of their beloved; *ceṣṭitam*—about the activities.

TRANSLATION

The *gopīs* then turned back, without hope that Govinda would ever return to them. Full of sorrow, they began to spend their days and nights chanting about the pastimes of their beloved.

TEXT 38

भगवानपि सम्प्राप्तो रामाक्रूरयुतो नृप ।
रथेन वायुवेगेन कालिन्दीमघनाशिनीम् ॥३८॥

bhagavān api samprāpto
rāmākrūra-yuto nṛpa
rathena vāyu-vegena
kālindīm agha-nāśinīm

bhagavān—the Supreme Lord; *api*—and; *samprāptaḥ*—arrived; *rāma-akrūra-yutaḥ*—together with Balarāma and Akrūra; *nṛpa*—O King (Parīkṣit); *rathena*—by the chariot; *vāyu*—like the wind; *vegena*—swift; *kālindīm*—at the river Kālindī (Yamunā); *agha*—sins; *nāśinīm*—which destroys.

TRANSLATION

My dear King, the Supreme Lord Kṛṣṇa, traveling as swiftly as the wind in that chariot with Lord Balarāma and Akrūra, arrived at the river Kālindī, which destroys all sins.

PURPORT

Śrīla Jīva Gosvāmī comments that Lord Kṛṣṇa secretly lamented His separation from the *gopīs*. These transcendental feelings of the Lord are part of His supreme pleasure potency.

TEXT 39

तत्रोपस्पृश्य पानीयं पीत्वा मृष्टं मणिप्रभम् ।
वृक्षषण्डमुपव्रज्य सरामो रथमाविशत् ॥३९॥

tatropaspṛśya pānīyaṁ
pītvā mṛṣṭaṁ maṇi-prabham
vṛkṣa-ṣaṇḍam upavrajya
sa-rāmo ratham āviśat

tatra—there; *upaspṛśya*—touching the water; *pānīyam*—in His hand; *pītvā*—drinking; *mṛṣṭam*—sweet; *maṇi*—like jewels; *prabham*—effulgent; *vṛkṣa*—of trees; *ṣaṇḍam*—a grove; *upavrajya*—moving up to; *sa-rāmaḥ*—with Balarāma; *ratham*—the chariot; *āviśat*—He mounted.

TRANSLATION

The river's sweet water was more effulgent than brilliant jewels. After Lord Kṛṣṇa had touched it for purification, He drank some from His hand. Then He had the chariot moved near a grove of trees and climbed back on, along with Balarāma.

TEXT 40

अक्रूरस्तावुपामन्त्र्य निवेश्य च रथोपरि ।
कालिन्द्या ह्रदमागत्य स्नानं विधिवदाचरत् ॥४०॥

akrūras tāv upāmantrya
niveśya ca rathopari
kālindyā hradam āgatya
snānaṁ vidhi-vad ācarat

akrūraḥ—Akrūra; *tau*—from the two of Them; *upāmantrya*—taking permission; *niveśya*—having Them sit down; *ca*—and; *ratha-upari*—on the chariot; *kālindyāḥ*—of the Yamunā; *hradam*—to a pond; *āgatya*—going; *snānam*—his bath; *vidhi-vat*—in accordance with scriptural injunction; *ācarat*—he performed.

TRANSLATION

Akrūra asked the two Lords to take Their seats on the chariot. Then, taking Their permission, he went to a pool in the Yamunā and took his bath as enjoined in the scriptures.

TEXT 41

निमज्ज्य तस्मिन् सलिले जपन् ब्रह्म सनातनम् ।
तावेव ददृशेऽक्रूरो रामकृष्णौ समन्वितौ ॥४१॥

nimajjya tasmin salile
japan brahma sanātanam
tāv eva dadṛśe 'krūro
rāma-kṛṣṇau samanvitau

nimajjya—immersing himself; *tasmin*—in that; *salile*—water; *japan*—reciting; *brahma*—Vedic *mantras; sanātanam*—eternal; *tau*—Them; *eva*—indeed; *dadṛśe*—saw; *akrūraḥ*—Akrūra; *rāma-kṛṣṇau*—Balarāma and Kṛṣṇa; *samanvitau*—together.

TRANSLATION

While immersing himself in the water and reciting eternal *mantras* from the *Vedas*, Akrūra suddenly saw Balarāma and Kṛṣṇa before him.

TEXTS 42–43

तौ रथस्थौ कथमिह सुतावानकदुन्दुभेः ।
तर्हि स्वित्स्यन्दने न स्त इत्युन्मज्ज्य व्यचष्ट सः ॥४२॥
तत्रापि च यथापूर्वमासीनौ पुनरेव सः ।
न्यमज्जद्दर्शनं यन्मे मृषा किं सलिले तयोः ॥४३॥

tau ratha-sthau katham iha
sutāv ānakadundubheḥ
tarhi svit syandane na sta
ity unmajjya vyacaṣṭa saḥ

tatrāpi ca yathā-pūrvam
āsīnau punar eva saḥ
nyamajjad darśanaṁ yan me
mṛṣā kiṁ salile tayoḥ

tau—They; *ratha-sthau*—present on the chariot; *katham*—how; *iha*—here; *sutau*—the two sons; *ānakadundubheḥ*—of Vasudeva; *tarhi*—then; *svit*—whether; *syandane*—on the chariot; *na staḥ*—They are not there; *iti*—thinking this; *unmajjya*—rising from the water; *vyacaṣṭa*—saw; *saḥ*—he; *tatra api*—in the same place; *ca*—and; *yathā*—as; *pūrvam*—previously; *āsīnau*—sitting; *punaḥ*—again; *eva*—indeed; *saḥ*—he; *nyamajjat*—entered the water; *darśanam*—the vision; *yat*—if; *me*—my; *mṛṣā*—false; *kim*—perhaps; *salile*—in the water; *tayoḥ*—of Them.

TRANSLATION

Akrūra thought, "How can the two sons of Ānakadundubhi, who are sitting in the chariot, be standing here in the water? They must have left the chariot." But when he came out of the river, there They were on the chariot, just as before. Asking himself "Was the vision I had of Them in the water an illusion?" Akrūra reentered the pool.

TEXTS 44–45

भूयस्तत्रापि सोऽद्राक्षीत्स्तूयमानमहीश्वरम् ।
सिद्धचारणगन्धर्वैरसुरैर्नतकन्धरैः ॥४४॥
सहस्रशिरसं देवं सहस्रफणमौलिनम् ।
नीलाम्बरं विसश्वेतं शृंगैः श्वेतमिव स्थितम् ॥४५॥

bhūyas tatrāpi so 'drākṣīt
stūyamānam ahīśvaram

siddha-cāraṇa-gandharvair
asurair nata-kandharaiḥ

sahasra-śirasaṁ devaṁ
sahasra-phaṇa-maulinam
nīlāmbaraṁ visa-śvetaṁ
śṛṅgaiḥ śvetam iva sthitam

bhūyaḥ—again; *tatra api*—in that same place; *saḥ*—he; *adrākṣīt*—saw; *stūyamānam*—being praised; *ahi-īśvaram*—the Lord of serpents (Ananta Śeṣa, the plenary expansion of Lord Balarāma who serves as the bed of Viṣṇu); *siddha-cāraṇa-gandharvaiḥ*—by Siddhas, Cāraṇas and Gandharvas; *asuraiḥ*—and by demons; *nata*—bowed; *kandharaiḥ*—whose necks; *sahasra*—thousands; *śirasam*—having heads; *devam*—the Supreme Lord; *sahasra*—thousands; *phaṇa*—having hoods; *maulinam*—and helmets; *nīla*—blue; *ambaram*—whose clothing; *visa*—like the filaments of a lotus stem; *śvetam*—white; *śṛṅgaiḥ*—with its peaks; *śvetam*—Kailāsa Mountain; *iva*—as if; *sthitam*—situated.

TRANSLATION

There Akrūra now saw Ananta Śeṣa, the Lord of the serpents, receiving praise from Siddhas, Cāraṇas, Gandharvas and demons, who all had their heads bowed. The Personality of Godhead whom Akrūra saw had thousands of heads, thousands of hoods and thousands of helmets. His blue garment and His fair complexion, as white as the filaments of a lotus stem, made Him appear like white Kailāsa Mountain with its many peaks.

TEXTS 46–48

तस्योत्संगे घनश्यामं पीतकौशेयवाससम् ।
पुरुषं चतुर्भुजं शान्तं पद्मपत्रारुणेक्षणम् ॥४६॥
चारुप्रसन्नवदनं चारुहासनिरीक्षणम् ।
सुभ्रून्नसं चारुकर्णं सुकपोलारुणाधरम् ॥४७॥
प्रलम्बपीवरभुजं तुंगांसोरःस्थलश्रियम् ।
कम्बुकण्ठं निम्ननाभिं वलिमत्पल्लवोदरम् ॥४८॥

tasyotsaṅge ghana-śyāmaṁ
pīta-kauśeya-vāsasam
puruṣaṁ catur-bhujaṁ śāntaṁ
padma-patrāruṇekṣaṇam

cāru-prasanna-vadanaṁ
cāru-hāsa-nirīkṣaṇam
su-bhrūnnasaṁ cāru-karṇaṁ
su-kapolāruṇādharam

pralamba-pīvara-bhujaṁ
tuṅgāṁsoraḥ-sthala-śriyam
kambu-kaṇṭhaṁ nimna-nābhiṁ
valimat-pallavodaram

tasya—of Him (Ananta Śeṣa); *utsaṅge*—on the lap; *ghana*—like a rain cloud; *śyāmam*—dark blue; *pīta*—yellow; *kauśeya*—silk; *vāsasam*—whose garment; *puruṣam*—the Supreme Lord; *catuḥ-bhujam*—with four arms; *śāntam*—peaceful; *padma*—of a lotus; *patra*—like the leaves; *aruṇa*—reddish; *īkṣaṇam*—whose eyes; *cāru*—attractive; *prasanna*—cheerful; *vadanam*—whose face; *cāru*—attractive; *hāsa*—smiling; *nirīkṣaṇam*—whose glance; *su*—beautiful; *bhrū*—whose eyebrows; *ut*—raised; *nasam*—whose nose; *cāru*—attractive; *karṇam*—whose ears; *su*—beautiful; *kapola*—whose cheeks; *aruṇa*—reddish; *adharam*—whose lips; *pralamba*—extended; *pīvara*—stout; *bhujam*—whose arms; *tuṅga*—raised; *aṁsa*—by His shoulders; *uraḥ-sthala*—and chest; *śriyam*—beautified; *kambu*—like a conchshell; *kaṇṭham*—whose throat; *nimna*—low; *nābhim*—whose navel; *vali*—lines; *mat*—having; *pallava*—like a leaf; *udaram*—whose abdomen.

TRANSLATION

Akrūra then saw the Supreme Personality of Godhead lying peacefully on the lap of Lord Ananta Śeṣa. The complexion of that Supreme Person was like a dark-blue cloud. He wore yellow garments and had four arms and reddish lotus-petal eyes. His face looked attractive and cheerful with its smiling, endearing glance and lovely eyebrows, its raised nose and finely formed ears, and its beautiful cheeks and reddish lips. The Lord's broad

shoulders and expansive chest were beautiful, and His arms long and stout. His neck resembled a conchshell, His navel was deep, and His abdomen bore lines like those on a banyan leaf.

TEXTS 49–50

बृहत्कटितटश्रोणिकरभोरुद्वयान्वितम् ।
चारुजानुयुगं चारुजङ्घायुगलसंयुतम् ॥४९॥
तुंगगुल्फारुणनखव्रातदीधितिभिर्वृतम् ।
नवांगुल्यंगुष्ठदलैर्विलसत्पादपंकजम् ॥५०॥

bṛhat-kaṭi-taṭa-śroṇi-
karabhoru-dvayānvitam
cāru-jānu-yugaṁ cāru-
jaṅghā-yugala-saṁyutam

tuṅga-gulphāruṇa-nakha-
vrāta-dīdhitibhir vṛtam
navāṅguly-aṅguṣṭha-dalair
vilasat-pāda-paṅkajam

bṛhat—large; *kaṭi-taṭa*—whose loins; *śroṇi*—and hips; *karabha*—like an elephant's trunk; *ūru*—of thighs; *dvaya*—a pair; *anvitam*—having; *cāru*—attractive; *jānu-yugam*—whose two knees; *cāru*—attractive; *jaṅghā*—of shanks; *yugala*—a pair; *saṁyutam*—having; *tuṅga*—high; *gulpha*—whose ankles; *aruṇa*—reddish; *nakha-vrāta*—from whose toenails; *dīdhitibhiḥ*—with effulgent rays; *vṛtam*—surrounded; *nava*—soft; *aṅguli-aṅguṣṭha*—the two big toes and other toes; *dalaiḥ*—like flower petals; *vilasat*—glowing; *pāda-paṅkajam*—whose lotus feet.

TRANSLATION

He had large loins and hips, thighs like an elephant's trunk, and shapely knees and shanks. His raised ankles reflected the brilliant effulgence emanating from the nails on His petallike toes, which beautified His lotus feet.

TEXTS 51–52

सुमहार्हमणिव्रातकिरीटकटकांगदैः ।
कटिसूत्रब्रह्मसूत्रहारनूपुरकुण्डलैः ॥५१॥
भ्राजमानं पद्मकरं शंखचक्रगदाधरम् ।
श्रीवत्सवक्षसं भ्राजत्कौस्तुभं वनमालिनम् ॥५२॥

su-mahārha-maṇi-vrāta-
kirīṭa-kaṭakāṅgadaiḥ
kaṭi-sūtra-brahma-sūtra-
hāra-nūpura-kuṇḍalaiḥ

bhrājamānaṁ padma-karaṁ
śaṅkha-cakra-gadā-dharam
śrīvatsa-vakṣasaṁ bhrājat-
kaustubhaṁ vana-mālinam

su-mahā—greatly; *arha*—precious; *maṇi-vrāta*—having many gems; *kirīṭa*—with helmets; *kaṭaka*—bracelets; *aṅgadaiḥ*—and armlets; *kaṭi-sūtra*—with belt; *brahma-sūtra*—sacred thread; *hāra*—necklaces; *nūpura*—ankle bells; *kuṇḍalaiḥ*—and earrings; *bhrājamānam*—effulgent; *padma*—carrying a lotus; *karam*—whose hand; *śaṅkha*—a conchshell; *cakra*—discus; *gadā*—and club; *dharam*—holding; *śrīvatsa*—carrying the mark known as Śrīvatsa; *vakṣasam*—whose chest; *bhrājat*—brilliant; *kaustubham*—with the Kaustubha gem; *vana-mālinam*—with a flower garland.

TRANSLATION

Adorned with a helmet, bracelets and armlets, which were all bedecked with many priceless jewels, and also with a belt, a sacred thread, necklaces, ankle bells and earrings, the Lord shone with dazzling effulgence. In one hand He held a lotus flower, in the others a conchshell, discus and club. Gracing His chest were the Śrīvatsa mark, the brilliant Kaustubha gem and a flower garland.

TEXTS 53–55

सुनन्दनन्दप्रमुखैः पर्षदैः सनकादिभिः ।
सुरेशैर्ब्रह्मरुद्राद्यैर्नवभिश्च द्विजोत्तमैः ॥५३॥
प्रह्लादनारदवसुप्रमुखैर्भागवतोत्तमैः ।
स्तूयमानं पृथग्भावैर्वचोभिरमलात्मभिः ॥५४॥
श्रिया पुष्टया गिरा कान्त्या कीर्त्या तुष्टयेलयोर्जया ।
विद्ययाविद्यया शक्त्या मायया च निषेवितम् ॥५५॥

sunanda-nanda-pramukhaiḥ
parṣadaiḥ sanakādibhiḥ
sureśair brahma-rudrādyair
navabhiś ca dvijottamaiḥ

prahrāda-nārada-vasu-
pramukhair bhāgavatottamaiḥ
stūyamānaṁ pṛthag-bhāvair
vacobhir amalātmabhiḥ

śriyā puṣṭyā girā kāntyā
kīrtyā tuṣṭyelayorjayā
vidyayāvidyayā śaktyā
māyayā ca niṣevitam

sunanda-nanda-pramukhaiḥ—headed by Sunanda and Nanda; *parṣadaiḥ*—by His personal attendants; *sanaka-ādibhiḥ*—by Sanaka Kumāra and his brothers; *sura-īśaiḥ*—by the chief demigods; *brahma-rudra-ādyaiḥ*—headed by Brahmā and Rudra; *navabhiḥ*—nine; *ca*—and; *dvija-uttamaiḥ*—by the chief *brāhmaṇas* (headed by Marīci); *prahrāda-nārada-vasu-pramukhaiḥ*—headed by Prahlāda, Nārada and Uparicara Vasu; *bhāgavata-uttamaiḥ*—by the most exalted devotees; *stūyamānam*—being praised; *pṛthak-bhāvaiḥ*—by each in a different loving attitude; *vacobhiḥ*—with words; *amala-ātmabhiḥ*—sanctified; *śriyā puṣṭyā girā kāntyā kīrtyā tuṣṭyā ilayā ūrjayā*—by His internal potencies Śrī, Puṣṭi, Gīr, Kānti, Kīrti, Tuṣṭi, Ilā and Ūrjā; *vidyayā avidyayā*—by His potencies of knowledge and ignorance; *śaktyā*—by His internal pleasure potency; *māyayā*—by His material creative potency; *ca*—and; *niṣevitam*—being served.

TRANSLATION

Encircling the Lord and worshiping Him were Nanda, Sunanda and His other personal attendants; Sanaka and the other Kumāras; Brahmā, Rudra and other chief demigods; the nine chief *brāhmaṇas;* and the best of the saintly devotees, headed by Prahlāda, Nārada and Uparicara Vasu. Each of these great personalities was worshiping the Lord by chanting sanctified words of praise in his own unique mood. Also in attendance were the Lord's principal internal potencies—Śrī, Puṣṭi, Gīr, Kānti, Kīrti, Tuṣṭi, Ilā and Ūrjā—as were His material potencies Vidyā, Avidyā and Māyā, and His internal pleasure potency, Śakti.

PURPORT

Śrīla Viśvanātha Cakravartī explains the Lord's potencies mentioned in these verses: "Śrī is the potency of wealth; Puṣṭi that of strength; Gīr, knowledge; Kānti, beauty; Kīrti, fame; and Tuṣṭi, renunciation. These are the Lord's six opulences. Ilā is His *bhū-śakti,* also known as *sandhinī,* the internal potency of whom the element earth is an expansion. Ūrjā is His internal potency for performing pastimes; she expands as the *tulasī* plant in this world. Vidyā and Avidyā [knowledge and ignorance] are external potencies who cause the living entities' liberation and bondage, respectively. Śakti is His internal pleasure potency, *hlādinī,* and Māyā is an internal potency who is the basis of Vidyā and Avidyā. The word *ca* implies the presence of the Lord's marginal energy, the *jīva-śakti,* who is subordinate to Māyā. Lord Viṣṇu was being served by all these personified potencies."

TEXTS 56–57

विलोक्य सुभृशं प्रीतो भक्त्या परमया युतः ।
हृष्यत्तनूरुहो भावपरिक्लिन्नात्मलोचनः ॥५६॥
गिरा गद्गदयास्तौषीत्सत्त्वमालम्ब्य सात्वतः ।
प्रणम्य मूर्ध्नावहितः कृताञ्जलिपुटः शनैः ॥५७॥

vilokya su-bhṛśaṁ prīto
bhaktyā paramayā yutaḥ
hṛṣyat-tanūruho bhāva-
pariklinnātma-locanaḥ

girā gadgadayāstauṣīt
sattvam ālambya sātvataḥ
praṇamya mūrdhnāvahitaḥ
kṛtāñjali-puṭaḥ śanaiḥ

vilokya—(Akrūra) seeing; *su-bhṛśam*—greatly; *prītaḥ*—pleased; *bhaktyā*—with devotion; *paramayā*—supreme; *yutaḥ*—enthused; *hṛṣyat*—standing on end; *tanū-ruhaḥ*—the hairs of his body; *bhāva*—out of loving ecstasy; *pariklinna*—wet; *ātma*—his body; *locanaḥ*—and eyes; *girā*—with words; *gadgadayā*—choking; *astauṣīt*—He offered homage; *sattvam*—soberness; *ālambya*—taking hold of; *sātvataḥ*—the great devotee; *praṇamya*—bowing down; *mūrdhnā*—with his head; *avahitaḥ*—attentively; *kṛta-añjali-puṭaḥ*—joining his palms in supplication; *śanaiḥ*—slowly.

TRANSLATION

As the great devotee Akrūra beheld all this, he became extremely pleased and felt enthused with transcendental devotion. His intense ecstasy caused His bodily hairs to stand on end and tears to flow from his eyes, drenching his entire body. Somehow managing to steady himself, Akrūra bowed his head to the ground. Then he joined his palms in supplication and, in a voice choked with emotion, very slowly and attentively began to pray.

Thus end the purports of the humble servant of His Divine Grace A. C. Bhaktivedanta Swami Prabhupāda to the Tenth Canto, Thirty-ninth Chapter, of the Śrīmad-Bhāgavatam, *entitled "Akrūra's Vision."*

CHAPTER FORTY

The Prayers of Akrūra

This chapter relates Akrūra's prayers to the Supreme Personality of Godhead.

Akrūra prayed, "Brahmā, who created this visible world, emanated from the lotus navel of the Supreme Lord. The five elements of physical nature, the five corresponding objects of perception, the ten senses, the ego, the total nature, the primeval creator and the demigods all originate from His bodily limbs. He cannot be known by sensory knowledge, and thus even Brahmā and the other demigods are ignorant of His real identity.

"Different classes of people worship the Supreme Personality of Godhead in different ways. Fruitive workers worship Him by performing Vedic sacrifices, philosophers by renouncing material work and pursuing spiritual knowledge, *yogīs* by meditating, Śaivites by worshiping Lord Śiva, Vaiṣṇavas by following the injunctions of such scriptures as the *Pañcarātra,* and other saintly persons by worshiping Him as the original form of the self, of the material substance and of the controlling demigods. Just as rivers flow from various directions into the ocean, the worship of those who dedicate themselves to these various entities finds its ultimate purpose within the Supreme Lord Viṣṇu.

"The form of the total universe, the Virāṭ-rūpa, is imagined to be the form of Lord Viṣṇu. Like aquatics moving about in water or like tiny insects burrowing in an *udumbara* fruit, all living beings move about within the Lord. These living beings, bewildered by His Māyā, wander along the path of material work, falsely identifying with body, home and so forth. Under the sway of illusion, a foolish person may overlook a reservoir of water covered by grass and leaves and instead run after a mirage. Similarly, living beings caught in the grip of ignorance abandon Lord Viṣṇu and become attached to their bodies, homes and so on. Such faithful servants of their senses cannot take shelter of the Supreme Lord's lotus feet. Only if, by His mercy, they get the association of saintly devotees will their material entanglement end. Only then can they develop Kṛṣṇa consciousness by serving the Lord's pure devotees."

TEXT 1

श्रीअक्रूर उवाच
नतोऽस्म्यहं त्वाखिलहेतुहेतुं
नारायणं पूरुषमाद्यमव्ययम् ।
यन्नाभिजातादरविन्दकोषाद्
ब्रह्माविरासीद्यत एष लोकः ॥१॥

śrī-akrūra uvāca
nato 'smy ahaṁ tvākhila-hetu-hetuṁ
nārāyaṇaṁ pūruṣam ādyam avyayam
yan-nābhi-jātād aravinda-koṣād
brahmāvirāsīd yata eṣa lokaḥ

śrī-akrūraḥ uvāca—Śrī Akrūra said; *nataḥ*—bowed down; *asmi*—am; *aham*—I; *tvā*—to You; *akhila*—of all; *hetu*—causes; *hetum*—the cause; *nārāyaṇam*—Lord Nārāyaṇa; *pūruṣam*—the Supreme Person; *ādyam*—original; *avyayam*—inexhaustible; *yat*—from whose; *nābhi*—navel; *jātāt*—which was generated; *aravinda*—of a lotus plant; *koṣāt*—from the whorl; *brahmā*—Brahmā; *avirāsīt*—appeared; *yataḥ*—from whom; *eṣaḥ*—this; *lokaḥ*—world.

TRANSLATION

Śrī Akrūra said: I bow down to You, the cause of all causes, the original and inexhaustible Supreme Person, Nārāyaṇa. From the whorl of the lotus born from Your navel, Brahmā appeared, and by his agency this universe has come into being.

TEXT 2

भूस्तोयमग्निः पवनं खमादिर्
महानजादिर्मन इन्द्रियाणि ।
सर्वेन्द्रियार्था विबुधाश्च सर्वे
ये हेतवस्ते जगतोऽङ्गभूताः ॥२॥

bhūs toyam agniḥ pavanaṁ kham ādir
mahān ajādir mana indriyāṇi
sarvendriyārthā vibudhāś ca sarve
ye hetavas te jagato 'ṅga-bhūtāḥ

bhūḥ—earth; *toyam*—water; *agniḥ*—fire; *pavanam*—air; *kham*—ether; *ādiḥ*—and its source, false ego; *mahān*—the *mahat-tattva; ajā*—the total material nature; *ādiḥ*—her source, the Supreme Lord; *manaḥ*—the mind; *indriyāṇi*—the senses; *sarva-indriya*—of all the senses; *arthāḥ*—the objects; *vibudhāḥ*—the demigods; *ca*—and; *sarve*—all; *ye*—which; *hetavaḥ*—causes; *te*—Your; *jagataḥ*—of the universe; *aṅga*—from the body; *bhūtāḥ*—generated.

TRANSLATION

Earth; water; fire; air; ether and its source, false ego; the *mahat-tattva;* the total material nature and her source, the Supreme Lord's *puruṣa* expansion; the mind; the senses; the sense objects; and the senses' presiding deities—all these causes of the cosmic manifestation are born from Your transcendental body.

TEXT 3

नैते स्वरूपं विदुरात्मनस्ते
ह्यजादयोऽनात्मतया गृहीताः ।
अजोऽनुबद्धः स गुणैरजाया
गुणात्परं वेद न ते स्वरूपम् ॥३॥

naite svarūpaṁ vidur ātmanas te
hy ajādayo 'nātmatayā gṛhītāḥ
ajo 'nubaddhaḥ sa guṇair ajāyā
guṇāt paraṁ veda na te svarūpam

na—do not; *ete*—these (elements of creation); *svarūpam*—the true identity; *viduḥ*—know; *ātmanaḥ*—of the Supreme Soul; *te*—You; *hi*—indeed; *ajā-ādayaḥ*—headed by the total material nature; *anātmatayā*—by the status of being nonliving matter; *gṛhītāḥ*—seized; *ajaḥ*—Lord

Brahmā; *anubaddhaḥ*—bound up; *saḥ*—he; *guṇaiḥ*—by the modes; *ajāyāḥ*—of material nature; *guṇāt*—to these modes; *param*—transcendental; *veda na*—he does not know; *te*—Your; *svarūpam*—true form.

TRANSLATION

The total material nature and these other elements of creation certainly cannot know You as You are, for they are manifested in the realm of dull matter. Since You are beyond the modes of nature, even Lord Brahmā, who is bound up in these modes, does not know Your true identity.

PURPORT

God is transcendental to material nature. Unless we also transcend the limited consciousness of material existence, we cannot know Him. Even the greatest living entity in the universe, Brahmā, cannot understand the Supreme unless he comes to the platform of pure Kṛṣṇa consciousness.

TEXT 4

त्वां योगिनो यजन्त्यद्धा महापुरुषमीश्वरम् ।
साध्यात्मं साधिभूतं च साधिदैवं च साधवः ॥४॥

tvāṁ yogino yajanty addhā
mahā-puruṣam īśvaram
sādhyātmaṁ sādhibhūtaṁ ca
sādhidaivaṁ ca sādhavaḥ

tvām—for You; *yoginaḥ*—*yogīs; yajanti*—perform sacrifice; *addhā*—certainly; *mahā-puruṣam*—for the Supreme Personality; *īśvaram*—the Godhead; *sa-adhyātmam*—(the witness of) the living entities; *sa-adhibhūtam*—of the material elements; *ca*—and; *sa-adhidaivam*—of the controlling demigods; *ca*—and; *sādhavaḥ*—purified persons.

TRANSLATION

Pure *yogīs* worship You, the Supreme Personality of Godhead, by conceiving of You in the threefold form comprising the living

entities, the material elements that constitute the living entities' bodies, and the controlling deities of those elements.

TEXT 5

त्रय्या च विद्यया केचित्त्वां वै वैतानिका द्विजाः ।
यजन्ते विततैर्यज्ञैर्नानारूपामराख्यया ॥५॥

trayyā ca vidyayā kecit
tvāṁ vai vaitānikā dvijāḥ
yajante vitatair yajñair
nānā-rūpāmarākhyayā

trayyā—of the three *Vedas; ca*—and; *vidyayā*—by the *mantras; kecit*—some; *tvām*—You; *vai*—indeed; *vaitānikāḥ*—who respect the regulations of the three sacred fires; *dvijāḥ*—*brāhmaṇas; yajante*—worship; *vitataiḥ*—elaborate; *yajñaiḥ*—with ritual sacrifices; *nānā*—various; *rūpa*—having forms; *amara*—of demigods; *ākhyayā*—by the designations.

TRANSLATION

***Brāhmaṇas* who follow the regulations concerning the three sacred fires worship You by chanting *mantras* from the three *Vedas* and performing elaborate fire sacrifices for the various demigods, who have many forms and names.**

PURPORT

Akrūra has now described how those who follow the paths of Sāṅkhya, *yoga* and the three *Vedas* worship the Supreme Lord in different ways. In the various places where the *Vedas* appear to recommend that one worship Indra, Varuṇa and other demigods, these demigods are stated to be supreme. But at the same time the *Vedas* state that there is one supreme controller, the Absolute Truth. That is Śrī Kṛṣṇa, the Personality of Godhead, who expands His potency through material creation into the forms of the demigods. Thus worship of the demigods goes to Him through the indirect method of *karma-kāṇḍa*, or fruitive religious rituals. Ultimately, however, one who wants to achieve eternal perfection should worship the Lord directly, in full Kṛṣṇa consciousness.

TEXT 6

एके त्वाखिलकर्माणि संन्यस्योपशमं गताः ।
ज्ञानिनो ज्ञानयज्ञेन यजन्ति ज्ञानविग्रहम् ॥६॥

eke tvākhila-karmāṇi
sannyasyopaśamaṁ gatāḥ
jñānino jñāna-yajñena
yajanti jñāna-vigraham

eke—some; *tvā*—to You; *akhila*—all; *karmāṇi*—activities; *sannyasya*—resigning; *upaśamam*—peace; *gatāḥ*—attaining; *jñāninaḥ*—pursuers of knowledge; *jñāna-yajñena*—by the sacrifice of cultivating knowledge; *yajanti*—they worship; *jñāna-vigraham*—the embodiment of knowledge.

TRANSLATION

In pursuit of spiritual knowledge, some persons renounce all material activities and, having thus become peaceful, perform the sacrifice of philosophic investigation to worship You, the original form of all knowledge.

PURPORT

Modern philosophers pursue knowledge without bothering to worship the Supreme Personality of Godhead, and thus they naturally end up with meager, if not trivial, results.

TEXT 7

अन्ये च संस्कृतात्मानो विधिनाभिहितेन ते ।
यजन्ति त्वन्मयास्त्वां वै बहुमूर्त्येकमूर्तिकम् ॥७॥

anye ca saṁskṛtātmāno
vidhinābhihitena te
yajanti tvan-mayās tvāṁ vai
bahu-mūrty-eka-mūrtikam

anye—others; *ca*—and; *saṁskṛta*—purified; *ātmānaḥ*—whose intelligence; *vidhinā*—by the injunctions (of such scriptures as the *Pañcarātra*);

abhihitena—presented; *te*—by You; *yajanti*—worship; *tvat-mayāḥ*—filled with thought of You; *tvām*—You; *vai*—indeed; *bahu-mūrti*—having many forms; *eka-mūrtikam*—having one form.

TRANSLATION

And yet others—those whose intelligence is pure—follow the injunctions of Vaiṣṇava scriptures promulgated by You. Absorbing their minds in thought of You, they worship You as the one Supreme Lord manifesting in multiple forms.

PURPORT

The word *saṁskṛtātmānaḥ,* "they whose intelligence is pure," is significant here. It implies that the worshipers mentioned before have not completely purified their intelligence of material contamination and thus worship the Lord indirectly. Those who are purified, however, directly worship the Lord, either as the Supreme Personality of Godhead, Lord Kṛṣṇa, or as one of His various plenary forms, such as Vāsudeva, Saṅkarṣaṇa, Pradyumna or Aniruddha, as indicated here.

TEXT 8

त्वामेवान्ये शिवोक्तेन मार्गेण शिवरूपिणम् ।
बह्वाचार्यविभेदेन भगवन्तमुपासते ॥८॥

tvām evānye śivoktena
mārgeṇa śiva-rūpiṇam
bahv-ācārya-vibhedena
bhagavantam upāsate

tvām—You; *eva*—also; *anye*—others; *śiva*—by Lord Śiva; *uktena*—spoken; *mārgeṇa*—by the path; *śiva-rūpiṇam*—in the form of Lord Śiva; *bahu-ācārya*—of many teachers; *vibhedena*—following the different presentations; *bhagavantam*—the Supreme Lord; *upāsate*—they worship.

TRANSLATION

There are still others, who worship You, the Supreme Lord, in the form of Lord Śiva. They follow the path described by him and interpreted in various ways by many teachers.

PURPORT

The words *tvām eva,* "You also," indicate that the path of worshiping Lord Śiva is indirect and therefore inferior. Akrūra himself is following the superior method by directly worshiping Kṛṣṇa, or Viṣṇu, with his prayers.

TEXT 9

सर्व एव यजन्ति त्वां सर्वदेवमयेश्वरम् ।
येऽप्यन्यदेवताभक्ता यद्यप्यन्यधियः प्रभो ॥९॥

sarva eva yajanti tvāṁ
sarva-deva-mayeśvaram
ye 'py anya-devatā-bhaktā
yady apy anya-dhiyaḥ prabho

sarve—all; *eva*—indeed; *yajanti*—worship; *tvām*—You; *sarva-deva*—all the demigods; *maya*—O You who comprise; *īśvaram*—the Supreme Lord; *ye*—they; *api*—even; *anya*—of other; *devatā*—deities; *bhaktāḥ*—devotees; *yadi api*—although; *anya*—turned elsewhere; *dhiyaḥ*—their attention; *prabho*—O master.

TRANSLATION

But all these people, my Lord, even those who have turned their attention away from You and are worshiping other deities, are actually worshiping You alone, O embodiment of all the demigods.

PURPORT

The idea here is that even those who worship the demigods are indirectly worshiping the Supreme Lord Viṣṇu. The understanding of such worshipers, however, is imperfect.

TEXT 10

यथाद्रिप्रभवा नद्यः पर्जन्यापूरिताः प्रभो ।
विशन्ति सर्वतः सिन्धुं तद्वत्त्वां गतयोऽन्ततः ॥१०॥

yathādri-prabhavā nadyaḥ
parjanyāpūritāḥ prabho
viśanti sarvataḥ sindhuṁ
tadvat tvāṁ gatayo 'ntataḥ

yathā—as; *adri*—from the mountains; *prabhavāḥ*—born; *nadyaḥ*—rivers; *parjanya*—by the rain; *āpūritāḥ*—filled; *prabho*—O master; *viśanti*—enter; *sarvataḥ*—from all sides; *sindhum*—the ocean; *tadvat*—similarly; *tvām*—You; *gatayaḥ*—these paths; *antataḥ*—finally.

TRANSLATION

As rivers born from the mountains and filled by the rain flow from all sides into the sea, so do all these paths in the end reach You, O master.

PURPORT

Lord Kṛṣṇa Himself speaks on this issue of worship in the *Bhagavad-gītā* (9.23-25):

ye 'py anya-devatā-bhaktā
yajante śraddhayānvitāḥ
te 'pi mām eva kaunteya
yajanty avidhi-pūrvakam

ahaṁ hi sarva-yajñānāṁ
bhoktā ca prabhur eva ca
na tu mām abhijānanti
tattvenātaś cyavanti te

yānti deva-vratā devān
pitṝn yānti pitṛ-vratāḥ
bhūtāni yānti bhūtejyā
yānti mad-yājino 'pi mām

"Those who are devotees of other gods and who worship them with faith actually worship only Me, O son of Kuntī, but they do so in a wrong way. I am the only enjoyer and master of all sacrifices. Therefore, those who do not recognize My true transcendental nature fall down. Those who worship the demigods will take birth among the demigods; those who worship the ancestors go to the ancestors; those who worship ghosts and spirits will take birth among such beings; and those who worship Me will live with Me."

TEXT 11

सत्त्वं रजस्तम इति भवतः प्रकृतेर्गुणाः ।
तेषु हि प्राकृताः प्रोता आब्रह्मस्थावरादयः ॥११॥

sattvaṁ rajas tama iti
bhavataḥ prakṛter guṇāḥ
teṣu hi prākṛtāḥ protā
ā-brahma-sthāvarādayaḥ

sattvam—goodness; *rajaḥ*—passion; *tamaḥ*—ignorance; *iti*—thus known; *bhavataḥ*—Your; *prakṛteḥ*—of the material nature; *guṇāḥ*—the qualities; *teṣu*—to them; *hi*—certainly; *prākṛtāḥ*—the conditioned living entities; *protāḥ*—woven; *ā-brahma*—up to Lord Brahmā; *sthāvara-ādayaḥ*—starting with the nonmoving creatures.

TRANSLATION

Goodness, passion and ignorance, the qualities of Your material nature, entangle all conditioned living beings, from Brahmā down to the nonmoving creatures.

TEXT 12

तुभ्यं नमस्ते त्वविषक्तदृष्टये
सर्वात्मने सर्वधियां च साक्षिणे ।
गुणप्रवाहोऽयमविद्यया कृतः
प्रवर्तते देवनृतिर्यगात्मसु ॥१२॥

tubhyaṁ namas te tv aviṣakta-dṛṣṭaye
sarvātmane sarva-dhiyāṁ ca sākṣiṇe
guṇa-pravāho 'yam avidyayā kṛtaḥ
pravartate deva-nṛ-tiryag-ātmasu

tubhyam—to You; *namaḥ*—obeisances; *te*—Your; *tu*—and; *aviṣakta*—aloof; *dṛṣṭaye*—whose vision; *sarva-ātmane*—to the Soul of all; *sarva*—of everyone; *dhiyām*—of the consciousness; *ca*—and; *sākṣiṇe*—to the witness; *guṇa*—of the material modes; *pravāhaḥ*—the flow; *ayam*—this; *avidyayā*—by the force of ignorance; *kṛtaḥ*—created; *pravartate*—goes on; *deva*—as demigods; *nṛ*—humans; *tiryak*—and animals; *ātmasu*—among those who assume the identities.

TRANSLATION

I offer My obeisances to You, who as the Supreme Soul of all beings witness everyone's consciousness with unbiased vision. The current of Your material modes, produced by the force of ignorance, flows strongly among the living beings who assume identities as demigods, humans and animals.

TEXTS 13–14

अग्निर्मुखं तेऽवनिरङ्घ्रिरीक्षणं
सूर्यो नभो नाभिरथो दिशः श्रुतिः ।
द्यौः कं सुरेन्द्रास्तव बाहवोऽर्णवाः
कुक्षिर्मरुत्प्राणबलं प्रकल्पितम् ॥१३॥
रोमाणि वृक्षौषधयः शिरोरुहा
मेघाः परस्यास्थिनखानि तेऽद्रयः ।
निमेषणं रात्र्यहनी प्रजापतिर्
मेढ्रस्तु वृष्टिस्तव वीर्यमिष्यते ॥१४॥

agnir mukhaṁ te 'vanir aṅghrir īkṣaṇaṁ
sūryo nabho nābhir atho diśaḥ śrutiḥ
dyauḥ kaṁ surendrās tava bāhavo 'rṇavāḥ
kukṣir marut prāṇa-balaṁ prakalpitam

romāṇi vṛkṣauṣadhayaḥ śiroruhā
meghāḥ parasyāsthi-nakhāni te 'drayaḥ
nimeṣaṇaṁ rātry-ahanī prajāpatir
meḍhras tu vṛṣṭis tava vīryam iṣyate

agniḥ—fire; *mukham*—face; *te*—Your; *avaniḥ*—the earth; *aṅghriḥ*—feet; *īkṣaṇam*—eye; *sūryaḥ*—the sun; *nabhaḥ*—the sky; *nābhiḥ*—navel; *atha u*—and also; *diśaḥ*—the directions; *śrutiḥ*—sense of hearing; *dyauḥ*—heaven; *kam*—head; *sura-indrāḥ*—the chief demigods; *tava*—Your; *bāhavaḥ*—arms; *arṇavāḥ*—the oceans; *kukṣiḥ*—abdomen; *marut*—the wind; *prāṇa*—vital air; *balam*—and physical strength; *prakalpitam*—conceived; *romāṇi*—bodily hairs; *vṛkṣa*—the trees; *oṣadhayaḥ*—the plants; *śiraḥ-ruhāḥ*—the hair on Your head; *meghāḥ*—the clouds; *parasya*—of the Supreme; *asthi*—bones; *nakhāni*—and nails; *te*—of You; *adrayaḥ*—the mountains; *nimeṣaṇam*—the blinking of Your eyes; *rātri-ahanī*—day and night; *prajāpatiḥ*—the progenitor of mankind; *meḍhraḥ*—genitals; *tu*—and; *vṛṣṭiḥ*—the rain; *tava*—Your; *vīryam*—semen; *iṣyate*—is considered.

TRANSLATION

Fire is said to be Your face, the earth Your feet, the sun Your eye, and the sky Your navel. The directions are Your sense of hearing, the chief demigods Your arms, and the oceans Your abdomen. Heaven is thought to be Your head, and the wind Your vital air and physical strength. The trees and plants are the hairs on Your body, the clouds the hair on Your head, and the mountains the bones and nails of You, the Supreme. The passage of day and night is the blinking of Your eyes, the progenitor of mankind Your genitals, and the rain Your semen.

TEXT 15

त्वय्यव्ययात्मन् पुरुषे प्रकल्पिता
लोकाः सपाला बहुजीवसंकुलाः ।
यथा जले सञ्जिहते जलौकसो
ऽप्युदुम्बरे वा मशका मनोमये ॥१५॥

tvayy avyayātman puruṣe prakalpitā
lokāḥ sa-pālā bahu-jīva-saṅkulāḥ
yathā jale sañjihate jalaukaso
'py udumbare vā maśakā mano-maye

tvayi—within You; *avyaya-ātman*—the inexhaustible one; *puruṣe*—the Supreme Personality of Godhead; *prakalpitāḥ*—created; *lokāḥ*—the worlds; *sa-pālāḥ*—together with their protecting demigods; *bahu*—with many; *jīva*—living beings; *saṅkulāḥ*—crowded; *yathā*—just as; *jale*—in water; *sañjihate*—move about; *jala-okasaḥ*—aquatic animals; *api*—indeed; *udumbare*—in an *udumbara* fruit (a kind of fig); *vā*—or; *maśakāḥ*—small biting insects; *manaḥ*—the mind (and other senses); *maye*—(in You) who comprise.

TRANSLATION

All the worlds, with their presiding demigods and teeming populations, originate in You, the inexhaustible Supreme Personality of Godhead. These worlds travel within You, the basis of the mind and senses, just as aquatics swim in the sea or tiny insects burrow within an *udumbara* fruit.

TEXT 16

यानि यानीह रूपाणि क्रीडनार्थं बिभर्षि हि ।
तैरामृष्टशुचो लोका मुदा गायन्ति ते यशः ॥१६॥

yāni yānīha rūpāṇi
krīḍanārthaṁ bibharṣi hi
tair āmṛṣṭa-śuco lokā
mudā gāyanti te yaśaḥ

yāni yāni—which various; *iha*—in this material world; *rūpāṇi*—forms; *krīḍana*—of play; *artham*—for the sake; *bibharṣi*—You manifest; *hi*—indeed; *taiḥ*—by them; *āmṛṣṭa*—cleansed; *śucaḥ*—of their unhappiness; *lokāḥ*—people; *mudā*—joyfully; *gāyanti*—sing; *te*—Your; *yaśaḥ*—glories.

TRANSLATION

To enjoy Your pastimes You manifest Yourself in various forms in this material world, and these incarnations cleanse away all the unhappiness of those who joyfully chant Your glories.

TEXTS 17–18

नमः कारणमत्स्याय प्रलयाब्धिचराय च ।
हयशीर्ष्णे नमस्तुभ्यं मधुकैटभमृत्यवे ॥१७॥
अकूपाराय बृहते नमो मन्दरधारिणे ।
क्षित्युद्धारविहाराय नमः शूकरमूर्तये ॥१८॥

namaḥ kāraṇa-matsyāya
pralayābdhi-carāya ca
hayaśīrṣṇe namas tubhyaṁ
madhu-kaiṭabha-mṛtyave

akūpārāya bṛhate
namo mandara-dhāriṇe
kṣity-uddhāra-vihārāya
namaḥ śūkara-mūrtaye

namaḥ—obeisances; *kāraṇa*—who is the original cause of creation; *matsyāya*—to the Supreme Lord's appearance as a fish; *pralaya*—of annihilation; *abdhi*—in the ocean; *carāya*—who moved about; *ca*—and; *haya-śīrṣṇe*—to the incarnation who appeared with the head of a horse; *namaḥ*—obeisances; *tubhyam*—to You; *madhu-kaiṭabha*—of the demons Madhu and Kaiṭabha; *mṛtyave*—to the killer; *akūpārāya*—to the tortoise; *bṛhate*—huge; *namaḥ*—obeisances; *mandara*—of Mandara Mountain; *dhāriṇe*—to the holder; *kṣiti*—of the earth; *uddhāra*—the lifting up; *vihārāya*—whose pleasure; *namaḥ*—obeisances; *śūkara*—of a boar; *mūrtaye*—to the form.

TRANSLATION

I offer my obeisances to You, the cause of the creation, Lord Matsya, who swam about in the ocean of dissolution, to Lord Hayagrīva, the killer of Madhu and Kaiṭabha, to the immense tortoise [Lord Kūrma], who supported Mandara Mountain, and to the boar incarnation [Lord Varāha], who enjoyed lifting the earth.

PURPORT

The *Viśva-kośa* dictionary states that the word *akūpārāya* indicates the king of tortoises.

TEXT 19

नमस्तेऽद्‌भुतसिंहाय साधुलोकभयापह ।
वामनाय नमस्तुभ्यं क्रान्तत्रिभुवनाय च ॥१९॥

namas te 'dbhuta-siṁhāya
sādhu-loka-bhayāpaha
vāmanāya namas tubhyaṁ
krānta-tribhuvanāya ca

namaḥ—obeisances; *te*—to You; *adbhuta*—amazing; *siṁhāya*—to the lion; *sādhu-loka*—of all saintly devotees; *bhaya*—of the fear; *apaha*—O remover; *vāmanāya*—to the dwarf; *namaḥ*—obeisances; *tubhyam*—to You; *krānta*—who stepped over; *tri-bhuvanāya*—the three planetary systems of the universe; *ca*—and.

TRANSLATION

Obeisances to You, the amazing lion [Lord Nṛsiṁha], who remove Your saintly devotees' fear, and to the dwarf Vāmana, who stepped over the three worlds.

TEXT 20

नमो भृगूणां पतये दृप्तक्षत्रवनच्छिदे ।
नमस्ते रघुवर्याय रावणान्तकराय च ॥२०॥

namo bhṛgūṇāṁ pataye
dṛpta-kṣatra-vana-cchide
namas te raghu-varyāya
rāvaṇānta-karāya ca

namaḥ—obeisances; *bhṛgūṇām*—of the descendants of Bhṛgu; *pataye*—to the chief (Lord Paraśurāma); *dṛpta*—conceited; *kṣatra*—of the members of the royal order; *vana*—the forest; *chide*—who cut down; *namaḥ*—obeisances; *te*—to You; *raghu-varyāya*—the best of the descendants of Raghu; *rāvaṇa*—of Rāvaṇa; *anta-karāya*—who put an end; *ca*—and.

TRANSLATION

Obeisances to You, Lord of the Bhṛgus, who cut down the forest of the conceited royal order, and to Lord Rāma, the best of the Raghu dynasty, who put an end to the demon Rāvaṇa.

TEXT 21

नमस्ते वासुदेवाय नमः संकर्षणाय च ।
प्रद्युम्नायानिरुद्धाय सात्वतां पतये नमः ॥२१॥

namas te vāsudevāya
namaḥ saṅkarṣaṇāya ca
pradyumnāyāniruddhāya
sātvatāṁ pataye namaḥ

namaḥ—obeisances; *te*—unto You; *vāsudevāya*—Lord Śrī Vāsudeva; *namaḥ*—obeisances; *saṅkarṣaṇāya*—to Lord Saṅkarṣaṇa; *ca*—and; *pradyumnāya*—to Lord Pradyumna; *aniruddhāya*—and to Lord Aniruddha; *sātvatām*—of the Yādavas; *pataye*—to the chief; *namaḥ*—obeisances.

TRANSLATION

Obeisances to You, Lord of the Sātvatas, and to Your forms of Vāsudeva, Saṅkarṣaṇa, Pradyumna and Aniruddha.

TEXT 22

नमो बुद्धाय शुद्धाय दैत्यदानवमोहिने ।
म्लेच्छप्रायक्षत्रहन्त्रे नमस्ते कल्किरूपिणे ॥२२॥

namo buddhāya śuddhāya
daitya-dānava-mohine
mleccha-prāya-kṣatra-hantre
namas te kalki-rūpiṇe

namaḥ—obeisances; *buddhāya*—to Lord Buddha; *śuddhāya*—the pure; *daitya-dānava*—of the demoniac descendants of Diti and Dānu; *mohine*—to the bewilderer; *mleccha*—of the outcaste meat-eaters; *prāya*—resembling; *kṣatra*—kings; *hantre*—to the killer; *namaḥ*—obeisances; *te*—to You; *kalki-rūpiṇe*—in the form of Kalki.

TRANSLATION

Obeisances to Your form as the faultless Lord Buddha, who will bewilder the Daityas and Dānavas, and to Lord Kalki, the annihilator of the meat-eaters posing as kings.

TEXT 23

भगवन् जीवलोकोऽयं मोहितस्तव मायया ।
अहं ममेत्यसद्ग्राहो भ्राम्यते कर्मवर्त्मसु ॥२३॥

bhagavan jīva-loko 'yaṁ
mohitas tava māyayā
ahaṁ mamety asad-grāho
bhrāmyate karma-vartmasu

bhagavan—O Supreme Lord; *jīva*—of living entities; *lokaḥ*—the world; *ayam*—this; *mohitaḥ*—bewildered; *tava*—Your; *māyayā*—by the illusory energy; *aham mama iti*—based on the conceptions of "I" and "my"; *asat*—false; *grāhaḥ*—whose conception; *bhrāmyate*—is made to wander; *karma*—of fruitive work; *vartmasu*—along the paths.

TRANSLATION

O Supreme Lord, the living entities in this world are bewildered by Your illusory energy. Becoming involved in the false concepts of "I" and "my," they are forced to wander along the paths of fruitive work.

TEXT 24

अहं चात्मात्मजागारदारार्थस्वजनादिषु ।
भ्रमामि स्वप्नकल्पेषु मूढः सत्यधिया विभो ॥२४॥

ahaṁ cātmātmajāgāra-
dārārtha-svajanādiṣu

bhramāmi svapna-kalpeṣu
mūḍhaḥ satya-dhiyā vibho

aham—I; *ca*—also; *ātma*—concerning my body; *ātma-ja*—children; *agāra*—home; *dāra*—wife; *artha*—wealth; *sva-jana*—followers; *ādiṣu*—and so on; *bhramāmi*—am deluded; *svapna*—a dream; *kalpeṣu*—who are just like; *mūḍhaḥ*—foolish; *satya*—that they are real; *dhiyā*—with the idea; *vibho*—O almighty Lord.

TRANSLATION

I too am deluded in this way, O almighty Lord, foolishly thinking my body, children, home, wife, money and followers to be real, though they are actually as unreal as a dream.

TEXT 25

अनित्यानात्मदुःखेषु विपर्ययमतिर्ह्यहम् ।
द्वन्द्वारामस्तमोविष्टो न जाने त्वात्मनः प्रियम् ॥२५॥

anityānātma-duḥkheṣu
viparyaya-matir hy aham
dvandvārāmas tamo-viṣṭo
na jāne tvātmanaḥ priyam

anitya—not eternal; *anātma*—not the real self; *duḥkheṣu*—in the sources of misery; *viparyaya*—backwards; *matiḥ*—whose mentality; *hi*—indeed; *aham*—I; *dvandva*—in duality; *ārāmaḥ*—taking pleasure; *tamaḥ*—in ignorance; *viṣṭaḥ*—absorbed; *na jāne*—I fail to recognize; *tvā*—You; *ātmanaḥ*—of myself; *priyam*—the dearmost.

TRANSLATION

Thus mistaking the temporary for the eternal, my body for my self, and sources of misery for sources of happiness, I have tried to take pleasure in material dualities. Covered in this way by ignorance, I could not recognize You as the real object of my love.

TEXT 26

यथाबुधो जलं हित्वा प्रतिच्छन्नं तदुद्भवैः ।
अभ्येति मृगतृष्णां वै तद्वत्त्वाहं पराङ्मुखः ॥२६॥

yathābudho jalaṁ hitvā
praticchannaṁ tad-udbhavaiḥ
abhyeti mṛga-tṛṣṇāṁ vai
tadvat tvāhaṁ parāṅ-mukhaḥ

yathā—as; *abudhaḥ*—someone who is unintelligent; *jalam*—water; *hitvā*—overlooking; *praticchannam*—covered; *tat-udbhavaiḥ*—by the plants growing in it; *abhyeti*—approaches; *mṛga-tṛṣṇām*—a mirage; *vai*—indeed; *tadvat*—in that same way; *tvā*—You; *aham*—I; *parāk-mukhaḥ*—turned away.

TRANSLATION

Just as a fool overlooks a body of water covered by the vegetation growing in it and chases a mirage, so I have turned away from You.

TEXT 27

नोत्सहेऽहं कृपणधीः काममकर्महतं मनः ।
रोद्धुं प्रमाथिभिश्चाक्षैर्ह्रियमाणमितस्ततः ॥२७॥

notsahe 'haṁ kṛpaṇa-dhīḥ
kāma-karma-hataṁ manaḥ
roddhuṁ pramāthibhiś cākṣair
hriyamāṇam itas tataḥ

na utsahe—am not able to find the strength; *aham*—I; *kṛpaṇa*—crippled; *dhīḥ*—whose intelligence; *kāma*—by material desires; *karma*—and material activities; *hatam*—disturbed; *manaḥ*—my mind; *roddhum*—to keep in check; *pramāthibhiḥ*—which are very powerful and willful; *ca*—and; *akṣaiḥ*—by the senses; *hriyamāṇam*—being dragged; *itaḥ tataḥ*—here and there.

TRANSLATION

My intelligence is so crippled that I cannot find the strength to curb my mind, which is disturbed by material desires and activities and constantly dragged here and there by my obstinate senses.

TEXT 28

सोऽहं तवाङ्घ्र्युपगतोऽस्म्यसतां दुरापं
तच्चाप्यहं भवदनुग्रह ईश मन्ये ।
पुंसो भवेद्यर्हि संसरणापवर्गस्
त्वय्यब्जनाभ सदुपासनया मतिः स्यात् ॥२८॥

so 'haṁ tavāṅghry-upagato 'smy asatāṁ durāpaṁ
tac cāpy ahaṁ bhavad-anugraha īśa manye
puṁso bhaved yarhi saṁsaraṇāpavargas
tvayy abja-nābha sad-upāsanayā matiḥ syāt

saḥ—being such; *aham*—I; *tava*—Your; *aṅghri*—feet; *upagataḥ asmi*—am approaching; *asatām*—for those who are impure; *durāpam*—impossible to attain; *tat*—that; *ca*—and; *api*—also; *aham*—I; *bhavat*—Your; *anugrahaḥ*—mercy; *īśa*—O Lord; *manye*—think; *puṁsaḥ*—of a person; *bhavet*—occurs; *yarhi*—when; *saṁsaraṇa*—of his rotation in the cycle of material existence; *apavargaḥ*—the cessation; *tvayi*—of You; *abja*—like a lotus; *nābha*—O You whose navel; *sat*—of pure devotees; *upāsanayā*—by worship; *matiḥ*—consciousness; *syāt*—develops.

TRANSLATION

Being thus fallen, I am approaching Your feet for shelter, O Lord, because although the impure can never attain Your feet, I think it is nevertheless possible by Your mercy. Only when one's material life has ceased, O lotus-naveled Lord, can one develop consciousness of You by serving Your pure devotees.

TEXT 29

नमो विज्ञानमात्राय सर्वप्रत्ययहेतवे ।
पुरुषेशप्रधानाय ब्रह्मणेऽनन्तशक्तये ॥२९॥

namo vijñāna-mātrāya
sarva-pratyaya-hetave
puruṣeśa-pradhānāya
brahmaṇe 'nanta-śaktaye

namaḥ—obeisances; *vijñāna*—of pure knowledge; *mātrāya*—to the embodiment; *sarva*—of all; *pratyaya*—forms of knowledge; *hetave*—to the source; *puruṣa*—of a person; *īśa*—the controlling forces; *pradhānāya*—to Him who predominates; *brahmaṇe*—to the Supreme Absolute Truth; *ananta*—unlimited; *śaktaye*—whose potencies.

TRANSLATION

Obeisances to the Supreme Absolute Truth, the possessor of unlimited energies. He is the embodiment of pure, transcendental knowledge, the source of all kinds of awareness, and the predominator of the forces of nature that rule over the living being.

TEXT 30

नमस्ते वासुदेवाय सर्वभूतक्षयाय च ।
हृषीकेश नमस्तुभ्यं प्रपन्नं पाहि मां प्रभो ॥३०॥

namas te vāsudevāya
sarva-bhūta-kṣayāya ca
hṛṣīkeśa namas tubhyaṁ
prapannaṁ pāhi māṁ prabho

namaḥ—obeisances; *te*—to You; *vāsudevāya*—the son of Vasudeva; *sarva*—of all; *bhūta*—living beings; *kṣayāya*—the residence; *ca*—and;

hṛṣīka-īśa—O Lord of the mind and senses; *namaḥ*—obeisances; *tubhyam*—to You; *prapannam*—who am surrendered; *pāhi*—please protect; *mām*—me; *prabho*—O master.

TRANSLATION

O son of Vasudeva, obeisances to You, within whom all living beings reside. O Lord of the mind and senses, again I offer You my obeisances. O master, please protect me, who am surrendered unto You.

Thus end the purports of the humble servant of His Divine Grace A. C. Bhaktivedanta Swami Prabhupāda to the Tenth Canto, Fortieth Chapter, of the Śrīmad-Bhāgavatam, *entitled "The Prayers of Akrūra."*

CHAPTER FORTY-ONE

Kṛṣṇa and Balarāma Enter Mathurā

This chapter describes how Lord Kṛṣṇa entered the city of Mathurā, killed a washerman and bestowed benedictions upon a weaver and a garland-maker named Sudāmā.

After showing His Viṣṇu form to Akrūra in the waters of the Yamunā and receiving Akrūra's prayers, Lord Kṛṣṇa withdrew that vision just as an actor winds up his performance. Akrūra emerged from the water and in great amazement approached the Lord, who asked him whether he had seen something wonderful while bathing. Akrūra replied, "Whatever wonderful things there are in the realms of water, earth or sky, all have their existence within You. Thus when one has seen You, nothing remains unseen." Akrūra then began driving the chariot again.

Kṛṣṇa, Balarāma and Akrūra reached Mathurā late in the afternoon. After meeting up with Nanda Mahārāja and the other cowherds, who had gone on ahead, Kṛṣṇa asked Akrūra to return home, promising to visit him there after He had killed Kaṁsa. Akrūra unhappily bid the Lord goodbye, went to King Kaṁsa to inform him that Kṛṣṇa and Balarāma had come, and went home.

Kṛṣṇa and Balarāma took the cowherd boys with Them to see the splendorous city. As they all entered Mathurā, the women of the city eagerly came out of their houses to see Kṛṣṇa. They had often heard about Him and had long since developed a deep attraction for Him. But now that they were actually seeing Him, they were overwhelmed with happiness, and all their distress due to His absence was eradicated.

Kṛṣṇa and Balarāma then came upon Kaṁsa's wicked washerman. Kṛṣṇa asked him for some of the first-class garments he was carrying, but he refused and even chastised the two Lords. At this Kṛṣṇa became very angry and beheaded the man with His fingertips. The washerman's assistants, seeing his untimely end, dropped their bundles of clothes on the spot and ran off in all directions. Kṛṣṇa and Balarāma then took some of the garments They especially fancied.

Next a weaver approached the two Lords and arrayed Them suitably, for which service he received from Kṛṣṇa opulence in this life and liberation in the next. Kṛṣṇa and Balarāma then went to the house of the garland-maker Sudāmā. Sudāmā offered Them his full obeisances, worshiped Them by bathing Their feet and offering Them such items as *arghya* and sandalwood paste, and chanted prayers in Their honor. Then he adorned Them with garlands of fragrant flowers. Pleased, the Lords offered him whatever benedictions he wished, and then They moved on.

TEXT 1

श्रीशुक उवाच
स्तुवतस्तस्य भगवान् दर्शयित्वा जले वपुः ।
भूयः समाहरत्कृष्णो नटो नाट्यमिवात्मनः ॥१॥

śrī-śuka uvāca
stuvatas tasya bhagavān
darśayitvā jale vapuḥ
bhūyaḥ samāharat kṛṣṇo
naṭo nāṭyam ivātmanaḥ

śrī-śukaḥ uvāca—Śukadeva Gosvāmī said; *stuvataḥ*—while praying; *tasya*—he, Akrūra; *bhagavān*—the Supreme Lord; *darśayitvā*—having shown; *jale*—in the water; *vapuḥ*—His personal form; *bhūyaḥ*—again; *samāharat*—withdrew; *kṛṣṇaḥ*—Śrī Kṛṣṇa; *naṭaḥ*—an actor; *nāṭyam*—the performance; *iva*—as; *ātmanaḥ*—his own.

TRANSLATION

Śukadeva Gosvāmī said: While Akrūra was still offering prayers, the Supreme Lord Kṛṣṇa withdrew His form that He had revealed in the water, just as an actor winds up his performance.

PURPORT

Lord Kṛṣṇa withdrew from Akrūra's sight the Viṣṇu form along with the vision of the spiritual sky and its eternal inhabitants.

TEXT 2

सोऽपि चान्तर्हितं वीक्ष्य जलादुन्मज्य सत्वरः ।
कृत्वा चावश्यकं सर्वं विस्मितो रथमागमत् ॥२॥

so 'pi cāntarhitaṁ vīkṣya
jalād unmajya satvaraḥ
kṛtvā cāvaśyakaṁ sarvaṁ
vismito ratham āgamat

saḥ—he, Akrūra; *api*—indeed; *ca*—and; *antarhitam*—disappeared; *vīkṣya*—seeing; *jalāt*—from the water; *unmajya*—emerging; *satvaraḥ*—quickly; *kṛtvā*—performing; *ca*—and; *āvaśyakam*—his prescribed duties; *sarvam*—all; *vismitaḥ*—surprised; *ratham*—to the chariot; *āgamat*—went.

TRANSLATION

When Akrūra saw the vision disappear, he came out of the water and quickly finished his various ritual duties. He then returned to the chariot, astonished.

TEXT 3

तमपृच्छद्धृषीकेशः किं ते दृष्टमिवाद्भुतम् ।
भूमौ वियति तोये वा तथा त्वां लक्षयामहे ॥३॥

tam apṛcchad dhṛṣīkeśaḥ
kiṁ te dṛṣṭam ivādbhutam
bhūmau viyati toye vā
tathā tvāṁ lakṣayāmahe

tam—of him; *apṛcchat*—asked; *hṛṣīkeśaḥ*—Lord Kṛṣṇa; *kim*—whether; *te*—by you; *dṛṣṭam*—seen; *iva*—indeed; *adbhutam*—something exceptional; *bhūmau*—on the earth; *viyati*—in the sky; *toye*—in the water; *vā*—or; *tathā*—so; *tvām*—you; *lakṣayāmahe*—We surmise.

TRANSLATION

Lord Kṛṣṇa asked Akrūra: Have you seen something wonderful on the earth, in the sky or in the water? From your appearance, We think you have.

TEXT 4

श्रीअक्रूर उवाच
अद्भुतानीह यावन्ति भूमौ वियति वा जले ।
त्वयि विश्वात्मके तानि किं मेऽदृष्टं विपश्यतः ॥४॥

śrī-akrūra uvāca
adbhutānīha yāvanti
bhūmau viyati vā jale
tvayi viśvātmake tāni
kiṁ me 'dṛṣṭaṁ vipaśyataḥ

śrī-akrūraḥ uvāca—Śrī Akrūra said; *adbhutāni*—wonderful things; *iha*—in this world; *yāvanti*—whatever; *bhūmau*—on the earth; *viyati*—in the sky; *vā*—or; *jale*—in the water; *tvayi*—in You; *viśva-ātmake*—who comprise everything; *tāni*—they; *kim*—what; *me*—by me; *adṛṣṭam*—not seen; *vipaśyataḥ*—seeing (You).

TRANSLATION

Śrī Akrūra said: Whatever wonderful things the earth, sky or water contain, all exist in You. Since You encompass everything, when I am seeing You, what have I not seen?

TEXT 5

यत्राद्भुतानि सर्वाणि भूमौ वियति वा जले ।
तं त्वानुपश्यतो ब्रह्मन् किं मे दृष्टमिहाद्भुतम् ॥५॥

yatrādbhutāni sarvāṇi
bhūmau viyati vā jale
taṁ tvānupaśyato brahman
kiṁ me dṛṣṭam ihādbhutam

yatra—in whom; *adbhutāni*—amazing things; *sarvāṇi*—all; *bhūmau*—on the earth; *viyati*—in the sky; *vā*—or; *jale*—in the water; *tam*—that person; *tvā*—You; *anupaśyataḥ*—seeing; *brahman*—O Supreme Absolute Truth; *kim*—what; *me*—by me; *dṛṣṭam*—seen; *iha*—in this world; *adbhutam*—amazing.

TRANSLATION

And now that I am seeing You, O Supreme Absolute Truth, in whom reside all amazing things on the earth, in the sky and in the water, what amazing things could I see in this world?

PURPORT

Akrūra has now realized that Lord Kṛṣṇa is not merely his nephew.

TEXT 6

इत्युक्त्वा चोदयामास स्यन्दनं गान्दिनीसुतः ।
मथुरामनयद् रामं कृष्णं चैव दिनात्यये ॥६॥

ity uktvā codayām āsa
syandanaṁ gāndinī-sutaḥ
mathurām anayad rāmaṁ
kṛṣṇaṁ caiva dinātyaye

iti—thus; *uktvā*—saying; *codayām āsa*—drove forward; *syandanam*—the chariot; *gāndinī-sutaḥ*—the son of Gāndinī, Akrūra; *mathurām*—to Mathurā; *anayat*—he brought; *rāmam*—Lord Balarāma; *kṛṣṇam*—Lord Kṛṣṇa; *ca*—and; *eva*—also; *dina*—of the day; *atyaye*—at the end.

TRANSLATION

With these words, Akrūra, the son of Gāndinī, began driving the chariot onward. At the end of the day he arrived in Mathurā with Lord Balarāma and Lord Kṛṣṇa.

TEXT 7

मार्गे ग्रामजना राजंस्तत्र तत्रोपसंगताः ।
वसुदेवसुतौ वीक्ष्य प्रीता दृष्टिं न चाददुः ॥७॥

mārge grāma-janā rājaṁs
tatra tatropasaṅgatāḥ
vasudeva-sutau vīkṣya
prītā dṛṣṭiṁ na cādaduḥ

mārge—on the road; *grāma*—of the villages; *janāḥ*—the people; *rājan*—O King (Parīkṣit); *tatra tatra*—here and there; *upasaṅgatāḥ*—approaching; *vasudeva-sutau*—at the two sons of Vasudeva; *vīkṣya*—looking; *prītāḥ*—pleased; *dṛṣṭim*—their vision; *na*—not; *ca*—and; *ādaduḥ*—could take back.

TRANSLATION

Wherever they passed along the road, O King, the village people came forward and looked upon the two sons of Vasudeva with great pleasure. In fact, the villagers could not withdraw their eyes from Them.

TEXT 8

तावद् व्रजौकसस्तत्र नन्दगोपादयोऽग्रतः ।
पुरोपवनमासाद्य प्रतीक्षन्तोऽवतस्थिरे ॥८॥

tāvad vrajaukasas tatra
nanda-gopādayo 'grataḥ
puropavanam āsādya
pratīkṣanto 'vatasthire

tāvat—by then; *vraja-okasaḥ*—the inhabitants of Vraja; *tatra*—there; *nanda-gopa-ādayaḥ*—headed by Nanda, the king of the cowherds; *agrataḥ*—before; *pura*—of the city; *upavanam*—a garden; *āsādya*—coming upon; *pratīkṣantaḥ*—waiting; *avatasthire*—they stayed there.

TRANSLATION

Nanda Mahārāja and the other residents of Vṛndāvana, having reached Mathurā ahead of the chariot, stopped at a garden on the outskirts of the city to wait for Kṛṣṇa and Balarāma.

PURPORT

Nanda and the others reached Mathurā first because the chariot carrying Kṛṣṇa and Balarāma was delayed by Akrūra's bathing.

TEXT 9

तान् समेत्याह भगवानक्रूरं जगदीश्वरः ।
गृहीत्वा पाणिना पाणिं प्रश्रितं प्रहसन्निव ॥९॥

tān sametyāha bhagavān
akrūraṁ jagad-īśvaraḥ
gṛhītvā pāṇinā pāṇiṁ
praśritaṁ prahasann iva

tān—with them; *sametya*—meeting; *āha*—said; *bhagavān*—the Supreme Personality of Godhead; *akrūram*—to Akrūra; *jagat-īśvaraḥ*—the Lord of the universe; *gṛhītvā*—taking; *pāṇinā*—with His hand; *pāṇim*—his hand; *praśritam*—who was humble; *prahasan*—smiling; *iva*—indeed.

TRANSLATION

After joining Nanda and the others, the Supreme Lord Kṛṣṇa, the controller of the universe, took humble Akrūra's hand in His own and, smiling, spoke as follows.

TEXT 10

भवान् प्रविशतामग्रे सहयानः पुरीं गृहम् ।
वयं त्विहावमुच्याथ ततो द्रक्ष्यामहे पुरीम् ॥१०॥

bhavān praviśatām agre
saha-yānaḥ purīṁ gṛham
vayaṁ tv ihāvamucyātha
tato drakṣyāmahe purīm

bhavān—you; *praviśatām*—should enter; *agre*—ahead; *saha*—together with; *yānaḥ*—the vehicle; *purīm*—the city; *gṛham*—and your home; *vayam*—we; *tu*—on the other hand; *iha*—here; *avamucya*—getting down; *atha*—then; *tataḥ*—afterwards; *drakṣyāmahe*—will see; *purīm*—the city.

TRANSLATION

Take the chariot and enter the city ahead of us. Then go home. After resting here a while, we will go to see the city.

TEXT 11

श्रीअक्रूर उवाच
नाहं भवद्‌भ्यां रहितः प्रवेक्ष्ये मथुरां प्रभो ।
त्यक्तुं नार्हसि मां नाथ भक्तं ते भक्तवत्सल ॥११॥

śrī-akrūra uvāca
nāhaṁ bhavadbhyāṁ rahitaḥ
pravekṣye mathurāṁ prabho
tyaktuṁ nārhasi māṁ nātha
bhaktaṁ te bhakta-vatsala

śrī-akrūraḥ uvāca—Śrī Akrūra said; *na*—cannot; *aham*—I; *bhavad-bhyām*—of the two of You; *rahitaḥ*—deprived; *pravekṣye*—enter; *ma-thurām*—Mathurā; *prabho*—O master; *tyaktum*—abandon; *na arhasi*—You should not; *mām*—me; *nātha*—O Lord; *bhaktam*—devotee; *te*—Your; *bhakta-vatsala*—O You who have parental affection for Your devotees.

TRANSLATION

Śrī Akrūra said: O master, without the two of You I shall not enter Mathurā. I am Your devotee, O Lord, so it is not fair for You to abandon me, since You are always affectionate to Your devotees.

TEXT 12

आगच्छ याम गेहान्नः सनाथान् कुर्वधोक्षज ।
सहाग्रजः सगोपालैः सुहृद्भिश्च सुहृत्तम ॥१२॥

āgaccha yāma gehān naḥ
sa-nāthān kurv adhokṣaja
sahāgrajaḥ sa-gopālaiḥ
suhṛdbhiś ca suhṛttama

āgaccha—please come; *yāma*—let us go; *gehān*—to the house; *naḥ*—our; *sa*—having; *nāthān*—a master; *kuru*—please make it; *adhokṣaja*—O transcendental Lord; *saha*—with; *agra-jaḥ*—Your elder brother; *sa-gopālaiḥ*—with the cowherd men; *suhṛdbhiḥ*—with Your friends; *ca*—and; *suhṛt-tama*—O supreme well-wisher.

TRANSLATION

Come, let us go to my house with Your elder brother, the cowherd men and Your companions. O best of friends, O transcendental Lord, in this way please grace my house with its master.

TEXT 13

पुनीहि पादरजसा गृहान्नो गृहमेधिनाम् ।
यच्छौचेनानुतृप्यन्ति पितरः साग्नयः सुराः ॥१३॥

punīhi pāda-rajasā
gṛhān no gṛha-medhinām
yac-chaucenānutṛpyanti
pitaraḥ sāgnayaḥ surāḥ

punīhi—please purify; *pāda*—of Your feet; *rajasā*—with the dust; *gṛhān*—the home; *naḥ*—of us; *gṛha-medhinām*—who are attached to household ritual duties; *yat*—by which; *śaucena*—purification; *anutṛpyanti*—will become satisfied; *pitaraḥ*—my forefathers; *sa*—together with; *agnayaḥ*—the sacrificial fires; *surāḥ*—and the demigods.

TRANSLATION

I am simply an ordinary householder attached to ritual sacrifices, so please purify my home with the dust of Your lotus feet. By that act of purification, my forefathers, the sacrificial fires and the demigods will all become satisfied.

TEXT 14

अवनिज्याङ्घ्रियुगलमासीत्श्लोक्यो बलिर्महान् ।
ऐश्वर्यमतुलं लेभे गतिं चैकान्तिनां तु या ॥१४॥

avanijyāṅghri-yugalam
āsīt ślokyo balir mahān
aiśvaryam atulaṁ lebhe
gatiṁ caikāntināṁ tu yā

avanijya—bathing; *aṅghri-yugalam*—the two feet; *āsīt*—became; *ślokyaḥ*—glorious; *baliḥ*—King Bali; *mahān*—the great; *aiśvaryam*—power; *atulam*—unequaled; *lebhe*—he achieved; *gatim*—the destination; *ca*—and; *ekāntinām*—of the unalloyed devotees of the Lord; *tu*—indeed; *yā*—which.

TRANSLATION

By bathing Your feet, the exalted Bali Mahārāja attained not only glorious fame and unequaled power but also the final destination of pure devotees.

TEXT 15

आपस्तेऽङ्घ्र्यवनेजन्यस्त्रीँल्लोकान् शुचयोऽपुनन् ।
शिरसाधत्त याः शर्वः स्वर्याताः सगरात्मजाः ॥१५॥

āpas te 'ṅghry-avanejanyas
trīṁl lokān śucayo 'punan
śirasādhatta yāḥ śarvaḥ
svar yātāḥ sagarātmajāḥ

āpaḥ—the water (namely, the river Gaṅgā); *te*—Your; *aṅghri*—of the feet; *avanejanyaḥ*—coming from the bathing; *trīn*—the three; *lokān*—worlds; *śucayaḥ*—being purely spiritual; *apunan*—has purified; *śirasā*—on his head; *ādhatta*—has taken; *yāḥ*—which; *śarvaḥ*—Lord Śiva; *svaḥ*—to heaven; *yātāḥ*—went; *sagara-ātmajāḥ*—the sons of King Sagara.

TRANSLATION

The water of the river Gaṅgā has purified the three worlds, having become transcendental by bathing Your feet. Lord Śiva accepted that water on his head, and by that water's grace the sons of King Sagara attained to heaven.

TEXT 16

देवदेव जगन्नाथ पुण्यश्रवणकीर्तन ।
यदूत्तमोत्तमःश्लोक नारायण नमोऽस्तु ते ॥१६॥

deva-deva jagan-nātha
puṇya-śravaṇa-kīrtana
yadūttamottamaḥ-śloka
nārāyaṇa namo 'stu te

deva-deva—O Lord of lords; *jagat-nātha*—O master of the universe; *puṇya*—pious; *śravaṇa*—hearing; *kīrtana*—and chanting (about whom); *yadu-uttama*—O best of the Yadus; *uttamaḥ-śloka*—O You who are glorified in excellent verses; *nārāyaṇa*—O Supreme Lord Nārāyaṇa; *namaḥ*—obeisances; *astu*—let there be; *te*—unto You.

TRANSLATION

O Lord of lords, master of the universe, O You whose glories it is most pious to hear and chant! O best of the Yadus, O You whose fame is recounted in excellent poetry! O Supreme Lord Nārāyaṇa, I offer You my obeisances.

TEXT 17

श्रीभगवानुवाच
आयास्ये भवतो गेहमहमार्यसमन्वितः ।
यदुचक्रद्रुहं हत्वा वितरिष्ये सुहृत्प्रियम् ॥१७॥

śrī-bhagavān uvāca
āyāsye bhavato geham
aham ārya-samanvitaḥ
yadu-cakra-druhaṁ hatvā
vitariṣye suhṛt-priyam

śrī-bhagavān uvāca—the Supreme Lord said; *āyāsye*—will come; *bhavataḥ*—to your; *geham*—house; *aham*—I; *ārya*—by My elder (brother, Balarāma); *samanvitaḥ*—accompanied; *yadu-cakra*—of the circle of Yadus; *druham*—the enemy (Kaṁsa); *hatvā*—killing; *vitariṣye*—I will grant; *suhṛt*—to My well-wishers; *priyam*—satisfaction.

TRANSLATION

The Supreme Lord said: I will come to Your house with My elder brother, but first I must satisfy My friends and well-wishers by killing the enemy of the Yadu clan.

PURPORT

Akrūra glorified Kṛṣṇa in Text 16 as *yadūttama,* "the best of the Yadus." Śrī Kṛṣṇa here confirms this by saying, in effect, "Since I am the best of the Yadus, I must kill the enemy of the Yadus, Kaṁsa, and then I will come to your house."

TEXT 18

श्रीशुक उवाच
एवमुक्तो भगवता सोऽक्रूरो विमना इव ।
पुरीं प्रविष्टः कंसाय कर्मावेद्य गृहं ययौ ॥१८॥

śrī-śuka uvāca
evam ukto bhagavatā
so 'krūro vimanā iva
purīṁ praviṣṭaḥ kaṁsāya
karmāvedya gṛhaṁ yayau

śrī-śukaḥ uvāca—Śukadeva Gosvāmī said; *evam*—thus; *uktaḥ*—addressed; *bhagavatā*—by the Lord; *saḥ*—he; *akrūraḥ*—Akrūra; *vimanāḥ*—disheartened; *iva*—somewhat; *purīm*—the city; *praviṣṭaḥ*—entering; *kaṁsāya*—to Kaṁsa; *karma*—about his activities; *āvedya*—informing; *gṛham*—to his home; *yayau*—went.

TRANSLATION

Śukadeva Gosvāmī said: Thus addressed by the Lord, Akrūra entered the city with a heavy heart. He informed King Kaṁsa of the success of his mission and then went home.

TEXT 19

अथापराह्ने भगवान् कृष्णः संकर्षणान्वितः ।
मथुरां प्राविशद् गोपैर्दिदृक्षुः परिवारितः ॥१९॥

athāparāhne bhagavān
kṛṣṇaḥ saṅkarṣaṇānvitaḥ
mathurāṁ prāviśad gopair
didṛkṣuḥ parivāritaḥ

atha—then; *apara-ahne*—in the afternoon; *bhagavān*—the Supreme Lord; *kṛṣṇaḥ*—Kṛṣṇa; *saṅkarṣaṇa-anvitaḥ*—together with Lord Balarāma; *mathurām*—Mathurā; *prāviśat*—entered; *gopaiḥ*—by the cowherd boys; *didṛkṣuḥ*—wanting to see; *parivāritaḥ*—joined.

TRANSLATION

Lord Kṛṣṇa desired to see Mathurā, so toward evening He took Lord Balarāma and the cowherd boys with Him and entered the city.

TEXTS 20–23

ददर्श तां स्फाटिकतुंगगोपुर-
द्वारां बृहद्धेमकपाटतोरणाम् ।
ताम्रारकोष्ठां परिखादुरासदाम्
उद्यानरम्योपवनोपशोभिताम् ॥२०॥
सौवर्णशृंगाटकहर्म्यनिष्कुटैः
श्रेणीसभाभिर्भवनैरुपस्कृताम् ।
वैदूर्यवज्रामलनीलविद्रुमैर्
मुक्ताहरिद्भिर्वलभीषु वेदिषु ॥२१॥
जुष्टेषु जालामुखरन्ध्रकुट्टिमेष्व्
आविष्टपारावतबर्हिनादिताम् ।
संसिक्तरथ्यापणमार्गचत्वरां
प्रकीर्णमाल्यांकुरलाजतण्डुलाम् ॥२२॥
आपूर्णकुम्भैर्दधिचन्दनोक्षितैः
प्रसूनदीपावलिभिः सपल्लवैः ।
सवृन्दरम्भाक्रमुकैः सकेतुभिः
स्वलंकृतद्वारगृहां सपट्टिकैः ॥२३॥

dadarśa tāṁ sphāṭika-tuṅga-gopura-
dvārāṁ bṛhad-dhema-kapāṭa-toraṇām
tāmrāra-koṣṭhāṁ parikhā-durāsadām
udyāna-ramyopavanopaśobhitām

sauvarṇa-śṛṅgāṭaka-harmya-niṣkuṭaiḥ
śreṇī-sabhābhir bhavanair upaskṛtām
vaidūrya-vajrāmala-nīla-vidrumair
muktā-haridbhir valabhīṣu vediṣu

juṣṭeṣu jālāmukha-randhra-kuṭṭimeṣv
āviṣṭa-pārāvata-barhi-nāditām
saṁsikta-rathyāpaṇa-mārga-catvarāṁ
prakīrṇa-mālyāṅkura-lāja-taṇḍulām

āpūrṇa-kumbhair dadhi-candanokṣitaiḥ
prasūna-dīpāvalibhiḥ sa-pallavaiḥ
sa-vṛnda-rambhā-kramukaiḥ sa-ketubhiḥ
sv-alaṅkṛta-dvāra-gṛhāṁ sa-paṭṭikaiḥ

dadarśa—He saw; *tām*—that (city); *sphāṭika*—of crystal; *tuṅga*—high; *gopura*—whose main gates; *dvārām*—and household gates; *bṛhat*—immense; *hema*—gold; *kapāṭa*—whose doors; *toraṇām*—and ornamental arches; *tāmra*—of copper; *āra*—and brass; *koṣṭhām*—whose storehouses; *parikhā*—with its canals; *durāsadām*—inviolable; *udyāna*—with public gardens; *ramya*—attractive; *upavana*—and parks; *upaśobhitām*—beautified; *sauvarṇa*—gold; *śṛṅgāṭaka*—with crossways; *harmya*—mansions; *niṣkuṭaiḥ*—and pleasure gardens; *śreṇī*—of guilds; *sabhābhiḥ*—with the assembly halls; *bhavanaiḥ*—and with houses; *upaskṛtām*—ornamented; *vaidūrya*—with *vaidūrya* gems; *vajra*—diamonds; *amala*—crystal quartz; *nīla*—sapphires; *vidrumaiḥ*—and coral; *muktā*—with pearls; *haridbhiḥ*—and emeralds; *valabhīṣu*—on the wood panels decorating the rafters in front of the houses; *vediṣu*—on columned balconies; *juṣṭeṣu*—bedecked; *jāla-āmukha*—of lattice windows; *randhra*—in the openings; *kuṭṭimeṣu*—and on gem-studded floors; *āviṣṭa*—sitting; *pārāvata*—with the pet doves; *barhi*—and the peacocks; *nāditām*—resounding; *saṁsikta*—sprinkled with water; *rathyā*—with royal avenues; *āpaṇa*—commercial streets; *mārga*—other roads; *catvarām*—and courtyards; *prakīrṇa*—scattered; *mālya*—with flower garlands; *aṅkura*—new sprouts; *lāja*—parched grains; *taṇḍulām*—and rice; *āpūrṇa*—full; *kumbhaiḥ*—with pots; *dadhi*—with yogurt; *candana*—and sandalwood paste; *ukṣitaiḥ*—smeared; *pra-sūna*—with flower petals; *dīpa-āvalibhiḥ*—and rows of lamps; *sa-pallavaiḥ*—with leaves; *sa-vṛnda*—with bunches of flowers; *rambhā*—with trunks of banana trees; *kramukaiḥ*—and trunks of betel-nut trees; *sa-ketubhiḥ*—with flags; *su-alaṅkṛta*—nicely decorated; *dvāra*—with doors; *gṛhām*—whose houses; *sa-paṭṭikaiḥ*—with ribbons.

TRANSLATION

The Lord saw Mathurā, with its tall gates and household entrances made of crystal, its immense archways and main doors of gold, its granaries and other storehouses of copper and brass, and its impregnable moats. Beautifying the city were pleasant gardens and parks. The main intersections were fashioned of gold, and there were mansions with private pleasure gardens, along with guildhalls and many other buildings. Mathurā resounded with the calls of peacocks and pet turtledoves, who sat in the small openings of the lattice windows and on the gem-studded floors, and also on the columned balconies and on the ornate rafters in front of the houses. These balconies and rafters were adorned with *vaidūrya* stones, diamonds, crystal quartz, sapphires, coral, pearls and emeralds. All the royal avenues and commercial streets were sprinkled with water, as were the side roads and courtyards, and flower garlands, newly grown sprouts, parched grains and rice had been scattered about everywhere. Gracing the houses' doorways were elaborately decorated pots filled with water, which were bedecked with mango leaves, smeared with yogurt and sandalwood paste, and encircled by flower petals and ribbons. Near the pots were flags, rows of lamps, bunches of flowers and the trunks of banana and betel-nut trees.

PURPORT

Śrīla Viśvanātha Cakravartī Ṭhākura gives this description of the elaborately decorated pots: "On either side of each doorway, above the scattered rice, is a pot. Encircling each pot are flower petals, on its neck are ribbons and in its mouth are leaves of mango and other trees. Above each pot, on a gold plate, are rows of lamps. A trunk of a banana tree stands on either side of each pot, and a betel-nut tree trunk stands in front and also behind. Flags lean against the pots."

TEXT 24

तां सम्प्रविष्टौ वसुदेवनन्दनौ
वृतौ वयस्यैर्नरदेववर्त्मना ।
द्रष्टुं समीयुस्त्वरिताः पुरस्त्रियो
हर्म्याणि चैवारुरुहुर्नृपोत्सुकाः ॥२४॥

tāṁ sampraviṣṭau vasudeva-nandanau
vṛtau vayasyair naradeva-vartmanā
draṣṭuṁ samīyus tvaritāḥ pura-striyo
harmyāṇi caivāruruhur nṛpotsukāḥ

tām—that (Mathurā); *sampraviṣṭau*—entering; *vasudeva*—of Vasudeva; *nandanau*—the two sons; *vṛtau*—surrounded; *vayasyaiḥ*—by Their young friends; *nara-deva*—of the King; *vartmanā*—by the road; *draṣṭum*—to see; *samīyuḥ*—came forward together; *tvaritāḥ*—hurriedly; *pura*—of the city; *striyaḥ*—the women; *harmyāṇi*—their houses; *ca*—and; *eva*—also; *āruruhuḥ*—they climbed on top of; *nṛpa*—O King (Parīkṣit); *utsukāḥ*—eager.

TRANSLATION

The women of Mathurā hurriedly assembled and went forth to see the two sons of Vasudeva as They entered the city on the King's road, surrounded by Their cowherd boyfriends. Some of the women, my dear King, eagerly climbed to the roofs of their houses to see Them.

TEXT 25

काश्चिद्विपर्यग्धृतवस्त्रभूषणा
विस्मृत्य चैकं युगलेष्वथापराः ।
कृतैकपत्रश्रवणैकनूपुरा
नांक्त्वा द्वितीयं त्वपराश्च लोचनम् ॥२५॥

kāścid viparyag-dhṛta-vastra-bhūṣaṇā
vismṛtya caikaṁ yugaleṣv athāparāḥ
kṛtaika-patra-śravaṇaika-nūpurā
nāṅktvā dvitīyaṁ tv aparāś ca locanam

kāścit—some of them; *viparyak*—backwards; *dhṛta*—putting on; *vastra*—their clothes; *bhūṣaṇāḥ*—and ornaments; *vismṛtya*—forgetting; *ca*—and; *ekam*—one; *yugaleṣu*—of the pairs; *atha*—and; *aparāḥ*—others; *kṛta*—placing; *eka*—only one; *patra*—earring; *śravaṇa*—on their ears; *eka*—or one; *nūpurāḥ*—set of ankle bells; *na aṅktvā*—not anointing; *dvitīyam*—the second; *tu*—but; *aparāḥ*—other ladies; *ca*—and; *locanam*—an eye.

TRANSLATION

Some of the ladies put their clothes and ornaments on backwards, others forgot one of their earrings or ankle bells, and others applied makeup to one of their eyes but not the other.

PURPORT

The ladies were very eager to see Kṛṣṇa, and in their haste and excitement they forgot themselves.

TEXT 26

अश्नन्त्य एकास्तदपास्य सोत्सवा
अभ्यज्यमाना अकृतोपमज्जनाः ।
स्वपन्त्य उत्थाय निशम्य निःस्वनं
प्रपाययन्त्योऽर्भमपोह्य मातरः ॥२६॥

aśnantya ekās tad apāsya sotsavā
abhyajyamānā akṛtopamajjanāḥ
svapantya utthāya niśamya niḥsvanaṁ
prapāyayantyo 'rbham apohya mātaraḥ

aśnantyaḥ—taking meals; *ekāḥ*—some; *tat*—that; *apāsya*—abandoning; *sa-utsavāḥ*—joyfully; *abhyajyamānāḥ*—being massaged; *akṛta*—not finishing; *upamajjanāḥ*—their bathing; *svapantyaḥ*—sleeping; *utthāya*—getting up; *niśamya*—having heard; *niḥsvanam*—the loud sounds; *prapāyayantyaḥ*—giving milk; *arbham*—to an infant; *apohya*—put aside; *mātaraḥ*—mothers.

TRANSLATION

Those who were taking their meals abandoned them, others went out without finishing their baths or massages, women who were sleeping at once rose when they heard the commotion, and mothers breast-feeding their infants simply put them aside.

TEXT 27

मनांसि तासामरविन्दलोचनः
प्रगल्भलीलाहसितावलोकैः ।
जहार मत्तद्विरदेन्द्रविक्रमो
दृशां ददच्छ्रीरमणात्मनोत्सवम् ॥२७॥

manāṁsi tāsām aravinda-locanaḥ
pragalbha-līlā-hasitāvalokaiḥ
jahāra matta-dviradendra-vikramo
dṛśāṁ dadac chrī-ramaṇātmanotsavam

manāṁsi—the minds; *tāsām*—their; *aravinda*—like lotuses; *locanaḥ*—He whose eyes; *pragalbha*—bold; *līlā*—with His pastimes; *hasita*—smiling; *avalokaiḥ*—with His glances; *jahāra*—He took away; *matta*—in rut; *dvirada-indra*—(like) a lordly elephant; *vikramaḥ*—whose gait; *dṛśām*—to their eyes; *dadat*—affording; *śrī*—of the goddess of fortune; *ramaṇa*—which is the source of pleasure; *ātmanā*—with His body; *utsavam*—a festival.

TRANSLATION

The lotus-eyed Lord, smiling as He recalled His bold pastimes, captivated those ladies' minds with His glances. He walked with the gait of a lordly elephant in rut, creating a festival for their eyes with His transcendental body, which is the source of pleasure for the divine goddess of fortune.

TEXT 28

दृष्ट्वा मुहुः श्रुतमनुद्रुतचेतसस्तं
तत्प्रेक्षणोत्स्मितसुधोक्षणलब्धमानाः ।
आनन्दमूर्तिमुपगुह्य दृशात्मलब्धं
हृष्यत्त्वचो जहुरनन्तमरिन्दमाधिम् ॥२८॥

dṛṣṭvā muhuḥ śrutam anudruta-cetasas taṁ
tat-prekṣaṇotsmita-sudhokṣaṇa-labdha-mānāḥ
ānanda-mūrtim upaguhya dṛśātma-labdhaṁ
hṛṣyat-tvaco jahur anantam arindamādhim

dṛṣṭvā—seeing; *muhuḥ*—repeatedly; *śrutam*—heard about; *anudruta*—melted; *cetasaḥ*—whose hearts; *tam*—Him; *tat*—His; *prekṣaṇa*—of the glances; *ut-smita*—and the broad smiles; *sudhā*—by the nectar; *ukṣaṇa*—from the sprinkling; *labdha*—receiving; *mānāḥ*—honor; *ānanda*—of ecstasy; *mūrtim*—the personal form; *upaguhya*—embracing; *dṛśā*—through their eyes; *ātma*—within themselves; *labdham*—gained; *hṛṣyat*—erupting; *tvacaḥ*—their skin; *jahuḥ*—they gave up; *anantam*—unlimited; *arim-dama*—O subduer of enemies (Parīkṣit); *ādhim*—mental distress.

TRANSLATION

The ladies of Mathurā had repeatedly heard about Kṛṣṇa, and thus as soon as they saw Him their hearts melted. They felt honored that He was sprinkling upon them the nectar of His glances and broad smiles. Taking Him into their hearts through their eyes, they embraced Him, the embodiment of all ecstasy, and as their bodily hairs stood on end, O subduer of enemies, they forgot the unlimited distress caused by His absence.

TEXT 29

प्रासादशिखरारूढाः प्रीत्युत्फुल्लमुखाम्बुजाः ।
अभ्यवर्षन् सौमनस्यैः प्रमदा बलकेशवौ ॥२९॥

prāsāda-śikharārūḍhāḥ
prīty-utphulla-mukhāmbujāḥ
abhyavarṣan saumanasyaiḥ
pramadā bala-keśavau

prāsāda—of the mansions; *śikhara*—to the roofs; *ārūḍhāḥ*—having climbed; *prīti*—with affection; *utphulla*—blooming; *mukha*—their faces; *ambujāḥ*—which were like lotuses; *abhyavarṣan*—they showered; *saumanasyaiḥ*—with flowers; *pramadāḥ*—the attractive women; *bala-keśavau*—Balarāma and Kṛṣṇa.

TRANSLATION

Their lotus faces blooming with affection, the ladies who had climbed to the roofs of the mansions rained down showers of flowers upon Lord Balarāma and Lord Kṛṣṇa.

TEXT 30

दध्यक्षतैः सोदपात्रैः स्रग्गन्धैरभ्युपायनैः ।
तावानर्चुः प्रमुदितास्तत्र तत्र द्विजातयः ॥३०॥

dadhy-akṣataiḥ soda-pātraiḥ
srag-gandhair abhyupāyanaiḥ
tāv ānarcuḥ pramuditās
tatra tatra dvijātayaḥ

dadhi—with yogurt; *akṣataiḥ*—unbroken barleycorns; *sa*—and; *uda-pātraiḥ*—with pots filled with water; *srak*—with garlands; *gandhaiḥ*—and fragrant substances; *abhyupāyanaiḥ*—and also with other items of worship; *tau*—the two of Them; *ānarcuḥ*—worshiped; *pramuditāḥ*—joyful; *tatra tatra*—in various places; *dvi-jātayaḥ*—*brāhmaṇas.*

TRANSLATION

***Brāhmaṇas* standing along the way honored the two Lords with presentations of yogurt, unbroken barleycorns, pots full of water, garlands, fragrant substances such as sandalwood paste, and other items of worship.**

TEXT 31

ऊचुः पौरा अहो गोप्यस्तपः किमचरन्महत् ।
या ह्येतावनुपश्यन्ति नरलोकमहोत्सवौ ॥३१॥

ūcuḥ paurā aho gopyas
tapaḥ kim acaran mahat
yā hy etāv anupaśyanti
nara-loka-mahotsavau

ūcuḥ—said; *paurāḥ*—the women of the city; *aho*—ah; *gopyaḥ*—the cowherd girls (of Vṛndāvana); *tapaḥ*—austerity; *kim*—what; *acaran*—have executed; *mahat*—great; *yāḥ*—who; *hi*—indeed; *etau*—these two; *anupaśyanti*—constantly see; *nara-loka*—for human society; *mahā-utsavau*—who are the greatest source of pleasure.

TRANSLATION

The women of Mathurā exclaimed: Oh, what severe austerities the *gopīs* must have performed to be able to regularly see Kṛṣṇa and Balarāma, who are the greatest source of pleasure for all mankind!

TEXT 32

रजकं कञ्चिदायान्तं रंगकारं गदाग्रजः ।
दृष्ट्वायाचत वासांसि धौतान्यत्युत्तमानि च ॥३२॥

rajakaṁ kañcid āyāntaṁ
raṅga-kāraṁ gadāgrajaḥ
dṛṣṭvāyācata vāsāṁsi
dhautāny aty-uttamāni ca

rajakam—washerman; *kañcit*—a certain; *āyāntam*—approaching; *raṅga-kāram*—engaged in dyeing; *gada-agrajaḥ*—Lord Śrī Kṛṣṇa, the elder brother of Gada; *dṛṣṭvā*—seeing; *ayācata*—requested; *vāsāṁsi*—garments; *dhautāni*—cleaned; *ati-uttamāni*—first class; *ca*—and.

TRANSLATION

Seeing a washerman approaching who had been dyeing some clothes, Kṛṣṇa asked him for the finest laundered garments he had.

TEXT 33

देह्यावयोः समुचितान्यंग वासांसि चार्हतोः ।
भविष्यति परं श्रेयो दातुस्ते नात्र संशयः ॥३३॥

dehy āvayoḥ samucitāny
aṅga vāsāṁsi cārhatoḥ
bhaviṣyati paraṁ śreyo
dātus te nātra saṁśayaḥ

dehi—please give; *āvayoḥ*—to Us two; *samucitāni*—suitable; *aṅga*—My dear; *vāsāṁsi*—clothes; *ca*—and; *arhatoḥ*—to the two who are deserving; *bhaviṣyati*—there will be; *param*—supreme; *śreyaḥ*—benefit; *dātuḥ*—for the giver; *te*—you; *na*—there is not; *atra*—in this matter; *saṁśayaḥ*—doubt.

TRANSLATION

[Lord Kṛṣṇa said:] Please give suitable garments to the two of Us, who certainly deserve them. If you grant this charity, you will undoubtedly receive the greatest benefit.

TEXT 34

स याचितो भगवता परिपूर्णेन सर्वतः ।
साक्षेपं रुषितः प्राह भृत्यो राज्ञः सुदुर्मदः ॥३४॥

sa yācito bhagavatā
paripūrṇena sarvataḥ
sākṣepaṁ ruṣitaḥ prāha
bhṛtyo rājñaḥ su-durmadaḥ

saḥ—he; *yācitaḥ*—requested; *bhagavatā*—by the Supreme Lord; *paripūrṇena*—who is absolutely complete; *sarvataḥ*—in all respects;

sa-ākṣepam—insultingly; *ruṣitaḥ*—angered; *prāha*—he spoke; *bhṛtyaḥ*—the servant; *rājñaḥ*—of the King; *su*—very much; *durmadaḥ*—falsely proud.

TRANSLATION

Thus requested by the Supreme Lord, who is perfectly complete in all respects, that arrogant servant of the King became angry and replied insultingly.

TEXT 35

ईदृशान्येव वासांसि नित्यं गिरिवनेचराः ।
परिधत्त किमुद्वृत्ता राजद्रव्याण्यभीप्सथ ॥३५॥

īdṛśāny eva vāsāṁsi
nityaṁ giri-vane-carāḥ
paridhatta kim udvṛttā
rāja-dravyāṇy abhīpsatha

īdṛśāni—of this sort; *eva*—indeed; *vāsāṁsi*—garments; *nityam*—always; *giri*—on the mountains; *vane*—and in the forests; *carāḥ*—those who travel; *paridhatta*—would put on; *kim*—whether; *udvṛttāḥ*—impudent; *rāja*—the King's; *dravyāṇi*—things; *abhīpsatha*—You want.

TRANSLATION

[The washerman said:] You impudent boys! You're accustomed to roaming the mountains and forests, and yet You would dare put on such clothes as these! These are the King's possessions You're asking for!

TEXT 36

याताशु बालिशा मैवं प्रार्थ्यं यदि जिजीविषा ।
बध्नन्ति घ्नन्ति लुम्पन्ति दृप्तं राजकुलानि वै ॥३६॥

yātāśu bāliśā maivaṁ
prārthyaṁ yadi jijīviṣā
badhnanti ghnanti lumpanti
dṛptaṁ rāja-kulāni vai

yāta—go; *āśu*—quickly; *bāliśāḥ*—fools; *mā*—do not; *evam*—like this; *prārthyam*—beg; *yadi*—if; *jijīviṣā*—You have the desire to live; *badhnanti*—they tie up; *ghnanti*—kill; *lumpanti*—and loot (his house); *dṛptam*—one who is bold; *rāja-kulāni*—the King's men; *vai*—indeed.

TRANSLATION

Fools, get out of here quickly! Don't beg like this if You want to stay alive. When someone is too bold, the King's men arrest him and kill him and take all his property.

TEXT 37

एवं विकत्थमानस्य कुपितो देवकीसुतः ।
रजकस्य कराग्रेण शिरः कायादपातयत् ॥३७॥

evaṁ vikatthamānasya
kupito devakī-sutaḥ
rajakasya karāgreṇa
śiraḥ kāyād apātayat

evam—thus; *vikatthamānasya*—who was brazenly speaking; *kupitaḥ*—angered; *devakī-sutaḥ*—Kṛṣṇa, the son of Devakī; *rajakasya*—of the washerman; *kara*—of one hand; *agreṇa*—with the front; *śiraḥ*—the head; *kāyāt*—from his body; *apātayat*—made fall.

TRANSLATION

As the washerman thus spoke brazenly, the son of Devakī became angry, and then merely with His fingertips He separated the man's head from his body.

TEXT 38

तस्यानुजीविनः सर्वे वासःकोशान् विसृज्य वै ।
दुद्रुवुः सर्वतो मार्गं वासांसि जगृहेऽच्युतः ॥३८॥

tasyānujīvinaḥ sarve
vāsaḥ-kośān visṛjya vai

dudruvuḥ sarvato mārgaṁ
vāsāṁsi jagṛhe 'cyutaḥ

tasya—his; *anujīvinaḥ*—employees; *sarve*—all; *vāsaḥ*—of clothes; *kośān*—the bundles; *visṛjya*—leaving behind; *vai*—indeed; *dudruvuḥ*—they fled; *sarvataḥ*—in all directions; *mārgam*—down the road; *vāsāṁsi*—garments; *jagṛhe*—took; *acyutaḥ*—Lord Kṛṣṇa.

TRANSLATION

The washerman's assistants all dropped their bundles of clothes and fled down the road, scattering in all directions. Lord Kṛṣṇa then took the clothes.

TEXT 39

वसित्वात्मप्रिये वस्त्रे कृष्णः संकर्षणस्तथा ।
शेषाण्यादत्त गोपेभ्यो विसृज्य भुवि कानिचित् ॥३९॥

vasitvātma-priye vastre
kṛṣṇaḥ saṅkarṣaṇas tathā
śeṣāṇy ādatta gopebhyo
visṛjya bhuvi kānicit

vasitvā—dressing Himself; *ātma-priye*—which He liked; *vastre*—in a pair of garments; *kṛṣṇaḥ*—Kṛṣṇa; *saṅkarṣaṇaḥ*—Balarāma; *tathā*—also; *śeṣāṇi*—the rest; *ādatta*—He gave; *gopebhyaḥ*—to the cowherd boys; *visṛjya*—throwing away; *bhuvi*—on the ground; *kānicit*—several.

TRANSLATION

Kṛṣṇa put on a pair of garments that especially pleased Him, and so did Balarāma. Then Kṛṣṇa distributed the remaining clothes among the cowherd boys, leaving some scattered on the ground.

TEXT 40

ततस्तु वायकः प्रीतस्तयोर्वेषमकल्पयत् ।
विचित्रवर्णैश्चैलेयैराकल्पैरनुरूपतः ॥४०॥

tatas tu vāyakaḥ prītas
tayor veṣam akalpayat
vicitra-varṇaiś caileyair
ākalpair anurūpataḥ

tataḥ—then; *tu*—moreover; *vāyakaḥ*—a weaver; *prītaḥ*—affectionate; *tayoḥ*—for the two of Them; *veṣam*—dress; *akalpayat*—arranged; *vicitra*—various; *varṇaiḥ*—with colors; *caileyaiḥ*—made of cloth; *ākalpaiḥ*—with ornaments; *anurūpataḥ*—suitably.

TRANSLATION

Thereupon a weaver came forward and, feeling affection for the Lords, nicely adorned Their attire with cloth ornaments of various colors.

PURPORT

Śrīla Jīva Gosvāmī explains that the weaver adorned the Lords with cloth armlets and earrings that looked just like jewels. The word *anurūpataḥ* indicates that the colors matched nicely.

TEXT 41

नानालक्षणवेषाभ्यां कृष्णरामौ विरेजतुः ।
स्वलंकृतौ बालगजौ पर्वणीव सितेतरौ ॥४१॥

nānā-lakṣaṇa-veṣābhyāṁ
kṛṣṇa-rāmau virejatuḥ
sv-alaṅkṛtau bāla-gajau
parvaṇīva sitetarau

nānā—various; *lakṣaṇa*—having fine qualities; *veṣābhyām*—with Their individual clothes; *kṛṣṇa-rāmau*—Kṛṣṇa and Balarāma; *virejatuḥ*—appeared resplendent; *su-alaṅkṛtau*—nicely decorated; *bāla*—young; *gajau*—elephants; *parvaṇi*—during a festival; *iva*—as if; *sita*—white; *itarau*—and the opposite (black).

TRANSLATION

Kṛṣṇa and Balarāma looked resplendent, each in His own unique, wonderfully ornamented outfit. They resembled a pair of young elephants, one white and the other black, decorated for a festive occasion.

TEXT 42

तस्य प्रसन्नो भगवान् प्रादात्सारूप्यमात्मनः ।
श्रियं च परमां लोके बलैश्वर्यस्मृतीन्द्रियम् ॥४२॥

tasya prasanno bhagavān
prādāt sārūpyam ātmanaḥ
śriyaṁ ca paramāṁ loke
balaiśvarya-smṛtīndriyam

tasya—with him; *prasannaḥ*—satisfied; *bhagavān*—the Supreme Lord; *prādāt*—granted; *sārūpyam*—the liberation of having the same form; *ātmanaḥ*—as Himself; *śriyam*—opulence; *ca*—and; *paramām*—supreme; *loke*—in this world; *bala*—physical strength; *aiśvarya*—influence; *smṛti*—strength of memory; *indriyam*—dexterity of the senses.

TRANSLATION

Pleased with the weaver, the Supreme Lord Kṛṣṇa blessed him that after death he would achieve the liberation of attaining a form like the Lord's, and that while in this world he would enjoy supreme opulence, physical strength, influence, memory and sensory vigor.

TEXT 43

ततः सुदाम्नो भवनं मालाकारस्य जग्मतुः ।
तौ दृष्ट्वा स समुत्थाय ननाम शिरसा भुवि ॥४३॥

tataḥ sudāmno bhavanaṁ
mālā-kārasya jagmatuḥ

tau dṛṣṭvā sa samutthāya
nanāma śirasā bhuvi

tataḥ—then; *sudāmnaḥ*—of Sudāmā; *bhavanam*—to the home; *mālā-kārasya*—of the garland-maker; *jagmatuḥ*—the two of Them went; *tau*—Them; *dṛṣṭvā*—seeing; *saḥ*—he; *samutthāya*—standing up; *nanāma*—bowed down; *śirasā*—with his head; *bhuvi*—on the ground.

TRANSLATION

The two Lords then went to the house of the garland-maker Sudāmā. When Sudāmā saw Them he at once stood up and then bowed down, placing his head on the ground.

TEXT 44

तयोरासनमानीय पाद्यं चार्घ्यार्हणादिभिः ।
पूजां सानुगयोश्चक्रे स्रक्ताम्बूलानुलेपनैः ॥४४॥

tayor āsanam ānīya
pādyaṁ cārghyārhaṇādibhiḥ
pūjāṁ sānugayoś cakre
srak-tāmbūlānulepanaiḥ

tayoḥ—for Them; *āsanam*—seats; *ānīya*—bringing; *pādyam*—water to wash the feet; *ca*—and; *arghya*—with water to wash the hands; *arhaṇa*—presents; *ādibhiḥ*—and so on; *pūjām*—worship; *sa-anugayoḥ*—of the two, together with Their companions; *cakre*—he performed; *srak*—with garlands; *tāmbūla*—betel-nut preparation (*pān*); *anulepanaiḥ*—and sandalwood paste.

TRANSLATION

After offering Them seats and bathing Their feet, Sudāmā worshiped Them and Their companions with *arghya*, garlands, *pān*, sandalwood paste and other presentations.

TEXT 45

प्राह नः सार्थकं जन्म पावितं च कुलं प्रभो ।
पितृदेवर्षयो मह्यं तुष्टा ह्यागमनेन वाम् ॥४५॥

prāha naḥ sārthakaṁ janma
pāvitaṁ ca kulaṁ prabho
pitṛ-devarṣayo mahyaṁ
tuṣṭā hy āgamanena vām

prāha—he said; *naḥ*—our; *sa-arthakam*—worthwhile; *janma*—the birth; *pāvitam*—purified; *ca*—and; *kulam*—the family; *prabho*—O Lord; *pitṛ*—my forefathers; *deva*—the demigods; *ṛṣayaḥ*—and the great sages; *mahyam*—with me; *tuṣṭāḥ*—are satisfied; *hi*—indeed; *āgamanena*—by the arrival; *vām*—of You two.

TRANSLATION

[Sudāmā said:] O Lord, my birth is now sanctified and my family free of contamination. Now that You both have come here, my forefathers, the demigods and the great sages are certainly all satisfied with me.

TEXT 46

भवन्तौ किल विश्वस्य जगतः कारणं परम् ।
अवतीर्णाविहांशेन क्षेमाय च भवाय च ॥४६॥

bhavantau kila viśvasya
jagataḥ kāraṇaṁ param
avatīrṇāv ihāṁśena
kṣemāya ca bhavāya ca

bhavantau—You two; *kila*—indeed; *viśvasya*—of the entire; *jagataḥ*—universe; *kāraṇam*—the cause; *param*—ultimate; *avatīrṇau*—having descended; *iha*—here; *aṁśena*—with Your plenary portions; *kṣemāya*—for the benefit; *ca*—and; *bhavāya*—for the prosperity; *ca*—also.

TRANSLATION

You two Lords are the ultimate cause of this entire universe. To bestow sustenance and prosperity upon this realm, You have descended with Your plenary expansions.

TEXT 47

न हि वां विषमा दृष्टिः सुहृदोर्जगदात्मनोः ।
समयोः सर्वभूतेषु भजन्तं भजतोरपि ॥४७॥

na hi vāṁ viṣamā dṛṣṭiḥ
suhṛdor jagad-ātmanoḥ
samayoḥ sarva-bhūteṣu
bhajantaṁ bhajator api

na—there is not; *hi*—indeed; *vām*—on Your part; *viṣamā*—biased; *dṛṣṭiḥ*—vision; *suhṛdoḥ*—who are well-wishing friends; *jagat*—of the universe; *ātmanoḥ*—the Soul; *samayoḥ*—equal; *sarva*—to all; *bhūteṣu*—living beings; *bhajantam*—those who worship You; *bhajatoḥ*—reciprocating with; *api*—even.

TRANSLATION

Because You are the well-wishing friends and Supreme Soul of the whole universe, You regard all with unbiased vision. Therefore, although You reciprocate Your devotees' loving worship, You always remain equally disposed toward all living beings.

TEXT 48

तावाज्ञापयतं भृत्यं किमहं करवाणि वाम् ।
पुंसोऽत्यनुग्रहो ह्येष भवद्भिर्यन्नियुज्यते ॥४८॥

tāv ājñāpayataṁ bhṛtyaṁ
kim ahaṁ karavāṇi vām
puṁso 'ty-anugraho hy eṣa
bhavadbhir yan niyujyate

tau—They; *ājñāpayatam*—should please order; *bhṛtyam*—Their servant; *kim*—what; *aham*—I; *karavāṇi*—should do; *vām*—for You; *puṁsaḥ*—for any person; *ati*—extreme; *anugrahaḥ*—mercy; *hi*—indeed; *eṣaḥ*—this; *bhavadbhiḥ*—by You; *yat*—in which; *niyujyate*—he is engaged.

TRANSLATION

Please order me, Your servant, to do whatever You wish. To be engaged by You in some service is certainly a great blessing for anyone.

TEXT 49

इत्यभिप्रेत्य राजेन्द्र सुदामा प्रीतमानसः ।
शस्तैः सुगन्धैः कुसुमैर्माला विरचिता ददौ ॥४९॥

ity abhipretya rājendra
sudāmā prīta-mānasaḥ
śastaiḥ su-gandhaiḥ kusumair
mālā viracitā dadau

iti—thus speaking; *abhipretya*—understanding Their intention; *rāja-indra*—O best of kings (Parīkṣit); *sudāmā*—Sudāmā; *prīta-mānasaḥ*—pleased at heart; *śastaiḥ*—fresh; *su-gandhaiḥ*—and fragrant; *kusumaiḥ*—with flowers; *mālāḥ*—garlands; *viracitāḥ*—made; *dadau*—he gave.

TRANSLATION

[Śukadeva Gosvāmī continued:] O best of kings, having spoken these words, Sudāmā could understand what Kṛṣṇa and Balarāma wanted. Thus with great pleasure he presented Them with garlands of fresh, fragrant flowers.

TEXT 50

ताभिः स्वलंकृतौ प्रीतौ कृष्णरामौ सहानुगौ ।
प्रणताय प्रपन्नाय ददतुर्वरदौ वरान् ॥५०॥

tābhiḥ sv-alaṅkṛtau prītau
kṛṣṇa-rāmau sahānugau
praṇatāya prapannāya
dadatur vara-dau varān

tābhiḥ—with those (garlands); *su-alaṅkṛtau*—beautifully ornamented; *prītau*—satisfied; *kṛṣṇa-rāmau*—Kṛṣṇa and Balarāma; *saha*—along with; *anugau*—Their companions; *praṇatāya*—who was bowing down; *prapannāya*—to the surrendered (Sudāmā); *dadatuḥ*—They gave; *vara-dau*—the two givers of benedictions; *varān*—a choice of benedictions.

TRANSLATION

Beautifully adorned with these garlands, Kṛṣṇa and Balarāma were delighted, and so were Their companions. The two Lords then offered the surrendered Sudāmā, who was bowing down before Them, whatever benedictions he desired.

TEXT 51

सोऽपि वव्रेऽचलां भक्तिं तस्मिन्नेवाखिलात्मनि ।
तद्भक्तेषु च सौहार्दं भूतेषु च दयां पराम् ॥५१॥

so 'pi vavre 'calāṁ bhaktiṁ
tasminn evākhilātmani
tad-bhakteṣu ca sauhārdaṁ
bhūteṣu ca dayāṁ parām

saḥ—he; *api*—and; *vavre*—chose; *acalām*—unshakable; *bhaktim*—devotion; *tasmin*—to Him; *eva*—alone; *akhila*—of everything; *ātmani*—the Supreme Soul; *tat*—toward His; *bhakteṣu*—devotees; *ca*—and; *sauhārdam*—friendship; *bhūteṣu*—toward living beings in general; *ca*—and; *dayām*—mercy; *parām*—transcendental.

TRANSLATION

Sudāmā chose unshakable devotion for Kṛṣṇa, the Supreme Soul of all existence; friendship with His devotees; and transcendental compassion for all living beings.

TEXT 52

इति तस्मै वरं दत्त्वा श्रियं चान्वयवर्धिनीम् ।
बलमायुर्यशः कान्तिं निर्जगाम सहाग्रजः ॥५२॥

iti tasmai varaṁ dattvā
śriyaṁ cānvaya-vardhinīm
balam āyur yaśaḥ kāntiṁ
nirjagāma sahāgrajaḥ

iti—thus; *tasmai*—to him; *varam*—the benediction; *dattvā*—giving; *śriyam*—opulence; *ca*—and; *anvaya*—his family; *vardhinīm*—expanding; *balam*—strength; *āyuḥ*—long life; *yaśaḥ*—fame; *kāntim*—beauty; *nirjagāma*—He left; *saha*—together with; *agra-jaḥ*—His elder brother, Lord Balarāma.

TRANSLATION

Not only did Lord Kṛṣṇa grant Sudāmā these benedictions, but He also awarded him strength, long life, fame, beauty and ever-increasing prosperity for his family. Then Kṛṣṇa and His elder brother took Their leave.

PURPORT

We can see a clear difference between Lord Kṛṣṇa's dealings with the nasty washerman and His dealings with the devoted florist Sudāmā. The Lord is as hard as a thunderbolt for those who defy Him and as soft as a rose for those who surrender to Him. Therefore we should all sincerely surrender to Lord Kṛṣṇa, since that is clearly in our self-interest.

Thus end the purports of the humble servant of His Divine Grace A. C. Bhaktivedanta Swami Prabhupāda to the Tenth Canto, Forty-first Chapter, of the Śrīmad-Bhāgavatam, *entitled "Kṛṣṇa and Balarāma Enter Mathurā."*

CHAPTER FORTY-TWO

The Breaking of the Sacrificial Bow

This chapter describes the benediction Kubjā received, the breaking of the sacrificial bow, the destruction of Kaṁsa's soldiers, the inauspicious omens Kaṁsa saw and the festivities at the wrestling arena.

After leaving Sudāmā's house, Lord Kṛṣṇa came upon Kubjā, a young hunchbacked maidservant of Kaṁsa's who was carrying a tray of fine ointments. The Lord asked her who she was and requested some ointment from her. Entranced by His beauty and joking words, Kubjā gave both Kṛṣṇa and Balarāma a good deal of ointment. In return, Kṛṣṇa stepped on her toes with His lotus feet, took hold of her chin and lifted, thus straightening her spine. The now beautiful and charming Kubjā then grabbed the edge of Kṛṣṇa's upper cloth and asked Him to come to her house. Kṛṣṇa replied that after He had taken care of some business He would certainly come and relieve her mental torment. Then the two Lords continued Their sightseeing tour of Mathurā.

As Kṛṣṇa and Balarāma walked along the King's road, the merchants worshiped Them with various offerings. Kṛṣṇa asked where the bow sacrifice was to take place, and when He arrived at the arena He saw the wonderful bow, which resembled Lord Indra's. Despite the guards' protests, Kṛṣṇa forcibly picked up the bow, easily strung it and in an instant broke it in half, producing an ear-splitting sound that filled the heavens and struck terror in the heart of Kaṁsa. The many guards attacked Kṛṣṇa, crying out "Seize Him! Kill Him!" But Kṛṣṇa and Balarāma simply picked up the two halves of the bow and beat the guards to death. Next the Lords annihilated a company of soldiers sent by Kaṁsa, and then They left the arena and continued Their tour.

When the people of the city saw the amazing prowess and beauty of Kṛṣṇa and Balarāma, they thought They must be two chief demigods. Indeed, as the residents of Mathurā gazed upon the Lords, they enjoyed all the blessings the *gopīs* had predicted.

At sunset Kṛṣṇa and Balarāma returned to the cowherds' camp for Their evening meal. They then passed the night resting comfortably. But King Kaṁsa was not so fortunate. When he heard how Kṛṣṇa and

Balarāma had easily broken the mighty bow and destroyed his soldiers, he spent the night in great anxiety. Both while awake and while dreaming he saw many ill omens portending his imminent death, and his fear ruined any chance for rest.

At dawn the wrestling festival began. Crowds of people from the city and outlying districts entered the arena and took their seats in the lavishly decorated galleries. Kaṁsa, his heart trembling, sat down on the royal dais and invited Nanda Mahārāja and the other cowherd men to come sit in their places, and they did so after offering him their gifts. The musical overture then began as the sounds of the wrestlers slapping their arms resounded.

TEXT 1

श्रीशुक उवाच
अथ व्रजन् राजपथेन माधवः
स्त्रियं गृहीतांगविलेपभाजनाम् ।
विलोक्य कुब्जां युवतीं वराननां
पप्रच्छ यान्तीं प्रहसन् रसप्रदः ॥१॥

śrī-śuka uvāca
atha vrajan rāja-pathena mādhavaḥ
striyaṁ gṛhītāṅga-vilepa-bhājanām
vilokya kubjāṁ yuvatīṁ varānanāṁ
papraccha yāntīṁ prahasan rasa-pradaḥ

śrī-śukaḥ uvāca—Śukadeva Gosvāmī said; *atha*—then; *vrajan*—walking; *rāja-pathena*—along the King's road; *mādhavaḥ*—Kṛṣṇa; *striyam*—a woman; *gṛhīta*—holding; *aṅga*—for the body; *vilepa*—with ointments; *bhājanām*—a tray; *vilokya*—seeing; *kubjām*—hunchbacked; *yuvatīm*—young; *vara-ānanām*—with an attractive face; *papraccha*—He inquired; *yāntīm*—going; *prahasan*—smiling; *rasa*—of the pleasure of love; *pradaḥ*—the bestower.

TRANSLATION

Śukadeva Gosvāmī said: As He walked down the King's road, Lord Mādhava then saw a young hunchbacked woman with an at-

tractive face approach, carrying a tray of fragrant ointments. The bestower of the ecstasy of love smiled and inquired from her as follows.

PURPORT

According to Śrīla Viśvanātha Cakravartī Ṭhākura, the young hunchbacked girl was actually a partial expansion of the Lord's wife Satyabhāmā. Satyabhāmā is the Lord's internal energy known as Bhū-śakti, and this expansion of hers, known as Pṛthivī, represents the earth, which was bent down by the great burden of countless wicked rulers. Lord Kṛṣṇa descended to remove these wicked rulers, and thus His pastime of straightening out the hunchback Trivakrā, as explained in these verses, represents His rectifying the burdened condition of the earth. At the same time, the Lord awarded Trivakrā a conjugal relationship with Himself.

In addition to the given meaning, the word *rasa-pradaḥ* indicates that the Lord amused His cowherd boyfriends by His dealings with the young hunchback.

TEXT 2

का त्वं वरोर्वेतदु हानुलेपनं
कस्यांगने वा कथयस्व साधु नः ।
देह्यावयोरंगविलेपमुत्तमं
श्रेयस्ततस्ते न चिराद् भविष्यति ॥२॥

kā tvaṁ varorv etad u hānulepanaṁ
kasyāṅgane vā kathayasva sādhu naḥ
dehy āvayor aṅga-vilepam uttamaṁ
śreyas tatas te na cirād bhaviṣyati

kā—who; *tvam*—you; *vara-ūru*—O beautiful-thighed one; *etat*—this; *u ha*—ah, indeed; *anulepanam*—ointment; *kasya*—for whom; *aṅgane*—My dear woman; *vā*—or; *kathayasva*—please tell; *sādhu*—honestly; *naḥ*—Us; *dehi*—please give; *āvayoḥ*—to Us two; *aṅga-vilepam*—body ointment; *uttamam*—excellent; *śreyaḥ*—benefit; *tataḥ*—thereafter; *te*—your; *na cirāt*—soon; *bhaviṣyati*—will be.

TRANSLATION

Who are you, O beautiful-thighed one? Ah, ointment! Who is it for, My dear lady? Please tell Us truthfully. Give Us both some of your finest ointment and you will soon gain a great boon.

PURPORT

The Lord jokingly addressed the lady as *varoru,* "O beautiful-thighed one." His joke was not malicious, since He was actually about to make her beautiful.

TEXT 3

सैरन्ध्र्युवाच
दास्यस्म्यहं सुन्दर कंससम्मता
त्रिवक्रनामा ह्यनुलेपकर्मणि ।
मद्भावितं भोजपतेरतिप्रियं
विना युवां कोऽन्यतमस्तदर्हति ॥३॥

sairandhry uvāca
dāsy asmy ahaṁ sundara kaṁsa-sammatā
trivakra-nāmā hy anulepa-karmaṇi
mad-bhāvitaṁ bhoja-pater ati-priyaṁ
vinā yuvāṁ ko 'nyatamas tad arhati

sairandhrī uvāca—the maidservant said; *dāsī*—a servant; *asmi*—am; *aham*—I; *sundara*—O handsome one; *kaṁsa*—by Kaṁsa; *sammatā*—respected; *trivakra-nāmā*—known as Trivakrā ("bent in three places"); *hi*—indeed; *anulepa*—with ointments; *karmaṇi*—for my work; *mat*—by me; *bhāvitam*—prepared; *bhoja-pateḥ*—to the chief of the Bhojas; *ati-priyam*—very dear; *vinā*—except for; *yuvām*—You two; *kaḥ*—who; *anyatamaḥ*—else; *tat*—that; *arhati*—deserves.

TRANSLATION

The maidservant replied: O handsome one, I am a servant of King Kaṁsa, who highly regards me for the ointments I make. My name is Trivakrā. Who else but You two deserve my ointments, which the lord of the Bhojas likes so much?

PURPORT

Śrīla Viśvanātha Cakravartī explains that Trivakrā, who is also known as Kubjā, used the singular address *sundara,* "O handsome one," to hint that she felt conjugal desire for Kṛṣṇa alone, and she used the dual form *yuvām,* "for both of You," to try to hide her conjugal sentiment. The hunchback's name, Trivakrā, indicates that her body was bent at the neck, chest and waist.

TEXT 4

रूपपेशलमाधुर्यहसितालापवीक्षितैः ।
धर्षितात्मा ददौ सान्द्रमुभयोरनुलेपनम् ॥४॥

rūpa-peśala-mādhurya-
hasitālāpa-vīkṣitaiḥ
dharṣitātmā dadau sāndram
ubhayor anulepanam

rūpa—by His beauty; *peśala*—charm; *mādhurya*—sweetness; *hasita*—smiles; *ālāpa*—talking; *vīkṣitaiḥ*—and glances; *dharṣita*—overwhelmed; *ātmā*—her mind; *dadau*—she gave; *sāndram*—plentiful; *ubhayoḥ*—to both of Them; *anulepanam*—ointment.

TRANSLATION

Her mind overwhelmed by Kṛṣṇa's beauty, charm, sweetness, smiles, words and glances, Trivakrā gave both Kṛṣṇa and Balarāma generous amounts of ointment.

PURPORT

This incident is also described in the *Viṣṇu Purāṇa* (5.20.7):

śrutvā tam āha sā kṛṣṇaṁ
gṛhyatām iti sādaram
anulepanaṁ pradadau
gātra-yogyam athobhayoḥ

"Hearing this, she respectfully replied to Lord Kṛṣṇa, 'Please take it,' and gave both of Them ointment suitable for applying to Their bodies."

TEXT 5

ततस्तावंगरागेण स्ववर्णेतरशोभिना ।
सम्प्राप्तपरभागेन शुशुभातेऽनुरञ्जितौ ॥५॥

tatas tāv aṅga-rāgeṇa
sva-varṇetara-śobhinā
samprāpta-para-bhāgena
śuśubhāte 'nurañjitau

tataḥ—then; *tau*—They; *aṅga*—of Their bodies; *rāgeṇa*—with the coloring cosmetics; *sva*—Their own; *varṇa*—with colors; *itara*—other than; *śobhinā*—adorning; *samprāpta*—which exhibited; *para*—the highest; *bhāgena*—excellence; *śuśubhāte*—They appeared beautiful; *anurañjitau*—anointed.

TRANSLATION

Anointed with these most excellent cosmetics, which adorned Them with hues that contrasted with Their complexions, the two Lords appeared extremely beautiful.

PURPORT

The *ācāryas* suggest that Kṛṣṇa spread yellow ointment upon His body, and Balarāma blue ointment upon His.

TEXT 6

प्रसन्नो भगवान् कुब्जां त्रिवक्रां रुचिराननाम् ।
ऋज्वीं कर्तुं मनश्चक्रे दर्शयन् दर्शने फलम् ॥६॥

prasanno bhagavān kubjāṁ
trivakrāṁ rucirānanām
ṛjvīṁ kartuṁ manaś cakre
darśayan darśane phalam

prasannaḥ—satisfied; *bhagavān*—the Supreme Lord; *kubjām*—the hunchback; *trivakrām*—Trivakrā; *rucira*—attractive; *ānanām*—whose face; *ṛjvīm*—straight; *kartum*—to make; *manaḥ cakre*—He decided; *darśayan*—showing; *darśane*—of seeing Him; *phalam*—the result.

TRANSLATION

Lord Kṛṣṇa was pleased with Trivakrā, so He decided to straighten that hunchbacked girl with the lovely face just to demonstrate the result of seeing Him.

TEXT 7

पद्भ्यामाक्रम्य प्रपदे द्व्यंगुल्युत्तानपाणिना ।
प्रगृह्य चिबुकेऽध्यात्ममुदनीनमदच्युतः ॥७॥

padbhyām ākramya prapade
dvy-aṅguly-uttāna-pāṇinā
pragṛhya cibuke 'dhyātmam
udanīnamad acyutaḥ

padbhyām—with both His feet; *ākramya*—pressing down; *prapade*—on her toes; *dvi*—having two; *aṅguli*—fingers; *uttāna*—pointing upwards; *pāṇinā*—with His hands; *pragṛhya*—taking hold of; *cibuke*—her chin; *adhyātmam*—her body; *udanīnamat*—He raised; *acyutaḥ*—Lord Kṛṣṇa.

TRANSLATION

Pressing down on her toes with both His feet, Lord Acyuta placed one upward-pointing finger of each hand under her chin and straightened up her body.

TEXT 8

सा तदर्जुसमानांगी बृहच्छ्रोणिपयोधरा ।
मुकुन्दस्पर्शनात्सद्यो बभूव प्रमदोत्तमा ॥८॥

sā tadarju-samānāṅgī
bṛhac-chroṇi-payodharā
mukunda-sparśanāt sadyo
babhūva pramadottamā

sā—she; *tadā*—then; *ṛju*—straight; *samāna*—even; *aṅgī*—her limbs; *bṛhat*—large; *śroṇi*—her hips; *payaḥ-dharā*—and breasts; *mukunda-sparśanāt*—by the touch of Lord Mukunda; *sadyaḥ*—suddenly; *ba-bhūva*—became; *pramadā*—a woman; *uttamā*—most perfect.

TRANSLATION

Simply by Lord Mukunda's touch, Trivakrā was suddenly transformed into an exquisitely beautiful woman with straight, evenly proportioned limbs and large hips and breasts.

TEXT 9

ततो रूपगुणौदार्यसम्पन्ना प्राह केशवम् ।
उत्तरीयान्तमाकृष्य स्मयन्ती जातहृच्छया ॥९॥

tato rūpa-guṇaudārya-
sampannā prāha keśavam
uttarīyāntam ākṛṣya
smayantī jāta-hṛc-chayā

tataḥ—then; *rūpa*—with beauty; *guṇa*—good character; *audārya*—and generosity; *sampannā*—endowed; *prāha*—she addressed; *keśavam*—Lord Kṛṣṇa; *uttarīya*—of His upper garment; *antam*—the end; *ākṛṣya*—pulling; *smayantī*—smiling; *jāta*—having developed; *hṛt-śayā*—lusty feelings.

TRANSLATION

Now endowed with beauty, character and generosity, Trivakrā began to feel lusty desires for Lord Keśava. Taking hold of the end of His upper cloth, she smiled and addressed Him as follows.

TEXT 10

एहि वीर गृहं यामो न त्वां त्यक्तुमिहोत्सहे ।
त्वयोन्मथितचित्तायाः प्रसीद पुरुषर्षभ ॥१०॥

ehi vīra gṛhaṁ yāmo
na tvāṁ tyaktum ihotsahe

tvayonmathita-cittāyāḥ
prasīda puruṣarṣabha

ehi—come; *vīra*—O hero; *gṛham*—to my house; *yāmaḥ*—let us go; *na*—not; *tvām*—You; *tyaktum*—to leave; *iha*—here; *utsahe*—I can bear; *tvayā*—by You; *unmathita*—agitated; *cittāyāḥ*—on her whose mind; *prasīda*—please have mercy; *puruṣa-ṛṣabha*—O best of men.

TRANSLATION

Come, O hero, let us go to my house. I cannot bear to leave You here. O best of males, please take pity on me, since You have agitated my mind.

PURPORT

Śrīla Viśvanātha Cakravartī supplies the following conversation:

Kṛṣṇa: Is it for the purpose of dining that you're inviting Me to your house?

Trivakrā: I simply can't leave You here.

Kṛṣṇa: But people here on the King's road will misconstrue what you're saying and laugh. Therefore please don't speak like this.

Trivakrā: I can't help being agitated. You made the mistake of touching me. It's not my fault.

TEXT 11

एवं स्त्रिया याच्यमानः कृष्णो रामस्य पश्यतः ।
मुखं वीक्ष्यानु गोपानां प्रहसंस्तामुवाच ह ॥११॥

evaṁ striyā yācyamānaḥ
kṛṣṇo rāmasya paśyataḥ
mukhaṁ vīkṣyānu gopānāṁ
prahasaṁs tām uvāca ha

evam—in this way; *striyā*—by the woman; *yācyamānaḥ*—being begged; *kṛṣṇaḥ*—Lord Kṛṣṇa; *rāmasya*—of Balarāma; *paśyataḥ*—who was looking on; *mukham*—at the face; *vīkṣya*—glancing; *anu*—then; *gopānām*—of the cowherd boys; *prahasan*—laughing; *tām*—to her; *uvāca ha*—He said.

TRANSLATION

Thus entreated by the woman, Lord Kṛṣṇa first glanced at the face of Balarāma, who was watching the incident, and then at the faces of the cowherd boys. Then with a laugh Kṛṣṇa replied to her as follows.

TEXT 12

एष्यामि ते गृहं सुभ्रु पुंसामाधिविकर्शनम् ।
साधितार्थोऽगृहाणां नः पान्थानां त्वं परायणम् ॥१२॥

eṣyāmi te gṛhaṁ su-bhru
puṁsām ādhi-vikarśanam
sādhitārtho 'gṛhāṇāṁ naḥ
pānthānāṁ tvaṁ parāyaṇam

eṣyāmi—I will go; *te*—your; *gṛham*—to the house; *su-bhru*—O you who have beautiful eyebrows; *puṁsām*—of men; *ādhi*—the mental distress; *vikarśanam*—which eradicates; *sādhita*—having accomplished; *arthaḥ*—My purpose; *agṛhāṇām*—who have no home; *naḥ*—for Us; *pānthānām*—who are traveling on the road; *tvam*—you; *para*—the best; *ayaṇam*—shelter.

TRANSLATION

O lady with beautiful eyebrows, as soon as I fulfill My purpose I will certainly visit your house, where men can relieve their anxiety. Indeed, you are the best refuge for Us homeless travelers.

PURPORT

By the word *agṛhāṇām*, Śrī Kṛṣṇa indicated not only that He had no fixed residence but also that He was not yet married.

TEXT 13

विसृज्य माध्व्या वाण्या ताम् व्रजन्मार्गे वणिक्पथैः ।
नानोपायनताम्बूलस्रग्गन्धैः साग्रजोऽर्चितः ॥१३॥

visṛjya mādhvyā vāṇyā tām
vrajan mārge vaṇik-pathaiḥ
nānopāyana-tāmbūla-
srag-gandhaiḥ sāgrajo 'rcitaḥ

visṛjya—leaving; *mādhvyā*—sweet; *vāṇyā*—with words; *tām*—her; *vrajan*—walking; *mārge*—along the road; *vaṇik-pathaiḥ*—by the merchants; *nānā*—with various; *upāyana*—respectful offerings; *tāmbūla*—betel nut; *srak*—garlands; *gandhaiḥ*—and fragrant substances; *sa*—together with; *agra-jaḥ*—His elder brother; *arcitaḥ*—worshiped.

TRANSLATION

Leaving her with these sweet words, Lord Kṛṣṇa walked further down the road. The merchants along the way worshiped Him and His elder brother by presenting Them with various respectful offerings, including *pān*, garlands and fragrant substances.

TEXT 14

तद्दर्शनस्मरक्षोभादात्मानं नाविदन् स्त्रियः ।
विस्रस्तवासःकवरवलया लेख्यमूर्तयः ॥१४॥

tad-darśana-smara-kṣobhād
ātmānaṁ nāvidan striyaḥ
visrasta-vāsaḥ-kavara-
valayā lekhya-mūrtayaḥ

tat—Him; *darśana*—because of seeing; *smara*—due to the effects of Cupid; *kṣobhāt*—by their agitation; *ātmānam*—themselves; *na avidan*—could not recognize; *striyaḥ*—the women; *visrasta*—disheveled; *vāsaḥ*—their clothes; *kavara*—the locks of their hair; *valayāḥ*—and their bangles; *lekhya*—(as if) drawn in a picture; *mūrtayaḥ*—their forms.

TRANSLATION

The sight of Kṛṣṇa aroused Cupid in the hearts of the city women. Thus agitated, they forgot themselves. Their clothes, braids and bangles became disheveled, and they stood as still as figures in a painting.

PURPORT

Śrīla Viśvanātha Cakravartī states that since the women of Mathurā immediately experienced symptoms of conjugal attraction when they saw Kṛṣṇa, they were the most advanced devotees in the city. The ten effects of Cupid are described as follows: *cakṣū-rāgaḥ prathamaṁ cittāsaṅgas tato 'tha saṅkalpaḥ nidrā-cchedas tanutā viṣaya-nivṛttis trapā-nāśaḥ/ unmādo mūrcchā mṛtir ity etāḥ smara-daśā daśaiva syuḥ.* "First comes attraction expressed through the eyes, then intense attachment in the mind, then determination, loss of sleep, becoming emaciated, disinterest in external things, shamelessness, madness, becoming stunned and death. These are the ten stages of Cupid's effects."

Śrīla Viśvanātha Cakravartī also points out that devotees who possess pure love of Godhead generally do not exhibit the symptom of death, since this is inauspicious in relation to Kṛṣṇa. They do, however, manifest the other nine symptoms, culminating in becoming stunned in ecstasy.

TEXT 15

ततः पौरान् पृच्छमानो धनुषः स्थानमच्युतः ।
तस्मिन् प्रविष्टो ददृशे धनुरैन्द्रमिवाद्भुतम् ॥१५॥

tataḥ paurān pṛcchamāno
dhanuṣaḥ sthānam acyutaḥ
tasmin praviṣṭo dadṛśe
dhanur aindram ivādbhutam

tataḥ—then; *paurān*—from the city residents; *pṛcchamānaḥ*—inquiring about; *dhanuṣaḥ*—of the bow; *sthānam*—the place; *acyutaḥ*—the infallible Supreme Lord; *tasmin*—there; *praviṣṭaḥ*—entering; *dadṛśe*—He saw; *dhanuḥ*—the bow; *aindram*—that of Lord Indra; *iva*—like; *adbhutam*—amazing.

TRANSLATION

Lord Kṛṣṇa then asked the local people where the arena was in which the bow sacrifice would take place. When He went there He saw the amazing bow, which resembled Lord Indra's.

TEXT 16

पुरुषैर्बहुभिर्गुप्तमर्चितं परमर्द्धिमत् ।
वार्यमाणो नृभिः कृष्णः प्रसह्य धनुराददे ॥१६॥

puruṣair bahubhir guptam
arcitaṁ paramarddhimat
vāryamāṇo nṛbhiḥ kṛṣṇaḥ
prasahya dhanur ādade

puruṣaiḥ—by men; *bahubhiḥ*—many; *guptam*—guarded; *arcitam*—being worshiped; *parama*—supreme; *ṛddhi*—opulence; *mat*—possessing; *vāryamāṇaḥ*—warded off; *nṛbhiḥ*—by the guards; *kṛṣṇaḥ*—Lord Kṛṣṇa; *prasahya*—by force; *dhanuḥ*—the bow; *ādade*—picked up.

TRANSLATION

That most opulent bow was guarded by a large company of men, who were respectfully worshiping it. Kṛṣṇa pushed His way forward and, despite the guards' attempts to stop Him, picked it up.

TEXT 17

करेण वामेन सलीलमुद्धृतं
सज्यं च कृत्वा निमिषेण पश्यताम् ।
नृणां विकृष्य प्रबभञ्ज मध्यतो
यथेक्षुदण्डं मदकर्युरुक्रमः ॥१७॥

kareṇa vāmena sa-līlam uddhṛtaṁ
sajyaṁ ca kṛtvā nimiṣeṇa paśyatām
nṛṇāṁ vikṛṣya prababhañja madhyato
yathekṣu-daṇḍaṁ mada-kary urukramaḥ

kareṇa—with His hand; *vāmena*—left; *sa-līlam*—playfully; *uddhṛtam*—lifted; *sajyam*—the stringing; *ca*—and; *kṛtvā*—doing; *nimiṣeṇa*—in the wink of an eye; *paśyatām*—as they watched; *nṛṇām*—the guards; *vikṛṣya*—pulling it taut; *prababhañja*—He broke it; *madhyataḥ*—in the middle; *yathā*—as; *ikṣu*—of sugarcane; *daṇḍam*—a stick; *mada-karī*—an excited elephant; *urukramaḥ*—Lord Kṛṣṇa.

TRANSLATION

Easily lifting the bow with His left hand, Lord Urukrama strung it in a fraction of a second as the King's guards looked on. He then powerfully pulled the string and snapped the bow in half, just as an excited elephant might break a stalk of sugarcane.

TEXT 18

धनुषो भज्यमानस्य शब्दः खं रोदसी दिशः ।
पूरयामास यं श्रुत्वा कंसस्त्रासमुपागमत् ॥१८॥

dhanuṣo bhajyamānasya
śabdaḥ khaṁ rodasī diśaḥ
pūrayām āsa yaṁ śrutvā
kaṁsas trāsam upāgamat

dhanuṣaḥ—of the bow; *bhajyamānasya*—which was breaking; *śabdaḥ*—the sound; *kham*—the earth; *rodasī*—the sky; *diśaḥ*—and all the directions; *pūrayām āsa*—filled; *yam*—which; *śrutvā*—hearing; *kaṁsaḥ*—King Kaṁsa; *trāsam*—fear; *upāgamat*—experienced.

TRANSLATION

The sound of the bow's breaking filled the earth and sky in all directions. Upon hearing it, Kaṁsa was struck with terror.

TEXT 19

तद्रक्षिणः सानुचरं कुपिता आततायिनः ।
गृहीतुकामा आवव्रुर्गृह्यतां वध्यतामिति ॥१९॥

tad-rakṣiṇaḥ sānucaraṁ
kupitā ātatāyinaḥ
gṛhītu-kāmā āvavrur
gṛhyatāṁ vadhyatām iti

tat—its; *rakṣiṇaḥ*—guards; *sa*—along with; *anucaram*—His companions; *kupitāḥ*—angered; *ātatāyinaḥ*—holding weapons; *gṛhītu*—to catch; *kāmāḥ*—wanting; *āvavruḥ*—surrounded; *gṛhyatām*—seize Him; *vadhyatām*—kill Him; *iti*—thus saying.

TRANSLATION

The enraged guards then took up their weapons and, wanting to seize Kṛṣṇa and His companions, surrounded them and shouted, "Grab Him! Kill Him!"

TEXT 20

अथ तान् दुरभिप्रायान् विलोक्य बलकेशवौ ।
क्रुद्धौ धन्वन आदाय शकले तांश्च जघ्नतुः ॥२०॥

atha tān durabhiprāyān
vilokya bala-keśavau
kruddhau dhanvana ādāya
śakale tāṁś ca jaghnatuḥ

atha—thereupon; *tān*—them; *durabhiprāyān*—with evil intent; *vilokya*—seeing; *bala-keśavau*—Balarāma and Kṛṣṇa; *kruddhau*—angry; *dhanvanaḥ*—of the bow; *ādāya*—taking; *śakale*—the two broken pieces; *tān*—them; *ca*—and; *jaghnatuḥ*—struck.

TRANSLATION

Seeing the guards coming upon Them with evil intent, Balarāma and Keśava took up the two halves of the bow and began striking them down.

TEXT 21

बलं च कंसप्रहितं हत्वा शालामुखात्ततः ।
निष्क्रम्य चेरतुर्हृष्टौ निरीक्ष्य पुरसम्पदः ॥२१॥

balaṁ ca kaṁsa-prahitaṁ
hatvā śālā-mukhāt tataḥ

niṣkramya ceratur hṛṣṭau
nirīkṣya pura-sampadaḥ

balam—an armed force; *ca*—and; *kaṁsa-prahitam*—sent by Kaṁsa; *hatvā*—having killed; *śālā*—of the sacrificial arena; *mukhāt*—by the gate; *tataḥ*—then; *niṣkramya*—exciting; *ceratuḥ*—the two of Them walked along; *hṛṣṭau*—happy; *nirīkṣya*—observing; *pura*—of the city; *sampadaḥ*—the riches.

TRANSLATION

After also killing a contingent of soldiers sent by Kaṁsa, Kṛṣṇa and Balarāma left the sacrificial arena by its main gate and continued Their walk about the city, happily looking at the opulent sights.

TEXT 22

तयोस्तदद्भुतं वीर्यं निशाम्य पुरवासिनः ।
तेजः प्रागल्भ्यं रूपं च मेनिरे विबुधोत्तमौ ॥२२॥

tayos tad adbhutaṁ vīryaṁ
niśāmya pura-vāsinaḥ
tejaḥ prāgalbhyaṁ rūpaṁ ca
menire vibudhottamau

tayoḥ—of Them; *tat*—that; *adbhutam*—amazing; *vīryam*—heroic deed; *niśāmya*—seeing; *pura-vāsinaḥ*—the residents of the city; *tejaḥ*—Their strength; *prāgalbhyam*—boldness; *rūpam*—beauty; *ca*—and; *menire*—they considered; *vibudha*—of demigods; *uttamau*—two of the best.

TRANSLATION

Having witnessed the amazing deed Kṛṣṇa and Balarāma had performed, and seeing Their strength, boldness and beauty, the people of the city thought They must be two prominent demigods.

TEXT 23

तयोर्विचरतोः स्वैरमादित्योऽस्तमुपेयिवान् ।
कृष्णरामौ वृतौ गोपैः पुराच्छकटमीयतुः ॥२३॥

tayor vicaratoḥ svairam
ādityo 'stam upeyivān
kṛṣṇa-rāmau vṛtau gopaiḥ
purāc chakaṭam īyatuḥ

tayoḥ—as They; *vicaratoḥ*—moved about; *svairam*—at Their will; *ādityaḥ*—the sun; *astam*—its setting; *upeyivān*—approached; *kṛṣṇa-rāmau*—Kṛṣṇa and Balarāma; *vṛtau*—accompanied; *gopaiḥ*—by the cowherd boys; *purāt*—from the city; *śakaṭam*—to the place where the wagons had been unharnessed; *īyatuḥ*—went.

TRANSLATION

As They strolled about at will, the sun began to set, so They left the city with the cowherd boys and returned to the cowherds' wagon encampment.

TEXT 24

गोप्यो मुकुन्दविगमे विरहातुरा या
आशासताशिष ऋता मधुपुर्यभूवन् ।
सम्पश्यतां पुरुषभूषणगात्रलक्ष्मीं
हित्वेतरान्नु भजतश्चकमेऽयनं श्रीः ॥२४॥

gopyo mukunda-vigame virahāturā yā
āśāsatāśiṣa ṛtā madhu-pury abhūvan
sampaśyatāṁ puruṣa-bhūṣaṇa-gātra-lakṣmīṁ
hitvetarān nu bhajataś cakame 'yanaṁ śrīḥ

gopyaḥ—the *gopīs; mukunda-vigame*—when Lord Mukunda was departing; *viraha*—by feelings of separation; *āturāḥ*—tormented; *yāḥ*—which; *āśāsata*—they had spoken; *āśiṣaḥ*—the benedictions; *ṛtāḥ*—true; *madhu-puri*—in Mathurā; *abhūvan*—have become; *sampaśyatām*—for those who are fully seeing; *puruṣa*—of men; *bhūṣaṇa*—of the ornament; *gātra*—of His body; *lakṣmīm*—the beauty; *hitvā*—abandoning; *itarān*—others; *nu*—indeed; *bhajataḥ*—who were worshiping her; *cakame*—hankered for; *ayanam*—shelter; *śrīḥ*—the goddess of fortune.

TRANSLATION

At the time of Mukunda's [Kṛṣṇa's] departure from Vṛndāvana, the *gopīs* had foretold that the residents of Mathurā would enjoy many benedictions, and now the *gopīs'* predictions were coming true, for those residents were gazing upon the beauty of Kṛṣṇa, the jewel among men. Indeed, the goddess of fortune desired the shelter of that beauty so much that she abandoned many other men, although they worshiped her.

TEXT 25

अवनिक्ताङ्घ्रियुगलौ भुक्त्वा क्षीरोपसेचनम् ।
ऊषतुस्तां सुखं रात्रिं ज्ञात्वा कंसचिकीर्षितम् ॥२५॥

avaniktāṅghri-yugalau
bhuktvā kṣīropasecanam
ūṣatus tāṁ sukhaṁ rātriṁ
jñātvā kaṁsa-cikīrṣitam

avanikta—bathed; *aṅghri-yugalau*—the two feet of each of Them; *bhuktvā*—eating; *kṣīra-upasecanam*—boiled rice sprinkled with milk; *ūṣatuḥ*—They stayed there; *tām*—for that; *sukham*—comfortably; *rātrim*—night; *jñātvā*—knowing; *kaṁsa-cikīrṣitam*—what Kaṁsa intended to do.

TRANSLATION

After Kṛṣṇa's and Balarāma's feet were bathed, the two Lords ate rice with milk. Then, although knowing what Kaṁsa intended to do, They spent the night there comfortably.

TEXTS 26–27

कंसस्तु धनुषो भंगं रक्षिणां स्वबलस्य च ।
वधं निशम्य गोविन्दरामविक्रीडितं परम् ॥२६॥
दीर्घप्रजागरो भीतो दुर्निमित्तानि दुर्मतिः ।
बहून्यचष्टोभयथा मृत्योर्दौत्यकराणि च ॥२७॥

kaṁsas tu dhanuṣo bhaṅgaṁ
rakṣiṇāṁ sva-balasya ca
vadhaṁ niśamya govinda-
rāma-vikrīḍitaṁ param

dīrgha-prajāgaro bhīto
durnimittāni durmatiḥ
bahūny acaṣṭobhayathā
mṛtyor dautya-karāṇi ca

kaṁsaḥ—King Kaṁsa; *tu*—but; *dhanuṣaḥ*—of the bow; *bhaṅgam*—the breaking; *rakṣiṇām*—of the guards; *sva*—his; *balasya*—of the army; *ca*—and; *vadham*—the killing; *niśamya*—hearing of; *govinda-rāma*—of Kṛṣṇa and Balarāma; *vikrīḍitam*—the playing; *param*—merely; *dīrgha*—for a long time; *prajāgaraḥ*—remaining awake; *bhītaḥ*—afraid; *durnimittāni*—bad omens; *durmatiḥ*—the wicked-minded; *bahūni*—many; *acaṣṭa*—saw; *ubhayathā*—in both states (sleep and wakefulness); *mṛtyoḥ*—of death; *dautya-karāṇi*—the messengers; *ca*—and.

TRANSLATION

Wicked King Kaṁsa, on the other hand, was terrified, having heard how Kṛṣṇa and Balarāma had broken the bow and killed his guards and soldiers, all simply as a game. He remained awake for a long time, and both while awake and while dreaming he saw many bad omens, messengers of death.

TEXTS 28–31

अदर्शनं स्वशिरसः प्रतिरूपे च सत्यपि ।
असत्यपि द्वितीये च द्वैरूप्यं ज्योतिषां तथा ॥२८॥

छिद्रप्रतीतिश्छायायां प्राणघोषानुपश्रुतिः ।
स्वर्णप्रतीतिर्वृक्षेषु स्वपदानामदर्शनम् ॥२९॥
स्वप्ने प्रेतपरिष्वंगः खरयानं विषादनम् ।
यायान्नलदमाल्येकस्तैलाभ्यक्तो दिगम्बरः ॥३०॥
अन्यानि चेत्थंभूतानि स्वप्नजागरितानि च ।
पश्यन्मरणसन्त्रस्तो निद्रां लेभे न चिन्तया ॥३१॥

adarśanaṁ sva-śirasaḥ
pratirūpe ca saty api
asaty api dvitīye ca
dvai-rūpyaṁ jyotiṣāṁ tathā

chidra-pratītiś chāyāyāṁ
prāṇa-ghoṣānupaśrutiḥ
svarṇa-pratītir vṛkṣeṣu
sva-padānām adarśanam

svapne preta-pariṣvaṅgaḥ
khara-yānaṁ viṣādanam
yāyān nalada-mäly ekas
tailābhyakto dig-ambaraḥ

anyāni cetthaṁ-bhūtāni
svapna-jāgaritāni ca
paśyan maraṇa-santrasto
nidrāṁ lebhe na cintayā

adarśanam—the invisibility; *sva*—of his own; *śirasaḥ*—head; *pratirūpe*—his reflection; *ca*—and; *sati*—being present; *api*—even; *asati*—there not being; *api*—even; *dvitīye*—a cause for duplication; *ca*—and; *dvai-rūpyam*—double image; *jyotiṣām*—of the heavenly bodies; *tathā*—also; *chidra*—of a hole; *pratītiḥ*—the seeing; *chāyāyām*—in his shadow; *prāṇa*—of his life air; *ghoṣa*—of the reverberation; *anupaśrutiḥ*—the failure to hear; *svarṇa*—of a golden color; *pratītiḥ*—the perception; *vṛkṣeṣu*—on trees; *sva*—his own; *padānām*—footprints; *adarśanam*—not seeing; *svapne*—while asleep; *preta*—by ghostly spirits;

pariṣvaṅgaḥ—being embraced; *khara*—upon a donkey; *yānam*—traveling; *viṣa*—poison; *adanam*—swallowing; *yāyāt*—was going about; *nalada*—of spikenards, rose-purple flowers native to India; *mālī*—wearing a garland; *ekaḥ*—someone; *taila*—with oil; *abhyaktaḥ*—smeared; *dik-ambaraḥ*—naked; *anyāni*—other (omens); *ca*—and; *ittham-bhūtāni*—like these; *svapna*—while asleep; *jāgaritāni*—while awake; *ca*—also; *paśyan*—seeing; *maraṇa*—of death; *santrastaḥ*—terrified; *nidrām*—sleep; *lebhe*—he could achieve; *na*—not; *cintayā*—because of his anxiety.

TRANSLATION

When he looked at his reflection he could not see his head; for no reason the moon and stars appeared double; he saw a hole in his shadow; he could not hear the sound of his life air; trees seemed covered with a golden hue; and he could not see his footprints. He dreamt that he was being embraced by ghosts, riding a donkey and drinking poison, and also that a naked man smeared with oil was passing by wearing a garland of *nalada* flowers. Seeing these and other such omens both while dreaming and while awake, Kaṁsa was terrified by the prospect of death, and out of anxiety he could not sleep.

TEXT 32

व्युष्टायां निशि कौरव्य सूर्ये चाद्भ्यः समुत्थिते ।
कारयामास वै कंसो मल्लक्रीडामहोत्सवम् ॥३२॥

vyuṣṭāyāṁ niśi kauravya
sūrye cādbhyaḥ samutthite
kārayām āsa vai kaṁso
malla-krīḍā-mahotsavam

vyuṣṭāyām—having passed; *niśi*—the night; *kauravya*—O descendant of Kuru (Parīkṣit); *sūrye*—the sun; *ca*—and; *adbhyaḥ*—from the water; *samutthite*—rising; *kārayām āsa*—had carried out; *vai*—indeed; *kaṁsaḥ*—Kaṁsa; *malla*—of wrestlers; *krīḍā*—of the sport; *mahā-utsavam*—the great festival.

TRANSLATION

When the night had finally passed and the sun rose up again from the water, Kaṁsa set about arranging for the grand wrestling festival.

TEXT 33

आनर्चुः पुरुषा रंगं तूर्यभेर्यश्च जघ्निरे ।
मञ्चाश्चालंकृताः स्रग्भिः पताकाचैलतोरणैः ॥३३॥

ānarcuḥ puruṣā raṅgaṁ
tūrya-bheryaś ca jaghnire
mañcāś cālaṅkṛtāḥ sragbhiḥ
patākā-caila-toraṇaiḥ

ānarcuḥ—worshiped; *puruṣāḥ*—the King's men; *raṅgam*—the arena; *tūrya*—musical instruments; *bheryaḥ*—drums; *ca*—and; *jaghnire*—they vibrated; *mañcāḥ*—the viewing platforms; *ca*—and; *alaṅkṛtāḥ*—were decorated; *sragbhiḥ*—with garlands; *patākā*—with flags; *caila*—cloth ribbons; *toraṇaiḥ*—and gateways.

TRANSLATION

The King's men performed the ritual worship of the wrestling arena, sounded their drums and other instruments and decorated the viewing galleries with garlands, flags, ribbons and arches.

TEXT 34

तेषु पौरा जानपदा ब्रह्मक्षत्रपुरोगमाः ।
यथोपजोषं विविशू राजानश्च कृतासनाः ॥३४॥

teṣu paurā jānapadā
brahma-kṣatra-purogamāḥ
yathopajoṣaṁ viviśū
rājānaś ca kṛtāsanāḥ

teṣu—upon these (platforms); *paurāḥ*—the city-dwellers; *jānapadāḥ*—and the people of the suburbs; *brahma*—by the *brāhmaṇas; kṣatra*—and the *kṣatriyas; puraḥ-gamāḥ*—headed; *yathā-upajoṣam*—as suited their comfort; *viviśuḥ*—came and sat; *rājānaḥ*—the kings; *ca*—also; *kṛta*—given; *āsanāḥ*—special seats.

TRANSLATION

The city-dwellers and residents of the outlying districts, led by *brāhmaṇas* and *kṣatriyas*, came and sat down comfortably in the galleries. The royal guests received special seats.

TEXT 35

कंसः परिवृतोऽमात्यै राजमञ्च उपाविशत् ।
मण्डलेश्वरमध्यस्थो हृदयेन विदूयता ॥३५॥

kaṁsaḥ parivṛto 'mātyai
rāja-mañca upāviśat
maṇḍaleśvara-madhya-stho
hṛdayena vidūyatā

kaṁsaḥ—Kaṁsa; *parivṛtaḥ*—surrounded; *amātyaiḥ*—by his ministers; *rāja-mañce*—on the King's platform; *upāviśat*—sat; *maṇḍala-īśvara*—of secondary rulers of various regions; *madhya*—in the midst; *sthaḥ*—situated; *hṛdayena*—with his heart; *vidūyatā*—trembling.

TRANSLATION

Surrounded by his ministers, Kaṁsa took his seat on the imperial dais. But even as he sat amidst his various provincial rulers, his heart trembled.

TEXT 36

वाद्यमानेषु तूर्येषु मल्लतालोत्तरेषु च ।
मल्लाः स्वलंकृताः दृप्ताः सोपाध्यायाः समासत ॥३६॥

vādyamāneṣu tūryeṣu
malla-tālottareṣu ca
mallāḥ sv-alaṅkṛtāḥ dṛptāḥ
sopādhyāyāḥ samāsata

vādyamāneṣu—as they were being played; *tūryeṣu*—the musical instruments; *malla*—suitable for wrestling; *tāla*—with meters; *uttareṣu*—prominent; *ca*—and; *mallāḥ*—the wrestlers; *su-alaṅkṛtāḥ*—well ornamented; *dṛptāḥ*—proud; *sa-upādhyāyāḥ*—together with their instructors; *samāsata*—came and sat down.

TRANSLATION

While the musical instruments loudly played in the rhythmic meters appropriate for wrestling matches, the lavishly ornamented wrestlers proudly entered the arena with their coaches and sat down.

TEXT 37

चाणूरो मुष्टिकः कूटः शलस्तोशल एव च ।
त आसेदुरुपस्थानं वल्गुवाद्यप्रहर्षिताः ॥३७॥

cāṇūro muṣṭikaḥ kūṭaḥ
śalas tośala eva ca
ta āsedur upasthānaṁ
valgu-vādya-praharṣitāḥ

cāṇūraḥ muṣṭikaḥ kūṭaḥ—the wrestlers Cāṇūra, Muṣṭika and Kūṭa; *śalaḥ tośalaḥ*—Śala and Tośala; *eva ca*—also; *te*—they; *āseduḥ*—sat down; *upasthānam*—on the mat of the wrestling ring; *valgu*—pleasing; *vādya*—by the music; *praharṣitāḥ*—enthused.

TRANSLATION

Enthused by the pleasing music, Cāṇūra, Muṣṭika, Kūṭa, Śala and Tośala sat down on the wrestling mat.

TEXT 38

नन्दगोपादयो गोपा भोजराजसमाहुताः ।
निवेदितोपायनास्त एकस्मिन्मञ्च आविशन् ॥३८॥

nanda-gopādayo gopā
bhoja-rāja-samāhutāḥ
niveditopāyanās ta
ekasmin mañca āviśan

nanda-gopa-ādayaḥ—headed by Nanda Gopa; *gopāḥ*—the cowherds; *bhoja-rāja*—by Kaṁsa, King of the Bhojas; *samāhutāḥ*—called forward; *nivedita*—presenting; *upāyanāḥ*—their offerings; *te*—they; *ekasmin*—in one; *mañce*—viewing gallery; *āviśan*—sat down.

TRANSLATION

Nanda Mahārāja and the other cowherds, summoned by the King of the Bhojas, presented him with their offerings and then took their seats in one of the galleries.

PURPORT

According to Śrīla Viśvanātha Cakravartī, the word *samāhutāḥ* indicates that King Kaṁsa respectfully called the leaders of Vraja forward so that they could make their offerings to the central government. According to the *ācārya,* Kaṁsa assured Nanda as follows: "My dear King of Vraja, you are the most important of my village rulers. Yet even though you have come to Mathurā from your cowherd village, you have not come to visit me. Is that because you are frightened? Don't think that your two sons are bad because They broke the bow. I invited Them here because I heard They were extremely powerful, and I've arranged this wrestling match as a test of Their strength. So please come forward without hesitation. Don't be afraid."

Śrīla Viśvanātha Cakravartī further states that Nanda Mahārāja noticed his two sons were not present. Apparently, out of disrespect for King Kaṁsa's order, They had taken the morning off and gone elsewhere.

Thus Kaṁsa delegated some cowherd men to go look for Them and advise Them to behave properly and come back to the wrestling arena. The *ācārya* also states that the reason Nanda and the other cowherd men sat in the galleries was that they could not find any sitting places on the royal dais.

Thus end the purports of the humble servant of His Divine Grace A. C. Bhaktivedanta Swami Prabhupāda to the Tenth Canto, Forty-second Chapter, of the Śrīmad-Bhāgavatam, *entitled "The Breaking of the Sacrificial Bow."*

CHAPTER FORTY-THREE

Kṛṣṇa Kills the Elephant Kuvalayāpīḍa

This chapter tells how Lord Kṛṣṇa killed the lordly elephant Kuvalayāpīḍa, how Kṛṣṇa and Balarāma entered the wrestling arena and what Kṛṣṇa said to the wrestler Cāṇūra.

After finishing Their early-morning rituals, Kṛṣṇa and Balarāma heard kettledrums heralding the start of the wrestling match, and They went to see the festivities. At the gate of the wrestling arena They encountered an elephant named Kuvalayāpīḍa, who attacked Kṛṣṇa at the urging of his keeper. The mighty elephant grabbed at Kṛṣṇa with his trunk, but the Lord struck back and then disappeared from the beast's sight among his legs. Enraged at not being able to see Kṛṣṇa, Kuvalayāpīḍa sought Him out with his sense of smell and seized Him. But the Lord pulled loose. In this way Kṛṣṇa teased and tormented Kuvalayāpīḍa, finally yanking out one of his tusks and beating him and his keepers to death.

Sprinkled with the elephant's blood and carrying one of his tusks on His shoulder as a weapon, Lord Kṛṣṇa appeared unprecedentedly beautiful as He entered the wrestling arena. There the various classes of people saw Him in different ways, according to their specific relationship with Him.

When King Kaṁsa heard how Kṛṣṇa and Balarāma had killed Kuvalayāpīḍa, he realized They were invincible and became filled with anxiety. The members of the audience, on the other hand, became joyful as they reminded one another about the Lords' amazing pastimes. The people declared that Kṛṣṇa and Balarāma must be two expansions of the Supreme Lord Nārāyaṇa who had descended into the house of Vasudeva.

Cāṇūra then stepped forward and challenged Kṛṣṇa and Balarāma to wrestle, saying King Kaṁsa wished to see such a match. Kṛṣṇa replied, "Although We are merely nomadic forest folk, We are nonetheless subjects of the King; thus We will not hesitate to please him with an exhibition of wrestling." As soon as Cāṇūra heard this, he suggested that Kṛṣṇa should wrestle him and that Balarāma should wrestle Muṣṭika.

TEXT 1

श्रीशुक उवाच
अथ कृष्णश्च रामश्च कृतशौचौ परन्तप ।
मल्लदुन्दुभिनिर्घोषं श्रुत्वा द्रष्टुमुपेयतुः ॥१॥

śrī-śuka uvāca
atha kṛṣṇaś ca rāmaś ca
kṛta-śaucau parantapa
malla-dundubhi-nirghoṣaṁ
śrutvā draṣṭum upeyatuḥ

śrī-śukaḥ uvāca—Śrī Śukadeva Gosvāmī said; *atha*—next; *kṛṣṇaḥ*—Kṛṣṇa; *ca*—and; *rāmaḥ*—Balarāma; *ca*—also; *kṛta*—having carried out; *śaucau*—purification; *param-tapa*—O chastiser of enemies; *malla*—of the wrestling match; *dundubhi*—of the kettledrums; *nirghoṣam*—the resounding vibration; *śrutvā*—hearing; *draṣṭum*—to see; *upeyatuḥ*—They approached.

TRANSLATION

Śukadeva Gosvāmī said: O chastiser of enemies, Kṛṣṇa and Balarāma, having executed all necessary purification, then heard the kettledrums resounding at the wrestling arena, and They went there to see what was happening.

PURPORT

Śrīla Śrīdhara Svāmī explains the words *kṛta-śaucau*, "having executed all necessary purification," as follows: "Two days previously, Kṛṣṇa and Balarāma had executed Their purification, Their relief from offense, [by performing heroic deeds. The Lords reasoned:] 'Even after We have made Our power known by breaking the bow and by performing other feats, Our parents have still not secured freedom. Kaṁsa is again trying to kill them. Therefore, although he is Our maternal uncle, it will not be wrong for Us to kill him.' They assured Their offenselessness by this reasoning."

TEXT 2

रंगद्वारं समासाद्य तस्मिन्नागमवस्थितम् ।
अपश्यत्कुवलयापीडं कृष्णोऽम्बष्ठप्रचोदितम् ॥२॥

raṅga-dvāraṁ samāsādya
tasmin nāgam avasthitam
apaśyat kuvalayāpīḍaṁ
kṛṣṇo 'mbaṣṭha-pracoditam

raṅga—of the arena; *dvāram*—the gate; *samāsādya*—reaching; *tasmin*—in that place; *nāgam*—an elephant; *avasthitam*—standing; *apaśyat*—He saw; *kuvalayāpīḍam*—named Kuvalayāpīḍa; *kṛṣṇaḥ*—Lord Kṛṣṇa; *ambaṣṭha*—by his keeper; *pracoditam*—urged on.

TRANSLATION

When Lord Kṛṣṇa reached the entrance to the arena, He saw the elephant Kuvalayāpīḍa blocking His way at the urging of his keeper.

PURPORT

The elephant-keeper revealed his malicious intent by blocking Lord Kṛṣṇa's entrance into the arena.

TEXT 3

बद्ध्वा परिकरं शौरिः समुह्य कुटिलालकान् ।
उवाच हस्तिपं वाचा मेघनादगभीरया ॥३॥

baddhvā parikaraṁ śauriḥ
samuhya kuṭilālakān
uvāca hastipaṁ vācā
megha-nāda-gabhīrayā

baddhvā—binding; *parikaram*—His clothes; *śauriḥ*—Lord Kṛṣṇa; *samuhya*—tying together; *kuṭila*—curled; *alakān*—the locks of His hair;

uvāca—He spoke; *hasti-pam*—to the elephant-keeper; *vācā*—with words; *megha*—of a cloud; *nāda*—like the sound; *gabhīrayā*—grave.

TRANSLATION

Securely binding up His clothes and tying back His curly locks, Lord Kṛṣṇa addressed the elephant-keeper with words as grave as the rumbling of a cloud.

PURPORT

Lord Kṛṣṇa was obviously preparing for a fight. According to Śrīla Viśvanātha Cakravartī Ṭhākura, the Lord put aside His jacket, tightened His belt and tied back His hair.

TEXT 4

अम्बष्ठाम्बष्ठ मार्गं नौ देह्यपक्रम मा चिरम् ।
नो चेत्सकुञ्जरं त्वाद्य नयामि यमसादनम् ॥४॥

ambaṣṭhāmbaṣṭha mārgaṁ nau
dehy apakrama mā ciram
no cet sa-kuñjaraṁ tvādya
nayāmi yama-sādanam

ambaṣṭha ambaṣṭha—O elephant-keeper, elephant-keeper; *mārgam*—way; *nau*—to Us; *dehi*—give; *apakrama*—move aside; *mā ciram*—without delay; *na u cet*—if not; *sa-kuñjaram*—together with your elephant; *tvā*—you; *adya*—today; *nayāmi*—I will send; *yama*—of the lord of death; *sādanam*—to the abode.

TRANSLATION

O driver, driver, move aside at once and let Us pass! If you don't, this very day I will send both you and your elephant to the abode of Yamarāja!

TEXT 5

एवं निर्भर्त्सितोऽम्बष्ठः कुपितः कोपितं गजम् ।
चोदयामास कृष्णाय कालान्तकयमोपमम् ॥५॥

evaṁ nirbhartsito 'mbaṣṭhaḥ
kupitaḥ kopitaṁ gajam
codayām āsa kṛṣṇāya
kālāntaka-yamopamam

evam—thus; *nirbhartsitaḥ*—threatened; *ambaṣṭhaḥ*—the elephant-keeper; *kupitaḥ*—angered; *kopitam*—the enraged; *gajam*—elephant; *codayām āsa*—he goaded; *kṛṣṇāya*—toward Kṛṣṇa; *kāla*—time; *antaka*—death; *yama*—and Yamarāja; *upamam*—comparable to.

TRANSLATION

Thus threatened, the elephant-keeper became angry. He goaded his furious elephant, who appeared equal to time, death and Yamarāja, into attacking Lord Kṛṣṇa.

TEXT 6

करीन्द्रस्तमभिद्रुत्य करेण तरसाग्रहीत् ।
कराद्विगलितः सोऽमुं निहत्याङ्घ्रिष्वलीयत ॥६॥

karīndras tam abhidrutya
kareṇa tarasāgrahīt
karād vigalitaḥ so 'muṁ
nihatyāṅghriṣv alīyata

kari—of elephants; *indraḥ*—the lord; *tam*—Him; *abhidrutya*—running toward; *kareṇa*—with his trunk; *tarasā*—violently; *agrahīt*—seized; *karāt*—from the trunk; *vigalitaḥ*—slipping away; *saḥ*—He, Kṛṣṇa; *amum*—him, Kuvalayāpīḍa; *nihatya*—striking; *aṅghriṣu*—among his legs; *alīyata*—He disappeared.

TRANSLATION

The lord of the elephants charged Kṛṣṇa and violently seized Him with his trunk. But Kṛṣṇa slipped away, struck him a blow and disappeared from his view among his legs.

PURPORT

Lord Kṛṣṇa struck the elephant with His fist and then disappeared among his legs.

TEXT 7

संक्रुद्धस्तमचक्षाणो घ्राणदृष्टिः स केशवम् ।
परामृशत्पुष्करेण स प्रसह्य विनिर्गतः ॥७॥

saṅkruddhas tam acakṣāṇo
ghrāṇa-dṛṣṭiḥ sa keśavam
parāmṛśat puṣkareṇa
sa prasahya vinirgataḥ

saṅkruddhaḥ—infuriated; *tam*—Him; *acakṣāṇaḥ*—not seeing; *ghrāṇa*—by his sense of smell; *dṛṣṭiḥ*—whose vision; *saḥ*—he, the elephant; *keśavam*—Lord Keśava; *parāmṛśat*—took hold of; *puṣkareṇa*—with the end of his trunk; *saḥ*—He, Kṛṣṇa; *prasahya*—by force; *vinirgataḥ*—came free.

TRANSLATION

Infuriated at being unable to see Lord Keśava, the elephant sought Him out with his sense of smell. Once again Kuvalayāpīḍa seized the Lord with the end of his trunk, only to have the Lord forcefully free Himself.

PURPORT

Lord Kṛṣṇa allowed the elephant to seize Him so that the beast would be encouraged to keep fighting. Once Kuvalayāpīḍa had thus become proud, Lord Kṛṣṇa again thwarted him with His superior potency.

TEXT 8

पुच्छे प्रगृह्यातिबलं धनुषः पञ्चविंशतिम् ।
विचकर्ष यथा नागं सुपर्ण इव लीलया ॥८॥

pucche pragṛhyāti-balaṁ
dhanuṣaḥ pañca-viṁśatim
vicakarṣa yathā nāgaṁ
suparṇa iva līlayā

pucche—by his tail; *pragṛhya*—grabbing him; *ati-balam*—the extremely powerful (elephant); *dhanuṣaḥ*—bow-lengths; *pañca-viṁśatim*—twenty-five; *vicakarṣa*—He dragged; *yathā*—as; *nāgam*—a snake; *suparṇaḥ*—Garuḍa; *iva*—as; *līlayā*—playfully.

TRANSLATION

Lord Kṛṣṇa then grabbed the powerful Kuvalayāpīḍa by the tail and playfully dragged him twenty-five bow-lengths as easily as Garuḍa might drag a snake.

TEXT 9

स पर्यावर्तमानेन सव्यदक्षिणतोऽच्युतः ।
बभ्राम भ्राम्यमाणेन गोवत्सेनेव बालकः ॥९॥

sa paryāvartamānena
savya-dakṣiṇato 'cyutaḥ
babhrāma bhrāmyamāṇena
go-vatseneva bālakaḥ

saḥ—He; *paryāvartamānena*—with him (the elephant) who was being moved around; *savya-dakṣiṇataḥ*—to the left and then the right; *acyutaḥ*—Lord Kṛṣṇa; *babhrāma*—moved also; *bhrāmyamāṇena*—together with him who was being moved; *go-vatsena*—with a calf; *iva*—just as; *bālakaḥ*—a young boy.

TRANSLATION

As Lord Acyuta held on to the elephant's tail, the animal tried to twist away to the left and to the right, making the Lord swerve in the opposite direction, as a young boy would swerve when pulling a calf by the tail.

TEXT 10

ततोऽभिमुखमभ्येत्य पाणिनाहत्य वारणम् ।
प्राद्रवन् पातयामास स्पृश्यमानः पदे पदे ॥१०॥

tato 'bhimukham abhyetya
pāṇināhatya vāraṇam
prādravan pātayām āsa
spṛśyamānaḥ pade pade

tataḥ—then; *abhimukham*—face to face; *abhyetya*—coming; *pāṇinā*—with His hand; *āhatya*—slapping; *vāraṇam*—the elephant; *prādravan*—running away; *pātayām āsa*—He made him fall; *spṛśyamānaḥ*—being touched; *pade pade*—with each step.

TRANSLATION

Kṛṣṇa then came face to face with the elephant and slapped him and ran away. Kuvalayāpīḍa pursued the Lord, managing to touch Him again and again with each step, but Kṛṣṇa outmaneuvered the elephant and made him trip and fall.

TEXT 11

स धावन् क्रीडया भूमौ पतित्वा सहसोत्थितः ।
तं मत्वा पतितं क्रुद्धो दन्ताभ्यां सोऽहनत्क्षितिम् ॥११॥

sa dhāvan krīḍayā bhūmau
patitvā sahasotthitaḥ
taṁ matvā patitaṁ kruddho
dantābhyāṁ so 'hanat kṣitim

saḥ—He; *dhāvan*—running; *krīḍayā*—playfully; *bhūmau*—on the ground; *patitvā*—falling; *sahasā*—suddenly; *utthitaḥ*—getting up; *tam*—Him; *matvā*—thinking; *patitam*—fallen; *kruddhaḥ*—angry; *dantābhyām*—with his tusks; *saḥ*—he, Kuvalayāpīḍa; *ahanat*—struck; *kṣitim*—the earth.

TRANSLATION

As Kṛṣṇa dodged about, He playfully fell on the ground and quickly got up again. The raging elephant, thinking Kṛṣṇa was down, tried to gore Him with his tusks but struck the earth instead.

TEXT 12

स्वविक्रमे प्रतिहते कुञ्जरेन्द्रोऽत्यमर्षितः ।
चोद्यमानो महामात्रैः कृष्णमभ्यद्रवद् रुषा ॥१२॥

sva-vikrame pratihate
kuñjarendro 'ty-amarṣitaḥ
codyamāno mahāmātraiḥ
kṛṣṇam abhyadravad ruṣā

sva—his; *vikrame*—prowess; *pratihate*—being thwarted; *kuñjara-indraḥ*—the lord of elephants; *ati*—extreme; *amarṣitaḥ*—with frustrated anger; *codyamānaḥ*—urged on; *mahāmātraiḥ*—by the elephant-keepers; *kṛṣṇam*—at Kṛṣṇa; *abhyadravat*—he charged; *ruṣā*—furiously.

TRANSLATION

His prowess foiled, the lordly elephant Kuvalayāpīḍa went into a frenzied rage out of frustration. But the elephant-keepers goaded him on, and he furiously charged Kṛṣṇa once again.

TEXT 13

तमापतन्तमासाद्य भगवान्मधुसूदनः ।
निगृह्य पाणिना हस्तं पातयामास भूतले ॥१३॥

tam āpatantam āsādya
bhagavān madhusūdanaḥ
nigṛhya pāṇinā hastaṁ
pātayām āsa bhū-tale

tam—him; *āpatantam*—attacking; *āsādya*—confronting; *bhagavān*—the Supreme Lord; *madhu-sūdanaḥ*—the killer of the demon Madhu; *nigṛhya*—firmly seizing; *pāṇinā*—with His hand; *hastam*—his trunk; *pātayām āsa*—He made him fall; *bhū-tale*—onto the ground.

TRANSLATION

The Supreme Lord, killer of the demon Madhu, confronted the elephant as he attacked. Seizing his trunk with one hand, Kṛṣṇa threw him to the ground.

TEXT 14

पतितस्य पदाक्रम्य मृगेन्द्र इव लीलया ।
दन्तमुत्पाट्य तेनेभं हस्तिपांश्चाहनद्धरिः ॥१४॥

patitasya padākramya
mṛgendra iva līlayā
dantam utpāṭya tenebhaṁ
hastipāṁś cāhanad dhariḥ

patitasya—of the fallen (elephant); *padā*—with His foot; *ākramya*—climbing upon him; *mṛgendraḥ*—a lion; *iva*—as if; *līlayā*—with ease; *dantam*—one of his tusks; *utpāṭya*—pulling out; *tena*—with it; *ibham*—the elephant; *hasti-pān*—the elephant-keepers; *ca*—also; *ahanat*—killed; *hariḥ*—Lord Kṛṣṇa.

TRANSLATION

Lord Hari then climbed onto the elephant with the ease of a mighty lion, pulled out a tusk, and with it killed the beast and his keepers.

TEXT 15

मृतकं द्विपमुत्सृज्य दन्तपाणिः समाविशत् ।
अंसन्यस्तविषाणोऽसृङ्मदबिन्दुभिरंकितः ।
विरूढस्वेदकणिकावदनाम्बुरुहो बभौ ॥१५॥

mṛtakaṁ dvipam utsṛjya
danta-pāṇiḥ samāviśat
aṁsa-nyasta-viṣāṇo 'sṛṅ-
mada-bindubhir aṅkitaḥ
virūḍha-sveda-kaṇikā-
vadanāmburuho babhau

mṛtakam—dead; *dvipam*—the elephant; *utsṛjya*—discarding; *danta*—his tusk; *pāṇiḥ*—in His hand; *samāviśat*—He entered (the arena); *aṁsa*—upon His shoulder; *nyasta*—placing; *viṣāṇaḥ*—the tusk; *asṛk*—of blood; *mada*—and the elephant's sweat; *bindubhiḥ*—with drops; *aṅkitaḥ*—sprinkled; *virūḍha*—exuding; *sveda*—of (His own) perspiration; *kaṇikā*—with fine drops; *vadana*—His face; *ambu-ruhaḥ*—lotuslike; *babhau*—shone.

TRANSLATION

Leaving the dead elephant aside, Lord Kṛṣṇa held on to the tusk and entered the wrestling arena. With the tusk resting on His shoulder, drops of the elephant's blood and sweat sprinkled all over Him, and His lotus face covered with fine drops of His own perspiration, the Lord shone with great beauty.

TEXT 16

वृतौ गोपैः कतिपयैर्बलदेवजनार्दनौ ।
रंगं विविशतू राजन् गजदन्तवरायुधौ ॥१६॥

vṛtau gopaiḥ katipayair
baladeva-janārdanau
raṅgaṁ viviśatū rājan
gaja-danta-varāyudhau

vṛtau—surrounded; *gopaiḥ*—by cowherd boys; *katipayaiḥ*—several; *baladeva-janārdanau*—Balarāma and Kṛṣṇa; *raṅgam*—the arena; *viviśatuḥ*—entered; *rājan*—O King (Parīkṣit); *gaja-danta*—the elephant's tusks; *vara*—chosen; *āyudhau*—whose weapons.

TRANSLATION

My dear King, Lord Baladeva and Lord Janārdana, each carrying one of the elephant's tusks as His chosen weapon, entered the arena with several cowherd boys.

TEXT 17

मल्लानामशनिर्नृणां नरवरः स्त्रीणां स्मरो मूर्तिमान्
गोपानां स्वजनोऽसतां क्षितिभुजां शास्ता स्वपित्रोः शिशुः ।
मृत्युर्भोजपतेर्विराडविदुषां तत्त्वं परं योगिनां
वृष्णीनां परदेवतेति विदितो रंगं गतः साग्रजः ॥१७॥

mallānām aśanir nṛṇāṁ nara-varaḥ strīṇāṁ smaro mūrtimān
gopānāṁ sva-jano 'satāṁ kṣiti-bhujāṁ śāstā sva-pitroḥ śiśuḥ
mṛtyur bhoja-pater virāḍ aviduṣāṁ tattvaṁ paraṁ yogināṁ
vṛṣṇīnāṁ para-devateti vidito raṅgaṁ gataḥ sāgrajaḥ

mallānām—for the wrestlers; *aśaniḥ*—lightning; *nṛṇām*—for the males; *nara-varaḥ*—the best of men; *strīṇām*—for the women; *smaraḥ*—Cupid; *mūrti-mān*—incarnate; *gopānām*—for the cowherds; *sva-janaḥ*—their relative; *asatām*—impious; *kṣiti-bhujām*—for the kings; *śāstā*—a punisher; *sva-pitroḥ*—for His parents; *śiśuḥ*—a child; *mṛtyuḥ*—death; *bhoja-pateḥ*—for the King of the Bhojas, Kaṁsa; *virāṭ*—the totality of the material universe; *aviduṣām*—for the unintelligent; *tattvam*—the Truth; *param*—Supreme; *yoginām*—for the *yogīs; vṛṣṇīnām*—for the members of the Vṛṣṇi dynasty; *para-devatā*—their most worshipable Deity; *iti*—in these ways; *viditaḥ*—understood; *raṅgam*—the arena; *gataḥ*—He entered; *sa*—along with; *agra-jaḥ*—His elder brother.

TRANSLATION

The various groups of people in the arena regarded Kṛṣṇa in different ways when He entered it with His elder brother. The wrestlers saw Kṛṣṇa as a lightning bolt, the men of Mathurā as the best of males, the women as Cupid in person, the cowherd men as their relative, the impious rulers as a chastiser, His parents as their child, the King of the Bhojas as death, the unintelligent as

the Supreme Lord's universal form, the *yogīs* as the Absolute Truth and the Vṛṣṇis as their supreme worshipable Deity.

PURPORT

Śrīla Śrīdhara Svāmī quotes the following verse, which explains the ten attitudes toward Kṛṣṇa described here:

raudro 'dbhutaś ca śṛṅgāro
hāsyaṁ vīro dayā tathā
bhayānakaś ca bībhatsaḥ
śāntaḥ sa-prema-bhaktikaḥ

"[There are ten different moods:] fury [perceived by the wrestlers], wonder [by the men], conjugal attraction [the women], laughter [the cowherds], chivalry [the kings], mercy [His parents], terror [Kaṁsa], ghastliness [the unintelligent], peaceful neutrality [the *yogīs*] and loving devotion [the Vṛṣṇis]."

Śrīla Viśvanātha Cakravartī points out that people like the wrestlers, Kaṁsa and the impious rulers perceive Kṛṣṇa as dangerous, angry or threatening because they fail to understand the actual position of the Personality of Godhead. Actually, Lord Kṛṣṇa is everyone's friend and well-wisher, but because we rebel against Him, He chastises us, and thus we may perceive Him as threatening. Kṛṣṇa, or God, is actually merciful, and when He punishes us, that is also His mercy.

Śrīla Bhaktisiddhānta Sarasvatī Ṭhākura quotes the following Vedic statement: *raso vai saḥ rasaṁ hy evāyaṁ labdhvānandī bhavati.* "He Himself is *rasa*, the taste or mellow of a particular relationship. And certainly one who achieves this *rasa* becomes *ānandī*, filled with bliss." (*Taittirīya Upaniṣad* 2.7.1)

Śrīla Bhaktisiddhānta Sarasvatī quotes a further verse to explain the word *rasa:*

vyatītya bhāvanā-vartma
yaś camatkāra-bhāra-bhūḥ
hṛdi sattvojjvale bāḍhaṁ
svadate sa raso mataḥ

"That which is beyond imagination, heavy with wonder and relished in the heart shining with goodness—such is known as *rasa.*"

As Śrīla Rūpa Gosvāmī elaborately explains in his *Bhakti-rasāmṛta-sindhu*, there are five main *rasas*—neutrality, servitude, friendship, parental love and conjugal love—and seven secondary *rasas*—amazement, humor, chivalry, compassion, fury, fear and dread. Thus altogether there are twelve *rasas*, and the supreme object of them all is Śrī Kṛṣṇa Himself. In other words, our love and affection are actually meant for Śrī Kṛṣṇa. Unfortunately, out of ignorance we stubbornly try to squeeze happiness and love out of material relationships, which are not directly connected to Kṛṣṇa, and thus life becomes a constant frustration. The solution is simple: surrender to Kṛṣṇa, love Kṛṣṇa, love Kṛṣṇa's devotees and be happy forever.

TEXT 18

हतं कुवलयापीडं दृष्ट्वा तावपि दुर्जयौ ।
कंसो मनस्यपि तदा भृशमुद्विविजे नृप ॥१८॥

hataṁ kuvalayāpīḍaṁ
dṛṣṭvā tāv api durjayau
kaṁso manasy api tadā
bhṛśam udvivije nṛpa

hatam—killed; *kuvalayāpīḍam*—the elephant Kuvalayāpīḍa; *dṛṣṭvā*—seeing; *tau*—the two of Them, Kṛṣṇa and Balarāma; *api*—and; *durjayau*—invincible; *kaṁsaḥ*—King Kaṁsa; *manasi*—in his mind; *api*—indeed; *tadā*—then; *bhṛśam*—exceedingly; *udvivije*—became anxious; *nṛpa*—O King (Parīkṣit).

TRANSLATION

When Kaṁsa saw that Kuvalayāpīḍa was dead and the two brothers were invincible, he was overwhelmed with anxiety, O King.

TEXT 19

तौ रेजतू रंगगतौ महाभुजौ
विचित्रवेषाभरणस्रगम्बरौ ।
यथा नटावुत्तमवेषधारिणौ
मनः क्षिपन्तौ प्रभया निरीक्षताम् ॥१९॥

tau rejatū raṅga-gatau mahā-bhujau
vicitra-veṣābharaṇa-srag-ambarau
yathā naṭāv uttama-veṣa-dhāriṇau
manaḥ kṣipantau prabhayā nirīkṣatām

tau—the two of Them; *rejatuḥ*—shone; *raṅga-gatau*—present in the arena; *mahā-bhujau*—the mighty-armed Lords; *vicitra*—variegated; *veṣa*—whose style of dress; *ābharaṇa*—ornaments; *srak*—garlands; *ambarau*—and garments; *yathā*—like; *naṭau*—two actors; *uttama*—excellent; *veṣa*—costumes; *dhāriṇau*—wearing; *manaḥ*—the minds; *kṣipantau*—striking; *prabhayā*—with Their effulgences; *nirīkṣatām*—of those who looked on.

TRANSLATION

Arrayed with variegated ornaments, garlands and garments, just like a pair of excellently costumed actors, the two mighty-armed Lords shone splendidly in the arena. Indeed, They overpowered the minds of all onlookers with Their effulgences.

TEXT 20

निरीक्ष्य तावुत्तमपूरुषौ जना
मञ्चस्थिता नागरराष्ट्रका नृप ।
प्रहर्षवेगोत्कलितेक्षणानना:
पपुर्न तृप्ता नयनैस्तदाननम् ॥२०॥

nirīkṣya tāv uttama-pūruṣau janā
mañca-sthitā nāgara-rāṣṭrakā nṛpa
praharṣa-vegotkaliteksaṇānanāḥ
papur na tṛptā nayanais tad-ānanam

nirīkṣya—seeing; *tau*—both of Them; *uttama-pūruṣau*—the Supreme Personalities; *janāḥ*—the people; *mañca*—in the viewing galleries; *sthitāḥ*—sitting; *nāgara*—the city-dwellers; *rāṣṭrakāḥ*—and the people from outlying districts; *nṛpa*—O King; *praharṣa*—of their joy; *vega*—by the force; *utkalita*—made to expand widely; *īkṣaṇa*—their eyes; *ānanāḥ*—and faces; *papuḥ*—they drank; *na*—not; *tṛptāḥ*—satiated; *nayanaiḥ*—with their eyes; *tat*—of Them; *ānanam*—the faces.

TRANSLATION

O King, as the citizens of the city and the people from outlying districts gazed upon those two Supreme Personalities from their seats in the galleries, the force of the people's happiness caused their eyes to open wide and their faces to blossom. They drank in the vision of the Lords' faces without becoming satiated.

TEXTS 21–22

पिबन्त इव चक्षुर्भ्यां लिहन्त इव जिह्वया ।
जिघ्रन्त इव नासाभ्यां श्लिष्यन्त इव बाहुभिः ॥२१॥
ऊचुः परस्परं ते वै यथादृष्टं यथाश्रुतम् ।
तद्रूपगुणमाधुर्यप्रागल्भ्यस्मारिता इव ॥२२॥

pibanta iva cakṣurbhyāṁ
lihanta iva jihvayā
jighranta iva nāsābhyāṁ
śliṣyanta iva bāhubhiḥ

ūcuḥ parasparaṁ te vai
yathā-dṛṣṭaṁ yathā-śrutam
tad-rūpa-guṇa-mādhurya-
prāgalbhya-smāritā iva

pibantaḥ—drinking; *iva*—as if; *cakṣurbhyām*—with their eyes; *lihantaḥ*—licking; *iva*—as if; *jihvayā*—with their tongues; *jighrantaḥ*—smelling; *iva*—as if; *nāsābhyām*—with their nostrils; *śliṣyantaḥ*—embracing; *iva*—as if; *bāhubhiḥ*—with their arms; *ūcuḥ*—they spoke; *parasparam*—among one another; *te*—they; *vai*—indeed; *yathā*—just as; *dṛṣṭam*—they had seen; *yathā*—just as; *śrutam*—they had heard; *tat*—Their; *rūpa*—of the beauty; *guṇa*—qualities; *mādhurya*—charm; *prāgalbhya*—and bravery; *smāritāḥ*—reminded; *iva*—as if.

TRANSLATION

The people seemed to be drinking Kṛṣṇa and Balarāma with their eyes, licking Them with their tongues, smelling Them with their nostrils and embracing Them with their arms. Reminded of

the Lords' beauty, character, charm and bravery, the members of the audience began describing these features to one another according to what they had seen and heard.

PURPORT

Naturally, those who assembled in Mathurā for the wrestling festival had heard the latest news of Kṛṣṇa's and Balarāma's adventures in the city—how the Lords had broken the sacrificial bow, defeated the police and killed the elephant Kuvalayāpīḍa. And now that the people were seeing Kṛṣṇa and Balarāma enter the arena, their greatest expectations were confirmed. Kṛṣṇa is the embodiment of all beauty, fame and opulence, and therefore those assembled in the wrestling arena became fully satisfied by glorifying what they had heard of Him and were now seeing.

TEXT 23

एतौ भगवतः साक्षाद्धरेर्नारायणस्य हि ।
अवतीर्णाविहांशेन वसुदेवस्य वेश्मनि ॥२३॥

etau bhagavataḥ sākṣād
dharer nārāyaṇasya hi
avatīrṇāv ihāṁśena
vasudevasya veśmani

etau—these two; *bhagavataḥ*—of the Supreme Lord; *sākṣāt*—directly; *hareḥ*—of Lord Hari; *nārāyaṇasya*—Nārāyaṇa; *hi*—certainly; *avatīrṇau*—have descended; *iha*—to this world; *aṁśena*—as expansions; *vasudevasya*—of Vasudeva; *veśmani*—in the home.

TRANSLATION

[The people said:] These two boys are certainly expansions of the Supreme Lord Nārāyaṇa who have descended to this world in the home of Vasudeva.

TEXT 24

एष वै किल देवक्यां जातो नीतश्च गोकुलम् ।
कालमेतं वसन् गूढो ववृधे नन्दवेश्मनि ॥२४॥

eṣa vai kila devakyāṁ
jāto nītaś ca gokulam
kālam etaṁ vasan gūḍho
vavṛdhe nanda-veśmani

eṣaḥ—this (Kṛṣṇa); *vai*—certainly; *kila*—indeed; *devakyām*—from the womb of Devakī; *jātaḥ*—born; *nītaḥ*—brought; *ca*—and; *gokulam*—to Gokula; *kālam*—time; *etam*—this much; *vasan*—living; *gūḍhaḥ*—hidden; *vavṛdhe*—He grew up; *nanda-veśmani*—in the house of Nanda Mahārāja.

TRANSLATION

This one [Kṛṣṇa] took birth from mother Devakī and was brought to Gokula, where He has remained concealed all this time, growing up in the house of King Nanda.

TEXT 25

पूतनानेन नीतान्तं चक्रवातश्च दानवः ।
अर्जुनौ गुह्यकः केशी धेनुकोऽन्ये च तद्विधाः ॥२५॥

pūtanānena nītāntaṁ
cakravātaś ca dānavaḥ
arjunau guhyakaḥ keśī
dhenuko 'nye ca tad-vidhāḥ

pūtanā—the witch Pūtanā; *anena*—by Him; *nītā*—brought; *antam*—to her end; *cakravātaḥ*—whirlwind; *ca*—and; *dānavaḥ*—the demon; *arjunau*—the twin Arjuna trees; *guhyakaḥ*—the demon Śaṅkhacūḍa; *keśī*—the horse demon, Keśī; *dhenukaḥ*—the jackass demon, Dhenuka; *anye*—others; *ca*—and; *tat-vidhāḥ*—like them.

TRANSLATION

He made Pūtanā and the whirlwind demon meet with death, pulled down the twin Arjuna trees and killed Śaṅkhacūḍa Keśī, Dhenuka and similar demons.

TEXTS 26–27

गावः सपाला एतेन दावाग्नेः परिमोचिताः ।
कालियो दमितः सर्प इन्द्रश्च विमदः कृतः ॥२६॥
सप्ताहमेकहस्तेन धृतोऽद्रिप्रवरोऽमुना ।
वर्षवाताशनिभ्यश्च परित्रातं च गोकुलम् ॥२७॥

gāvaḥ sa-pālā etena
dāvāgneḥ parimocitāḥ
kāliyo damitaḥ sarpa
indraś ca vimadaḥ kṛtaḥ

saptāham eka-hastena
dhṛto 'dri-pravaro 'munā
varṣa-vātāśanibhyaś ca
paritrātaṁ ca gokulam

gāvaḥ—the cows; *sa*—together with; *pālāḥ*—their tenders; *etena*—by Him; *dāva-agneḥ*—from the forest fire; *parimocitāḥ*—saved; *kāliyaḥ*—Kāliya; *damitaḥ*—subdued; *sarpaḥ*—the serpent; *indraḥ*—Indra; *ca*—and; *vimadaḥ*—prideless; *kṛtaḥ*—made; *sapta-aham*—for seven days; *eka-hastena*—with one hand; *dhṛtaḥ*—held; *adri*—of mountains; *pra-varaḥ*—the most eminent; *amunā*—by Him; *varṣa*—from rain; *vāta*—wind; *aśanibhyaḥ*—and hail; *ca*—also; *paritrātam*—delivered; *ca*—and; *gokulam*—the residents of Gokula.

TRANSLATION

He saved the cows and the cowherds from a forest fire and subdued the serpent Kāliya. He removed Lord Indra's false pride by holding up the best of mountains with one hand for an entire week, thus protecting the inhabitants of Gokula from rain, wind and hail.

TEXT 28

गोप्योऽस्य नित्यमुदितहसितप्रेक्षणं मुखम् ।
पश्यन्त्यो विविधांस्तापांस्तरन्ति स्माश्रमं मुदा ॥२८॥

gopyo 'sya nitya-mudita-
hasita-prekṣaṇaṁ mukham
paśyantyo vividhāṁs tāpāṁs
taranti smāśramaṁ mudā

gopyaḥ—the young *gopīs; asya*—His; *nitya*—always; *mudita*—cheerful; *hasita*—smiling; *prekṣaṇam*—whose glance; *mukham*—the face; *paśyantyaḥ*—seeing; *vividhān*—of various kinds; *tāpān*—distress; *taranti sma*—transcended; *aśramam*—free from fatigue; *mudā*—happily.

TRANSLATION

The *gopīs* overcame all kinds of distress and experienced great happiness by seeing His face, which is always cheerful with smiling glances and ever free of fatigue.

TEXT 29

वदन्त्यनेन वंशोऽयं यदोः सुबहुविश्रुतः ।
श्रियं यशो महत्वं च लप्स्यते परिरक्षितः ॥२९॥

vadanty anena vaṁśo 'yaṁ
yadoḥ su-bahu-viśrutaḥ
śriyaṁ yaśo mahatvaṁ ca
lapsyate parirakṣitaḥ

vadanti—they say; *anena*—by Him; *vaṁśaḥ*—the dynasty; *ayam*—this; *yadoḥ*—descending from King Yadu; *su-bahu*—very much; *viśrutaḥ*—famous; *śriyam*—riches; *yaśaḥ*—glory; *mahatvam*—power; *ca*—and; *lapsyate*—it will achieve; *parirakṣitaḥ*—protected on all sides.

TRANSLATION

It is said that under His full protection the Yadu dynasty will become extremely famous and attain wealth, glory and power.

TEXT 30

अयं चास्याग्रजः श्रीमान् रामः कमललोचनः ।
प्रलम्बो निहतो येन वत्सको ये बकादयः ॥३०॥

ayaṁ cāsyāgrajaḥ śrīmān
rāmaḥ kamala-locanaḥ
pralambo nihato yena
vatsako ye bakādayaḥ

ayam—this; *ca*—and; *asya*—His; *agra-jaḥ*—elder brother; *śrī-mān*—the possessor of all opulences; *rāmaḥ*—Lord Balarāma; *kamala-locanaḥ*—the lotus-eyed; *pralambaḥ*—the demon Pralamba; *nihataḥ*—killed; *yena*—by whom; *vatsakaḥ*—Vatsāsura; *ye*—who; *baka*—Bakāsura; *ādayaḥ*—and others.

TRANSLATION

This lotus-eyed elder brother of His, Lord Balarāma, is the proprietor of all transcendental opulences. He has killed Pralamba, Vatsaka, Baka and other demons.

PURPORT

In fact two of the demons mentioned here were killed by Kṛṣṇa, not Balarāma. The reason for the mistake is that as news of Kṛṣṇa's exploits spread among ordinary people, the facts became somewhat muddled. The same tendency can be observed in modern newspapers.

TEXT 31

जनेष्वेवं ब्रुवाणेषु तूर्येषु निनदत्सु च ।
कृष्णरामौ समाभाष्य चाणूरो वाक्यमब्रवीत् ॥३१॥

janeṣv evaṁ bruvāṇeṣu
tūryeṣu ninadatsu ca
kṛṣṇa-rāmau samābhāṣya
cāṇūro vākyam abravīt

janeṣu—as the people; *evam*—thus; *bruvāṇeṣu*—were speaking; *tūryeṣu*—as the musical instruments; *ninadatsu*—were resounding; *ca*—and; *kṛṣṇa-rāmau*—Kṛṣṇa and Balarāma; *samābhāṣya*—addressing; *cāṇūraḥ*—the demonic wrestler Cāṇūra; *vākyam*—words; *abravīt*—said.

TRANSLATION

While the people talked in this way and the musical instruments resounded, the wrestler Cāṇūra addressed Kṛṣṇa and Balarāma with the following words.

PURPORT

Cāṇūra could not tolerate that the audience was praising Kṛṣṇa so highly. Therefore he had to say something to the two brothers.

TEXT 32

हे नन्दसूनो हे राम भवन्तौ वीरसम्मतौ ।
नियुद्धकुशलौ श्रुत्वा राज्ञाहूतौ दिदृक्षुणा ॥३२॥

he nanda-sūno he rāma
bhavantau vīra-sammatau
niyuddha-kuśalau śrutvā
rājñāhūtau didṛkṣuṇā

he nanda-sūno—O son of Nanda; *he rāma*—O Rāma; *bhavantau*—You two; *vīra*—by heroes; *sammatau*—are well respected; *niyuddha*—in wrestling; *kuśalau*—skillful; *śrutvā*—hearing; *rājñā*—by the King; *āhūtau*—called for; *didṛkṣuṇā*—who wanted to see.

TRANSLATION

O son of Nanda, O Rāma, You two are well respected by courageous men and are both skillful at wrestling. Having heard of Your prowess, the King has called You here, wanting to see for himself.

TEXT 33

प्रियं राज्ञः प्रकुर्वत्यः श्रेयो विन्दन्ति वै प्रजाः ।
मनसा कर्मणा वाचा विपरीतमतोऽन्यथा ॥३३॥

priyaṁ rājñaḥ prakurvatyaḥ
śreyo vindanti vai prajāḥ

manasā karmaṇā vācā
viparītam ato 'nyathā

priyam—the pleasure; *rājñaḥ*—of the King; *prakurvatyaḥ*—executing; *śreyaḥ*—good fortune; *vindanti*—acquire; *vai*—indeed; *prajāḥ*—citizens; *manasā*—with their minds; *karmaṇā*—with their deeds; *vācā*—with their words; *viparītam*—opposite; *ataḥ*—to this; *anyathā*—otherwise.

TRANSLATION

Subjects of the King who try to please him with their thoughts, acts and words are sure to achieve good fortune, but those who fail to do so will suffer the opposite fate.

TEXT 34

नित्यं प्रमुदिता गोपा वत्सपाला यथास्फुटम् ।
वनेषु मल्लयुद्धेन क्रीडन्तश्चारयन्ति गाः ॥३४॥

nityaṁ pramuditā gopā
vatsa-pālā yathā-sphuṭam
vaneṣu malla-yuddhena
krīḍantaś cārayanti gāḥ

nityam—always; *pramuditāḥ*—very happy; *gopāḥ*—cowherds; *vatsa-pālāḥ*—tending the calves; *yathā-sphuṭam*—obviously; *vaneṣu*—in the various forests; *malla-yuddhena*—with wrestling; *krīḍantaḥ*—playing; *cārayanti*—they graze; *gāḥ*—the cows.

TRANSLATION

It is well known that cowherd boys are always joyful as they tend their calves, and that the boys playfully wrestle with each other while grazing their animals in the various forests.

PURPORT

Here Cāṇūra explains how the two brothers came to be expert at wrestling.

TEXT 35

तस्माद् राज्ञः प्रियं यूयं वयं च करवाम हे ।
भूतानि नः प्रसीदन्ति सर्वभूतमयो नृपः ॥३५॥

tasmād rājñaḥ priyaṁ yūyaṁ
vayaṁ ca karavāma he
bhūtāni naḥ prasīdanti
sarva-bhūta-mayo nṛpaḥ

tasmāt—therefore; *rājñaḥ*—the King's; *priyam*—pleasure; *yūyam*—You two; *vayam*—we; *ca*—also; *karavāma he*—let us do; *bhūtāni*—all living beings; *naḥ*—with us; *prasīdanti*—will be satisfied; *sarva-bhūta*—all beings; *mayaḥ*—comprising; *nṛpaḥ*—the king.

TRANSLATION

Therefore let's do what the King wants. Everyone will be pleased with us, for the king embodies all living beings.

TEXT 36

तन्निशम्याब्रवीत्कृष्णो देशकालोचितं वचः ।
नियुद्धमात्मनोऽभीष्टं मन्यमानोऽभिनन्द्य च ॥३६॥

tan niśamyābravīt kṛṣṇo
deśa-kālocitaṁ vacaḥ
niyuddham ātmano 'bhīṣṭaṁ
manyamāno 'bhinandya ca

tat—that; *niśamya*—hearing; *abravīt*—spoke; *kṛṣṇaḥ*—Lord Kṛṣṇa; *deśa*—for the place; *kāla*—and time; *ucitam*—appropriate; *vacaḥ*—words; *niyuddham*—wrestling; *ātmanaḥ*—to Himself; *abhīṣṭam*—desirable; *manyamānaḥ*—considering; *abhinandya*—welcoming; *ca*—and.

TRANSLATION

Hearing this, Lord Kṛṣṇa, who liked to wrestle and welcomed the challenge, replied with words appropriate to the time and place.

TEXT 37

प्रजा भोजपतेरस्य वयं चापि वनेचराः ।
करवाम प्रियं नित्यं तन्नः परमनुग्रहः ॥३७॥

prajā bhoja-pater asya
vayaṁ cāpi vane-carāḥ
karavāma priyaṁ nityaṁ
tan naḥ param anugrahaḥ

prajāḥ—subjects; *bhoja-pateḥ*—of the King of the Bhojas; *asya*—of him; *vayam*—We; *ca*—also; *api*—even though; *vane-carāḥ*—wandering in the forest; *karavāma*—We must execute; *priyam*—his pleasure; *nityam*—always; *tat*—that; *naḥ*—for Us; *param*—the greatest; *anugrahaḥ*—benefit.

TRANSLATION

[Lord Kṛṣṇa said:] Although forest-dwellers, We are also subjects of the Bhoja king. We must gratify his desires, for such behavior will confer upon Us the greatest benefit.

TEXT 38

बाला वयं तुल्यबलैः क्रीडिष्यामो यथोचितम् ।
भवेन्नियुद्धं माधर्मः स्पृशेन्मल्लसभासदः ॥३८॥

bālā vayaṁ tulya-balaiḥ
krīḍiṣyāmo yathocitam
bhaven niyuddhaṁ mādharmaḥ
spṛśen malla-sabhā-sadaḥ

bālāḥ—young boys; *vayam*—We; *tulya*—equal; *balaiḥ*—with those whose strength; *krīḍiṣyāmaḥ*—We will play; *yathā ucitam*—in a fitting manner; *bhavet*—should occur; *niyuddham*—the wrestling match; *mā*—not; *adharmaḥ*—irreligion; *spṛśet*—should touch; *malla-sabhā*—of the assembly in the wrestling arena; *sadaḥ*—the members.

TRANSLATION

We are just young boys and should play with those of equal strength. The wrestling match must go on properly so that irreligion does not taint the respectable members of the audience.

TEXT 39

चाणूर उवाच
न बालो न किशोरस्त्वं बलश्च बलिनां वरः ।
लीलयेभो हतो येन सहस्रद्विपसत्त्वभृत् ॥३९॥

cāṇūra uvāca
na bālo na kiśoras tvaṁ
balaś ca balināṁ varaḥ
līlayebho hato yena
sahasra-dvipa-sattva-bhṛt

cāṇūraḥ uvāca—Cāṇūra said; *na*—not; *bālaḥ*—a boy; *na*—not; *kiśoraḥ*—a youth; *tvam*—You; *balaḥ*—Balarāma; *ca*—and; *balinām*—of the strong; *varaḥ*—the best; *līlayā*—as play; *ibhaḥ*—the elephant; *hataḥ*—killed; *yena*—by whom; *sahasra*—of one thousand; *dvipa*—elephants; *sattva*—of the strength; *bhṛt*—the bearer.

TRANSLATION

Cāṇūra said: You aren't really a child or even a young man, and neither is Balarāma, the strongest of the strong. After all, You playfully killed an elephant who had the strength of a thousand other elephants.

TEXT 40

तस्माद् भवद्भ्यां बलिभिर्योद्धव्यं नानयोऽत्र वै ।
मयि विक्रम वार्ष्णेय बलेन सह मुष्टिकः ॥४०॥

tasmād bhavadbhyāṁ balibhir
yoddhavyaṁ nānayo 'tra vai
mayi vikrama vārṣṇeya
balena saha muṣṭikaḥ

tasmāt—therefore; *bhavadbhyām*—You two; *balibhiḥ*—with those who are strong; *yoddhavyam*—should fight; *na*—there is not; *anayaḥ*—injustice; *atra*—in this; *vai*—certainly; *mayi*—to me; *vikrama*—(show) Your prowess; *vārṣṇeya*—O descendant of Vṛṣṇi; *balena saha*—with Balarāma; *muṣṭikaḥ*—Muṣṭika (should fight).

TRANSLATION

Therefore You two should fight powerful wrestlers. There's certainly nothing unfair about that. You, O descendant of Vṛṣṇi, can show Your prowess against me, and Balarāma can fight with Muṣṭika.

Thus end the purports of the humble servant of His Divine Grace A. C. Bhaktivedanta Swami Prabhupāda to the Tenth Canto, Forty-third Chapter, of the Śrīmad-Bhāgavatam, *entitled "Kṛṣṇa Kills the Elephant Kuvalayāpīḍa."*

CHAPTER FORTY-FOUR

The Killing of Kaṁsa

This chapter tells how Kṛṣṇa and Balarāma killed the wrestlers, how Kṛṣṇa killed Kaṁsa and consoled Kaṁsa's wives, and how the two Lords were reunited with Their mother and father.

Deciding to wrestle, Lord Kṛṣṇa faced off against Cāṇūra, and Lord Baladeva took on Muṣṭika. Battling arm to arm, head to head, knee to knee and chest to chest, the opponents attacked each other so fiercely that they appeared to be harming even their own bodies. The ladies in the arena, seeing the violent battle, began to condemn the King and all the members of the assembly: "A respectable audience should never have allowed a wrestling match between such huge wrestlers, whose limbs are as tough as lightning bolts, and such tender young boys, who are just entering youth. An intelligent person should never enter an assembly if he sees injustice being done there." Because Vasudeva and Devakī did not fully understand the power of Kṛṣṇa and Balarāma, they became extremely unhappy when they heard the women of the audience speak these words.

Śrī Kṛṣṇa then grabbed Cāṇūra's arms, whirled him around several times and threw him to the ground, killing him. Muṣṭika met a similar fate: after being struck powerfully by Lord Baladeva's palm, he began vomiting blood and then fell down dead. Thereupon the wrestlers named Kūṭa, Śala and Tośala came forward, but Kṛṣṇa and Balarāma easily killed them with the blows of Their fists and feet. The remaining wrestlers, fearing for their lives, all fled.

Except for Kaṁsa, everyone present cheered Kṛṣṇa and Balarāma. The King, in a rage, stopped the festive music and ordered that Vasudeva, Nanda, Ugrasena and all the cowherds be severely punished and that Kṛṣṇa and Balarāma be driven from the assembly. Kṛṣṇa became furious when He heard Kaṁsa speak this way, and He instantly leapt onto the lofty royal dais. He grabbed Kaṁsa by the hair, hurled him down onto the floor of the wrestling ring and threw Himself on top of him. In this way, Kaṁsa met his death. Because out of fear Kaṁsa had always thought of

Kṛṣṇa, after his death he gained the liberation of having a form like the Lord's.

Kaṁsa's eight brothers then attacked Kṛṣṇa, but Balarāma easily killed each of them with His club, just as a lion kills defenseless animals. Kettledrums resounded in the sky as the joyful demigods rained down flowers and chanted the glories of Lord Kṛṣṇa and Lord Balarāma.

The wives of Kaṁsa, grieving for their husband, lamented that he had died because of his violence toward other living beings and his lack of respect for Kṛṣṇa, the Supreme Soul, who creates, maintains and destroys the entire universe. The Lord consoled the widows, had the funeral rites performed for Kaṁsa and his brothers and then released His mother and father from bondage. Kṛṣṇa offered obeisances at His parents' feet, but they, now understanding Him to be the Supreme Personality of Godhead, did not embrace Him.

TEXT 1

श्रीशुक उवाच
एवं चर्चितसंकल्पो भगवान्मधुसूदनः ।
आससादाथ चाणूरं मुष्टिकं रोहिणीसुतः ॥१॥

śrī-śuka uvāca
evaṁ carcita-saṅkalpo
bhagavān madhusūdanaḥ
āsasādātha cāṇūraṁ
muṣṭikaṁ rohiṇī-sutaḥ

śrī-śukaḥ uvāca—Śukadeva Gosvāmī said; *evam*—thus; *carcita*—fixing; *saṅkalpaḥ*—His determination; *bhagavān*—the Supreme Lord; *madhusūdanaḥ*—Kṛṣṇa; *āsasāda*—confronted; *atha*—then; *cāṇūram*—Cāṇūra; *muṣṭikam*—Muṣṭika; *rohiṇī-sutaḥ*—the son of Rohiṇī, Lord Balarāma.

TRANSLATION

Śukadeva Gosvāmī said: Thus addressed, Lord Kṛṣṇa made up His mind to accept the challenge. He paired off with Cāṇūra, and Lord Balarāma with Muṣṭika.

TEXT 2

हस्ताभ्यां हस्तयोर्बद्ध्वा पद्भ्यामेव च पादयोः ।
विचकर्षतुरन्योन्यं प्रसह्य विजिगीषया ॥२॥

hastābhyāṁ hastayor baddhvā
padbhyām eva ca pādayoḥ
vicakarṣatur anyonyaṁ
prasahya vijigīṣayā

hastābhyām—with their hands; *hastayoḥ*—by the hands; *baddhvā*—seizing; *padbhyām*—with their legs; *eva ca*—also; *pādayoḥ*—by the legs; *vicakarṣatuḥ*—they (Kṛṣṇa paired with Cāṇūra, and Balarāma with Muṣṭika) dragged; *anyonyam*—each other; *prasahya*—with force; *vijigīṣayā*—with desire for victory.

TRANSLATION

Seizing each other's hands and locking legs with each other, the opponents struggled powerfully, eager for victory.

TEXT 3

अरत्नी द्वे अरत्निभ्यां जानुभ्यां चैव जानुनी ।
शिरः शीर्ष्णोरसोरस्तावन्योन्यमभिजघ्नतुः ॥३॥

aratnī dve aratnibhyāṁ
jānubhyāṁ caiva jānunī
śiraḥ śīrṣṇorasoras tāv
anyonyam abhijaghnatuḥ

aratnī—against the opponent's fists; *dve*—two; *aratnibhyām*—their fists; *jānubhyām*—their knees; *ca eva*—also; *jānunī*—against the opponent's knees; *śiraḥ*—head; *śīrṣṇā*—with head; *urasā*—with chest; *uraḥ*—chest; *tau*—they in pairs; *anyonyam*—each other; *abhijaghnatuḥ*—struck.

TRANSLATION

They each struck fists against fists, knees against knees, head against head and chest against chest.

PURPORT

The word *aratni* in this verse may indicate the elbow as well as the fist. Thus blows were perhaps also struck with the elbow, a technique seen today in various martial arts.

TEXT 4

परिभ्रामणविक्षेपपरिरम्भावपातनैः ।
उत्सर्पणापसर्पणैश्चान्योन्यं प्रत्यरुन्धताम् ॥४॥

paribhrāmaṇa-vikṣepa-
parirambhāvapātanaiḥ
utsarpaṇāpasarpaṇaiś
cānyonyaṁ pratyarundhatām

paribhrāmaṇa—with wheeling the other about; *vikṣepa*—shoving; *parirambha*—crushing; *avapātanaiḥ*—and throwing down; *utsarpaṇa*—releasing and running in front; *apasarpaṇaiḥ*—going behind; *ca*—and; *anyonyam*—each other; *pratyarundhatām*—they resisted.

TRANSLATION

Each fighter contended with his opponent by dragging him about in circles, shoving and crushing him, throwing him down and running before and behind him.

PURPORT

Śrīla Śrīdhara Svāmī explains that the word *parirambha* indicates crushing one's opponent with one's arms.

TEXT 5

उत्थापनैरुन्नयनैश्चालनैः स्थापनैरपि ।
परस्परं जिगीषन्तावपचक्रतुरात्मनः ॥५॥

utthāpanair unnayanaiś
cālanaiḥ sthāpanair api

parasparaṁ jigīṣantāv
apacakratur ātmanaḥ

utthāpanaiḥ—with lifting up; *unnayanaiḥ*—carrying; *cālanaiḥ*—pushing away; *sthāpanaiḥ*—holding stationary; *api*—also; *parasparam*—each other; *jigīṣantau*—wanting victory; *apacakratuḥ*—they harmed; *ātmanaḥ*—(even) themselves.

TRANSLATION

Forcefully lifting and carrying each other, pushing each other away and holding each other down, the fighters hurt even their own bodies in their great eagerness for victory.

PURPORT

Śrīla Jīva Gosvāmī explains that although Kṛṣṇa and Balarāma did not, of course, harm Themselves, it appeared that way to Cāṇūra, Muṣṭika and others of mundane vision. In other words, the Lords were fully absorbed in the pastime of being wrestlers.

TEXT 6

तद् बलाबलवद्युद्धं समेताः सर्वयोषितः ।
ऊचुः परस्परं राजन् सानुकम्पा वरूथशः ॥६॥

tad balābalavad yuddhaṁ
sametāḥ sarva-yoṣitaḥ
ūcuḥ parasparaṁ rājan
sānukampā varūthaśaḥ

tat—that; *bala-abala*—the strong and the weak; *vat*—involving; *yuddham*—fight; *sametāḥ*—assembled; *sarva*—all; *yoṣitaḥ*—the women; *ūcuḥ*—said; *parasparam*—to one another; *rājan*—O King (Parīkṣit); *sa-anukampāḥ*—feeling compassion; *varūthaśaḥ*—in groups.

TRANSLATION

My dear King, all the women present, considering the match an unfair fight between the strong and the weak, felt extreme anxiety

due to compassion. They assembled in groups around the arena and spoke to one another as follows.

TEXT 7

महानयं बताधर्म एषां राजसभासदाम् ।
ये बलाबलवद्युद्धं राज्ञोऽन्विच्छन्ति पश्यतः ॥७॥

mahān ayaṁ batādharma
eṣāṁ rāja-sabhā-sadām
ye balābalavad yuddhaṁ
rājño 'nvicchanti paśyataḥ

mahān—great; *ayam*—this; *bata*—alas; *adharmaḥ*—act of irreligion; *eṣām*—on the part of these; *rāja-sabhā*—in the King's assembly; *sadām*—persons present; *ye*—who; *bala-abala-vat*—between strong and weak; *yuddham*—a fight; *rājñaḥ*—while the King; *anvicchanti*—they also desire; *paśyataḥ*—is watching.

TRANSLATION

Alas, what a greatly irreligious act the members of this royal assembly are committing! As the King watches this fight between the strong and the weak, they also want to see it.

PURPORT

The idea the ladies are expressing is that even if the King somehow wanted to see such an unfair match, why should the respectable members of the assembly also desire to see it? These feelings are natural. Even nowadays, if in a public place we find a violent fight going on between a very strong, large person and a weaker, smaller person, we are aroused to indignation. Compassionate women are especially offended and enraged by such unfair violence.

TEXT 8

क्व वज्रसारसर्वांगौ मल्लौ शैलेन्द्रसन्निभौ ।
क्व चातिसुकुमारांगौ किशोरौ नाप्तयौवनौ ॥८॥

kva vajra-sāra-sarvāṅgau
mallau śailendra-sannibhau
kva cāti-sukumārāṅgau
kiśorau nāpta-yauvanau

kva—where, on the one hand; *vajra*—of lightning; *sāra*—with the strength; *sarva*—all; *aṅgau*—whose limbs; *mallau*—two wrestlers; *śaila*—mountains; *indra*—like the chief; *sannibhau*—whose appearance; *kva*—where; *ca*—and, on the other hand; *ati*—very; *su-kumāra*—tender; *aṅgau*—whose limbs; *kiśorau*—two youths; *na āpta*—not having yet attained; *yauvanau*—Their maturity.

TRANSLATION

What comparison can there be between these two professional wrestlers, with limbs as strong as lightning bolts and bodies resembling mighty mountains, and these two young, immature boys with exceedingly tender limbs?

TEXT 9

धर्मव्यतिक्रमो ह्यस्य समाजस्य ध्रुवं भवेत् ।
यत्राधर्मः समुत्तिष्ठेन्न स्थेयं तत्र कर्हिचित् ॥९॥

dharma-vyatikramo hy asya
samājasya dhruvaṁ bhavet
yatrādharmaḥ samuttiṣṭhen
na stheyaṁ tatra karhicit

dharma—of religious principles; *vyatikramaḥ*—transgression; *hi*—indeed; *asya*—by this; *samājasya*—company; *dhruvam*—certainly; *bhavet*—must be; *yatra*—wherein; *adharmaḥ*—irreligion; *samuttiṣṭhet*—has fully arisen; *na stheyam*—one should not remain; *tatra*—there; *karhicit*—for any duration of time at all.

TRANSLATION

Religious principles have certainly been violated in this assembly. One should not remain for even a moment in a place where irreligion is flourishing.

TEXT 10

न सभां प्रविशेत्प्राज्ञः सभ्यदोषाननुस्मरन् ।
अब्रुवन् विब्रुवन्नज्ञो नरः किल्बिषमश्नुते ॥१०॥

na sabhāṁ praviśet prājñaḥ
sabhya-doṣān anusmaran
abruvan vibruvann ajño
naraḥ kilbiṣam aśnute

na—not; *sabhām*—an assembly; *praviśet*—should enter; *prājñaḥ*—the wise person; *sabhya*—of the assembly members; *doṣān*—sinful discrepancies; *anusmaran*—keeping in mind; *abruvan*—not speaking; *vibruvan*—speaking wrongly; *ajñaḥ*—ignorant (or pretending to be so); *naraḥ*—a man; *kilbiṣam*—sin; *aśnute*—incurs.

TRANSLATION

A wise person should not enter an assembly if he knows the participants there are committing acts of impropriety. And if, having entered such an assembly, he fails to speak the truth, speaks falsely or pleads ignorance, he will certainly incur sin.

TEXT 11

वल्गतः शत्रुमभितः कृष्णस्य वदनाम्बुजम् ।
वीक्ष्यतां श्रमवार्युप्तं पद्मकोशमिवाम्बुभिः ॥११॥

valgataḥ śatrum abhitaḥ
kṛṣṇasya vadanāmbujam
vīkṣyatāṁ śrama-vāry-uptaṁ
padma-kośam ivāmbubhiḥ

valgataḥ—leaping; *śatrum*—of His enemy; *abhitaḥ*—on all sides; *kṛṣṇasya*—of Kṛṣṇa; *vadana*—the face; *ambujam*—lotuslike; *vīkṣyatām*—you should see; *śrama*—of fatigue; *vāri*—with the moisture; *uptam*—covered; *padma*—of a lotus flower; *kośam*—the whorl; *iva*—like; *ambubhiḥ*—with droplets of water.

TRANSLATION

Just see the lotus face of Kṛṣṇa as He darts around His foe! That face, covered with drops of perspiration brought on by the strenuous fight, resembles the whorl of a lotus covered with dew.

TEXT 12

किं न पश्यत रामस्य मुखमाताम्रलोचनम् ।
मुष्टिकं प्रति सामर्षं हाससंरम्भशोभितम् ॥१२॥

kiṁ na paśyata rāmasya
mukham ātāmra-locanam
muṣṭikaṁ prati sāmarṣaṁ
hāsa-saṁrambha-śobhitam

kim—why; *na paśyata*—do you not see; *rāmasya*—of Lord Balarāma; *mukham*—the face; *ātāmra*—like copper; *locanam*—with eyes; *muṣṭikam*—Muṣṭika; *prati*—toward; *sa-amarṣam*—with anger; *hāsa*—by His laughter; *saṁrambha*—and His absorption; *śobhitam*—beautified.

TRANSLATION

Don't you see the face of Lord Balarāma, with its eyes copper-red from His anger toward Muṣṭika and its beauty enhanced by His laughter and His absorption in the fight?

TEXT 13

पुण्या बत व्रजभुवो यदयं नृलिंग-
गूढः पुराणपुरुषो वनचित्रमाल्यः ।
गाः पालयन् सहबलः क्वणयंश्च वेणुं
विक्रीडयाञ्चति गिरित्ररमार्चिताङ्घ्रिः ॥१३॥

puṇyā bata vraja-bhuvo yad ayaṁ nṛ-liṅga-
gūḍhaḥ purāṇa-puruṣo vana-citra-mālyaḥ
gāḥ pālayan saha-balaḥ kvaṇayaṁś ca veṇuṁ
vikrīḍayāñcati giritra-ramārcitāṅghriḥ

puṇyāḥ—pious; *bata*—indeed; *vraja-bhuvaḥ*—the various regions of the land of Vraja; *yat*—in which; *ayam*—this; *nṛ*—human; *liṅga*—by characteristics; *gūḍhaḥ*—disguised; *purāṇa-puruṣaḥ*—the primeval Personality of Godhead; *vana*—composed of flowers and other items of the forest; *citra*—of wonderful variety; *mālyaḥ*—whose garlands; *gāḥ*—the cows; *pālayan*—herding; *saha*—together with; *balaḥ*—Lord Balarāma; *kvaṇayan*—vibrating; *ca*—and; *veṇum*—His flute; *vikrīḍayā*—with various pastimes; *añcati*—He moves about; *giritra*—by Lord Śiva; *ramā*—and the goddess of fortune; *arcita*—worshiped; *aṅghriḥ*—His feet.

TRANSLATION

How pious are the tracts of land in Vraja, for there the primeval Personality of Godhead, disguising Himself with human traits, wanders about, enacting His many pastimes! Adorned with wonderfully variegated forest garlands, He whose feet are worshiped by Lord Śiva and goddess Ramā vibrates His flute as He tends the cows in the company of Balarāma.

PURPORT

In this verse the devoted ladies in the audience point out the difference between Mathurā and Vṛndāvana. They want to indicate that in Vṛndāvana Kṛṣṇa simply enjoys with His girlfriends and boyfriends, whereas here in Mathurā the Lord is subjected to harassment by the bullying tactics of professional wrestlers. Thus the ladies are condemning the city of Mathurā because of their pain at seeing Kṛṣṇa in what they consider an unfair wrestling match. Of course, Mathurā is also one of the Lord's eternal abodes, but here the women in the assembly express their love in a critical mood.

TEXT 14

गोप्यस्तपः किमचरन् यदमुष्य रूपं
लावण्यसारमसमोर्ध्वमनन्यसिद्धम् ।
दृग्भिः पिबन्त्यनुसवाभिनवं दुरापम्
एकान्तधाम यशसः श्रिय ऐश्वरस्य ॥१४॥

gopyas tapaḥ kim acaran yad amuṣya rūpaṁ
lāvaṇya-sāram asamordhvam ananya-siddham
dṛgbhiḥ pibanty anusavābhinavaṁ durāpam
ekānta-dhāma yaśasaḥ śriya aiśvarasya

gopyaḥ—the *gopīs; tapaḥ*—austerities; *kim*—what; *acaran*—performed; *yat*—from which; *amuṣya*—of such a one (Lord Kṛṣṇa); *rūpam*—the form; *lāvaṇya-sāram*—the essence of loveliness; *asama-ūrdhvam*—not paralleled or surpassed; *ananya-siddham*—not perfected by any other ornament (self-perfect); *dṛgbhiḥ*—by the eyes; *pibanti*—they drink; *anusava-abhinavam*—constantly new; *durāpam*—difficult to obtain; *ekānta-dhāma*—the only abode; *yaśasaḥ*—of fame; *śriyaḥ*—of beauty; *aiśvarasya*—of opulence.

TRANSLATION

What austerities must the *gopīs* have performed! With their eyes they always drink the nectar of Lord Kṛṣṇa's form, which is the essence of loveliness and is not to be equaled or surpassed. That loveliness is the only abode of beauty, fame and opulence. It is self-perfect, ever fresh and extremely rare.

PURPORT

The word meanings and translation for this verse are from Śrīla Prabhupāda's *Caitanya-caritāmṛta* (*Ādi* 4.156).

TEXT 15

या दोहनेऽवहनने मथनोपलेप-
प्रेंखेंखनार्भरुदितोक्षणमार्जनादौ ।
गायन्ति चैनमनुरक्तधियोऽश्रुकण्ठ्यो
धन्या व्रजस्त्रिय उरुक्रमचित्तयानाः ॥१५॥

yā dohane 'vahanane mathanopalepa-
preṅkheṅkhanārbha-ruditokṣaṇa-mārjanādau
gāyanti cainam anurakta-dhiyo 'śru-kaṇṭhyo
dhanyā vraja-striya urukrama-citta-yānāḥ

yāḥ—who (the *gopīs*); *dohane*—while milking; *avahanane*—threshing; *mathana*—churning; *upalepa*—smearing; *preṅkha*—on swings; *iṅkhana*—swinging; *arbha-rudita*—(taking care of) crying babies; *ukṣaṇa*—sprinkling; *mārjana*—cleaning; *ādau*—and so on; *gāyanti*—they sing; *ca*—and; *enam*—about Him; *anurakta*—very much attached; *dhiyaḥ*—whose minds; *aśru*—with tears; *kaṇṭhyaḥ*—whose throats; *dhanyāḥ*—fortunate; *vraja-striyaḥ*—the ladies of Vraja; *urukrama*—of Lord Kṛṣṇa; *citta*—by consciousness; *yānāḥ*—whose acquisition of all desired objects.

TRANSLATION

The ladies of Vraja are the most fortunate of women because, with their minds fully attached to Kṛṣṇa and their throats always choked up with tears, they constantly sing about Him while milking the cows, winnowing grain, churning butter, gathering cow dung for fuel, riding on swings, taking care of their crying babies, sprinkling the ground with water, cleaning their houses, and so on. By their exalted Kṛṣṇa consciousness they automatically acquire all desirable things.

TEXT 16

प्रातर्व्रजाद् व्रजत आविशतश्च सायं
गोभिः समं क्वणयतोऽस्य निशम्य वेणुम् ।
निर्गम्य तूर्णमबलाः पथि भूरिपुण्याः
पश्यन्ति सस्मितमुखं सदयावलोकम् ॥१६॥

prātar vrajād vrajata āviśataś ca sāyaṁ
gobhiḥ samaṁ kvaṇayato 'sya niśamya veṇum
nirgamya tūrṇam abalāḥ pathi bhūri-puṇyāḥ
paśyanti sa-smita-mukhaṁ sa-dayāvalokam

prātaḥ—in the early morning; *vrajāt*—from Vraja; *vrajataḥ*—of Him who is going; *āviśataḥ*—entering; *ca*—and; *sāyam*—in the evening; *gobhiḥ samam*—together with the cows; *kvaṇayataḥ*—who is playing; *asya*—His; *niśamya*—hearing; *veṇum*—the flute; *nirgamya*—coming out; *tūrṇam*—quickly; *abalāḥ*—the women; *pathi*—on the road; *bhūri*—

extremely; *puṇyāḥ*—pious; *paśyanti*—they see; *sa*—with; *smita*—smiling; *mukham*—face; *sa-daya*—merciful; *avalokam*—with glances.

TRANSLATION

When the *gopīs* hear Kṛṣṇa playing His flute as He leaves Vraja in the morning with His cows or returns with them at sunset, the young girls quickly come out of their houses to see Him. They must have performed many pious activities to be able to see Him as He walks on the road, His smiling face mercifully glancing upon them.

TEXT 17

एवं प्रभाषमाणासु स्त्रीषु योगेश्वरो हरिः ।
शत्रुं हन्तुं मनश्चक्रे भगवान् भरतर्षभ ॥१७॥

evaṁ prabhāṣamāṇāsu
strīṣu yogeśvaro hariḥ
śatruṁ hantuṁ manaś cakre
bhagavān bharatarṣabha

evam—in this manner; *prabhāṣamāṇāsu*—while they were speaking; *strīṣu*—the women; *yoga-īśvaraḥ*—the master of all mystic power; *hariḥ*—Lord Kṛṣṇa; *śatrum*—His enemy; *hantum*—to kill; *manaḥ cakre*—made up His mind; *bhagavān*—the Supreme Lord; *bharata-ṛṣabha*—O hero of the Bhāratas.

TRANSLATION

[Śukadeva Gosvāmī continued:] As the women spoke thus, O hero of the Bhāratas, Lord Kṛṣṇa, the master of all mystic power, made up His mind to kill His opponent.

TEXT 18

सभयाः स्त्रीगिरः श्रुत्वा पुत्रस्नेहशुचातुरौ ।
पितरावन्वतप्येतां पुत्रयोरबुधौ बलम् ॥१८॥

sa-bhayāḥ strī-giraḥ śrutvā
putra-sneha-śucāturau
pitarāv anvatapyetāṁ
putrayor abudhau balam

sa-bhayāḥ—fearful; *strī*—of the women; *giraḥ*—the words; *śrutvā*—hearing; *putra*—for their sons; *sneha*—by their affection; *śuca*—with sorrow; *āturau*—overwhelmed; *pitarau*—Their parents (Devakī and Vasudeva); *anvatapyetām*—felt remorse; *putrayoḥ*—of their two sons; *abudhau*—not knowing; *balam*—the strength.

TRANSLATION

Out of affection for the two Lords, Their parents [Devakī and Vasudeva] became overwhelmed with sorrow when they heard the women's fearful statements. They grieved, not knowing their sons' strength.

PURPORT

Naturally, Kṛṣṇa's parents would lament in this situation, thinking "Why didn't we keep our sons at home? Why did we allow Them to participate in this corrupt exhibition?"

TEXT 19

तैस्तैर्नियुद्धविधिभिर्विविधैरच्युतेतरौ ।
युयुधाते यथान्योन्यं तथैव बलमुष्टिकौ ॥१९॥

tais tair niyuddha-vidhibhir
vividhair acyutetarau
yuyudhāte yathānyonyaṁ
tathaiva bala-muṣṭikau

taiḥ taiḥ—with all these; *niyuddha*—of wrestling; *vidhibhiḥ*—techniques; *vividhaiḥ*—various; *acyuta-itarau*—Lord Acyuta and His opponent; *yuyudhāte*—fought; *yathā*—as; *anyonyam*—with each other; *tathā eva*—just so; *bala-muṣṭikau*—Lord Balarāma and Muṣṭika.

TRANSLATION

Lord Balarāma and Muṣṭika, expertly displaying numerous wrestling techniques, battled each other in the same way that Lord Kṛṣṇa and His opponent did.

TEXT 20

भगवद्गात्रनिष्पातैर्वज्रनिष्पेषनिष्ठुरैः ।
चाणूरो भज्यमानांगो मुहुर्ग्लानिमवाप ह ॥२०॥

bhagavad-gātra-niṣpātair
vajra-niṣpeṣa-niṣṭhuraiḥ
cāṇūro bhajyamānāṅgo
muhur glānim avāpa ha

bhagavat—of the Supreme Lord; *gātra*—by the limbs; *niṣpātaiḥ*—due to the blows; *vajra*—of lightning; *niṣpeṣa*—like a crushing stroke; *niṣṭhuraiḥ*—hard; *cāṇūraḥ*—Cāṇūra; *bhajyamāna*—being broken; *aṅgaḥ*—his entire body; *muhuḥ*—more and more; *glānim*—pain and fatigue; *avāpa ha*—felt.

TRANSLATION

The harsh blows from the Supreme Lord's limbs fell like crushing lightning bolts upon Cāṇūra, breaking every part of his body and causing him more and more pain and fatigue.

PURPORT

Cāṇūra's elbows, arms, knees and other limbs were all weakening.

TEXT 21

स श्येनवेग उत्पत्य मुष्टीकृत्य करावुभौ ।
भगवन्तं वासुदेवं क्रुद्धो वक्षस्यबाधत ॥२१॥

sa śyena-vega utpatya
muṣṭī-kṛtya karāv ubhau
bhagavantaṁ vāsudevaṁ
kruddho vakṣasy abādhata

saḥ—he, Cāṇūra; *śyena*—of a hawk; *vegaḥ*—with the speed; *utpatya*—falling upon Him; *muṣṭī*—into fists; *kṛtya*—making; *karau*—his hands; *ubhau*—both; *bhagavantam*—the Supreme Lord; *vāsudevam*—Kṛṣṇa; *kruddhaḥ*—angry; *vakṣasi*—upon His chest; *abādhata*—struck.

TRANSLATION

Furious, Cāṇūra attacked Lord Vāsudeva with the speed of a hawk and struck His chest with both fists.

PURPORT

It appears that Cāṇūra, realizing he was being defeated, became furious and made a final attempt to defeat Lord Kṛṣṇa. The demon certainly had the spirit of a good fighter, but if he hoped for victory, he was certainly in the wrong place at the wrong time with the wrong person.

TEXTS 22–23

नाचलत्तत्प्रहारेण मालाहत इव द्विपः ।
बाह्वोर्निगृह्य चाणूरं बहुशो भ्रामयन् हरिः ॥२२॥
भूपृष्ठे पोथयामास तरसा क्षीणजीवितम् ।
विस्रस्ताकल्पकेशस्रगिन्द्रध्वज इवापतत् ॥२३॥

nācalat tat-prahāreṇa
mālāhata iva dvipaḥ
bāhvor nigṛhya cāṇūraṁ
bahuśo bhrāmayan hariḥ

bhū-pṛṣṭhe pothayām āsa
tarasā kṣīṇa-jīvitam
visrastākalpa-keśa-srag
indra-dhvaja ivāpatat

na acalat—He (Lord Kṛṣṇa) did not move; *tat-prahāreṇa*—because of his blows; *mālā*—with a garland; *āhata*—struck; *iva*—as; *dvipaḥ*—an elephant; *bāhvoḥ*—by the two arms; *nigṛhya*—seizing; *cāṇūram*—Cāṇūra; *bahuśaḥ*—several times; *bhrāmayan*—whirling him around; *hariḥ*—Lord Kṛṣṇa; *bhū*—of the earth; *pṛṣṭhe*—onto the surface; *pothayām āsa*—hurled; *tarasā*—forcefully; *kṣīṇa*—becoming lost; *jīvitam*—his life; *visrasta*—scattered; *ākalpa*—his clothing; *keśa*—hair; *srak*—and flower garland; *indra-dhvajaḥ*—a tall festival column; *iva*—as if; *apatat*—he fell.

TRANSLATION

No more shaken by the demon's mighty blows than an elephant struck with a flower garland, Lord Kṛṣṇa grabbed Cāṇūra by his arms, swung him around several times and hurled him onto the ground with great force. His clothes, hair and garland scattering, the wrestler fell down dead like a huge festival column collapsing.

PURPORT

Śrīla Śrīdhara Svāmī explains the words *indra-dhvaja* as follows: "In Bengal, on the occasion of a certain festival, people erect a tall column in the form of a man and decorate it with flags, banners, etc. He [Cāṇūra] fell just as such a pole might fall."

TEXTS 24–25

तथैव मुष्टिकः पूर्वं स्वमुष्ट्याभिहतेन वै ।
बलभद्रेण बलिना तलेनाभिहतो भृशम् ॥२४॥
प्रवेपितः स रुधिरमुद्वमन्मुखतोऽर्दितः ।
व्यसुः पपातोर्व्युपस्थे वाताहत इवाङ्घ्रिपः ॥२५॥

tathaiva muṣṭikaḥ pūrvaṁ
sva-muṣṭyābhihatena vai
balabhadreṇa balinā
talenābhihato bhṛśam

pravepitaḥ sa rudhiram
udvaman mukhato 'rditaḥ

vyasuḥ papātorvy-upasthe
vātāhata ivāṅghripaḥ

tathā—also; *eva*—similarly; *muṣṭikaḥ*—Muṣṭika; *pūrvam*—previously; *sva-muṣṭyā*—with his fist; *abhihatena*—who had been struck; *vai*—indeed; *balabhadreṇa*—by Lord Balarāma; *balinā*—the powerful; *talena*—with His palm; *abhihataḥ*—struck; *bhṛśam*—violently; *pravepitaḥ*—trembling; *saḥ*—he, Muṣṭika; *rudhiram*—blood; *udvaman*—vomiting; *mukhataḥ*—from his mouth; *arditaḥ*—tormented; *vyasuḥ*—lifeless; *papāta*—he fell; *urvī*—of the earth; *upasthe*—onto the lap; *vāta*—by the wind; *āhataḥ*—struck down; *iva*—like; *aṅghripaḥ*—a tree.

TRANSLATION

Similarly, Muṣṭika struck Lord Balabhadra with his fist and was slain. Receiving a violent blow from the mighty Lord's palm, the demon trembled all over in great pain, vomited blood and then fell lifeless onto the ground, like a tree blown down by the wind.

TEXT 26

ततः कूटमनुप्राप्तं रामः प्रहरतां वरः ।
अवधील्लीलया राजन् सावज्ञं वाममुष्टिना ॥२६॥

tataḥ kūṭam anuprāptaṁ
rāmaḥ praharatāṁ varaḥ
avadhīl līlayā rājan
sāvajñaṁ vāma-muṣṭinā

tataḥ—then; *kūṭam*—the demonic wrestler Kūṭa; *anuprāptam*—appearing on the scene; *rāmaḥ*—Lord Balarāma; *praharatām*—of fighters; *varaḥ*—the best; *avadhīt*—killed; *līlayā*—playfully; *rājan*—O King, Parīkṣit; *sa-avajñam*—neglectfully; *vāma*—left; *muṣṭinā*—with His fist.

TRANSLATION

Confronted next by the wrestler Kūṭa, Lord Balarāma the best of fighters, playfully and nonchalantly killed him with His left fist, O King.

TEXT 27

तर्ह्येव हि शलः कृष्णप्रपदाहतशीर्षकः ।
द्विधा विदीर्णस्तोशलक उभावपि निपेततुः ॥२७॥

tarhy eva hi śalaḥ kṛṣṇa-
prapadāhata-śīrṣakaḥ
dvidhā vidīrṇas tośalaka
ubhāv api nipetatuḥ

tarhi eva—and then; *hi*—indeed; *śalaḥ*—the wrestler Śala; *kṛṣṇa*—of Lord Kṛṣṇa; *prapada*—by the toes; *āhata*—struck; *śīrṣakaḥ*—his head; *dvidhā*—in two; *vidīrṇaḥ*—torn; *tośalaka*—Tośala; *ubhau api*—both of them; *nipetatuḥ*—fell down.

TRANSLATION

Then Kṛṣṇa struck the wrestler Śala in the head with His toes and tore him in half. The Lord dealt with Tośala in the same way, and both wrestlers fell down dead.

TEXT 28

चाणूरे मुष्टिके कूटे शले तोशलके हते ।
शेषाः प्रदुद्रुवुर्मल्लाः सर्वे प्राणपरीप्सवः ॥२८॥

cāṇūre muṣṭike kūṭe
śale tośalake hate
śeṣāḥ pradudruvur mallāḥ
sarve prāṇa-parīpsavaḥ

cāṇūre muṣṭike kūṭe—Cāṇūra, Muṣṭika and Kūṭa; *śale tośalake*—Śala and Tośala; *hate*—being killed; *śeṣāḥ*—those remaining; *pradudruvuḥ*—ran away; *mallāḥ*—wrestlers; *sarve*—all; *prāṇa*—their lives; *parīpsavaḥ*—hoping to save.

TRANSLATION

Cāṇūra, Muṣṭika, Kūṭa, Śala and Tośala having been killed, the remaining wrestlers all fled for their lives.

TEXT 29

गोपान् वयस्यानाकृष्य तैः संसृज्य विजह्रतुः ।
वाद्यमानेषु तूर्येषु वल्गन्तौ रुतनूपुरौ ॥२९॥

gopān vayasyān ākṛṣya
taiḥ saṁsṛjya vijahratuḥ
vādyamāneṣu tūryeṣu
valgantau ruta-nūpurau

gopān—the cowherd boys; *vayasyān*—Their young friends; *ākṛṣya*—gathering together; *taiḥ*—with them; *saṁsṛjya*—joining up; *vijahratuḥ*—They sported; *vādyamāneṣu*—while they played; *tūryeṣu*—the musical instruments; *valgantau*—the two of Them dancing about; *ruta*—resounding; *nūpurau*—Their ankle bells.

TRANSLATION

Kṛṣṇa and Balarāma then called Their young cowherd boyfriends to join Them, and in their company the Lords danced about and sported, Their ankle bells resounding as musical instruments played.

PURPORT

Nowadays we see that in championship boxing matches, as soon as there is a victory, all the friends and relatives of the victorious boxer rush into the ring to congratulate him, and often the champion will dance about in great happiness. Exactly in this mood, Kṛṣṇa and Balarāma danced about, celebrating Their victory with Their friends and relatives.

TEXT 30

जनाः प्रजहृषुः सर्वे कर्मणा रामकृष्णयोः ।
ऋते कंसं विप्रमुख्याः साधवः साधु साध्विति ॥३०॥

janāḥ prajahṛṣuḥ sarve
karmaṇā rāma-kṛṣṇayoḥ

ṛte kaṁsaṁ vipra-mukhyāḥ
sādhavaḥ sādhu sādhv iti

janāḥ—the people; *prajahṛṣuḥ*—rejoiced; *sarve*—all; *karmaṇā*—at the deed; *rāma-kṛṣṇayoḥ*—of Balarāma and Kṛṣṇa; *ṛte*—except; *kaṁsam*—Kaṁsa; *vipra*—of the *brāhmaṇas; mukhyāḥ*—the best; *sādhavaḥ*—the saintly persons; *sādhu sādhu iti*—(exclaimed) "Excellent! Excellent!"

TRANSLATION

Everyone except Kaṁsa rejoiced at the wonderful feat Kṛṣṇa and Balarāma had performed. The exalted *brāhmaṇas* and great saints exclaimed, "Excellent! Excellent!"

PURPORT

It is understood that as the best of the *brāhmaṇas* and saints were exclaiming "Excellent! Excellent!" the worst of the *brāhmaṇas*, namely Kaṁsa's priests, were seriously grieving.

TEXT 31

हतेषु मल्लवर्येषु विद्रुतेषु च भोजराट् ।
न्यवारयत्स्वतूर्याणि वाक्यं चेदमुवाच ह ॥३१॥

hateṣu malla-varyeṣu
vidruteṣu ca bhoja-rāṭ
nyavārayat sva-tūryāṇi
vākyaṁ cedam uvāca ha

hateṣu—being killed; *malla-varyeṣu*—the best wrestlers; *vidruteṣu*—having run away; *ca*—and; *bhoja-rāṭ*—the Bhoja king, Kaṁsa; *nyavārayat*—stopped; *sva*—his own; *tūryāṇi*—musical instruments; *vākyam*—words; *ca*—and; *idam*—these; *uvāca ha*—spoke.

TRANSLATION

The Bhoja king, seeing that his best wrestlers had all been killed or had fled, stopped the musical performance originally meant for his pleasure and spoke the following words.

TEXT 32

निःसारयत दुर्वृत्तौ वसुदेवात्मजौ पुरात् ।
धनं हरत गोपानां नन्दं बध्नीत दुर्मतिम् ॥३२॥

niḥsārayata durvṛttau
vasudevātmajau purāt
dhanaṁ harata gopānāṁ
nandaṁ badhnīta durmatim

niḥsārayata—expel; *durvṛttau*—who behave wickedly; *vasudeva-ātma-jau*—the two sons of Vasudeva; *purāt*—from the city; *dhanam*—the wealth; *harata*—take away; *gopānām*—of the cowherds; *nandam*—Nanda Mahārāja; *badhnīta*—tie up; *durmatim*—the fool, whose heart is crooked.

TRANSLATION

Drive the two wicked sons of Vasudeva out of the city! Confiscate the cowherds' property and arrest that fool Nanda!

TEXT 33

वसुदेवस्तु दुर्मेधा हन्यतामाश्वसत्तमः ।
उग्रसेनः पिता चापि सानुगः परपक्षगः ॥३३॥

vasudevas tu durmedhā
hanyatām āśv asattamaḥ
ugrasenaḥ pitā cāpi
sānugaḥ para-pakṣa-gaḥ

vasudevaḥ—Vasudeva; *tu*—and furthermore; *durmedhā*—the foolish-minded; *hanyatām*—should be killed; *āśu*—immediately; *asat-tamaḥ*—the worst of the impure; *ugrasenaḥ*—Ugrasena; *pitā*—my father; *ca api*—also; *sa*—together with; *anugaḥ*—his followers; *para*—of the enemy; *pakṣa-gaḥ*—taking the side.

TRANSLATION

Kill that most evil fool Vasudeva! And also kill my father, Ugrasena, along with his followers, who have all sided with our enemies!

TEXT 34

एवं विकत्थमाने वै कंसे प्रकुपितोऽव्ययः ।
लघिम्नोत्पत्य तरसा मञ्चमुत्तुंगमारुहत् ॥३४॥

evaṁ vikatthamāne vai
kaṁse prakupito 'vyayaḥ
laghimnotpatya tarasā
mañcam uttuṅgam āruhat

evam—thus; *vikatthamāne*—exclaiming with audacity; *vai*—indeed; *kaṁse*—Kaṁsa; *prakupitaḥ*—becoming extremely angry; *avyayaḥ*—the infallible Lord; *laghimnā*—with ease; *utpatya*—jumping up; *tarasā*—swiftly; *mañcam*—the royal platform; *uttuṅgam*—tall; *āruhat*—climbed onto.

TRANSLATION

As Kaṁsa thus raved so audaciously, the infallible Lord Kṛṣṇa, intensely angry, quickly and easily jumped up onto the high royal dais.

TEXT 35

तमाविशन्तमालोक्य मृत्युमात्मन आसनात् ।
मनस्वी सहसोत्थाय जगृहे सोऽसिचर्मणी ॥३५॥

tam āviśantam ālokya
mṛtyum ātmana āsanāt
manasvī sahasotthāya
jagṛhe so 'si-carmaṇī

tam—Him, Kṛṣṇa; *āviśantam*—entering (into his private sitting area); *ālokya*—seeing; *mṛtyum*—death; *ātmanaḥ*—his own; *āsanāt*—from his seat; *manasvī*—the intelligent; *sahasā*—immediately; *utthāya*—standing up; *jagṛhe*—took up; *saḥ*—he; *asi*—his sword; *carmaṇī*—and his shield.

TRANSLATION

Seeing Lord Kṛṣṇa approaching like death personified, the quick-witted Kaṁsa instantly rose from his seat and took up his sword and shield.

TEXT 36

तं खड्गपाणिं विचरन्तमाशु
श्येनं यथा दक्षिणसव्यमम्बरे ।
समग्रहीद्दुर्विषहोग्रतेजा
यथोरगं तार्क्ष्यसुतः प्रसह्य ॥३६॥

taṁ khaḍga-pāṇiṁ vicarantam āśu
śyenaṁ yathā dakṣiṇa-savyam ambare
samagrahīd durviṣahogra-tejā
yathoragaṁ tārkṣya-sutaḥ prasahya

tam—him, Kaṁsa; *khaḍga*—with sword; *pāṇim*—in his hand; *vicarantam*—moving about; *āśu*—quickly; *śyenam*—a hawk; *yathā*—like; *dakṣiṇa-savyam*—right and left; *ambare*—in the sky; *samagrahīt*—seized; *durviṣaha*—irresistible; *ugra*—and fearsome; *tejāḥ*—whose strength; *yathā*—as; *uragam*—a snake; *tārkṣya-sutaḥ*—the son of Tārkṣya, Garuḍa; *prasahya*—by force.

TRANSLATION

Sword in hand, Kaṁsa moved quickly from side to side like a hawk in the sky. But Lord Kṛṣṇa, whose fearsome strength is irresistible, powerfully seized the demon just as the son of Tārkṣya might capture a snake.

TEXT 37

प्रगृह्य केशेषु चलत्किरीटं
निपात्य रंगोपरि तुंगमञ्चात् ।
तस्योपरिष्टात्स्वयमब्जनाभः
पपात विश्वाश्रय आत्मतन्त्रः ॥३७॥

pragṛhya keśeṣu calat-kirīṭaṁ
nipātya raṅgopari tuṅga-mañcāt
tasyopariṣṭāt svayam abja-nābhaḥ
papāta viśvāśraya ātma-tantraḥ

pragṛhya—grabbing; *keśeṣu*—by the hair; *calat*—knocking off; *kirī-ṭam*—whose crown; *nipātya*—throwing down; *raṅga-upari*—onto the surface of the wrestling ring; *tuṅga*—high; *mañcāt*—from the platform; *tasya*—of him; *upariṣṭāt*—on top; *svayam*—Himself; *abja-nābhaḥ*—the lotus-naveled Supreme Lord; *papāta*—threw; *viśva*—of the entire universe; *āśrayaḥ*—the support; *ātma-tantraḥ*—independent.

TRANSLATION

Grabbing Kaṁsa by the hair and knocking off his crown, the lotus-naveled Lord threw him off the elevated dais onto the wrestling mat. Then the independent Lord, the support of the entire universe, threw Himself upon the King.

PURPORT

In *Kṛṣṇa, the Supreme Personality of Godhead,* Śrīla Prabhupāda describes the death of Kaṁsa as follows: "Kṛṣṇa at once straddled his chest and began to strike him over and over again. Simply from the strokes of His fist, Kaṁsa lost his vital force."

TEXT 38

तं सम्परेतं विचकर्ष भूमौ
हरिर्यथेभं जगतो विपश्यतः ।

हा हेति शब्दः सुमहांस्तदाभूद्
उदीरितः सर्वजनैर्नरेन्द्र ॥३८॥

taṁ samparetaṁ vicakarṣa bhūmau
harir yathebhaṁ jagato vipaśyataḥ
hā heti śabdaḥ su-mahāṁs tadābhūd
udīritaḥ sarva-janair narendra

tam—him; *samparetam*—dead; *vicakarṣa*—dragged; *bhūmau*—along the ground; *hariḥ*—a lion; *yathā*—as; *ibham*—an elephant; *jagataḥ*—all the people; *vipaśyataḥ*—as they looked on; *hā hā iti*—"Oh, oh!"; *śabdaḥ*—the sound; *su-mahān*—mighty; *tadā*—then; *abhūt*—arose; *udīritaḥ*—spoken; *sarva-janaiḥ*—by all the people; *nara-indra*—O ruler of men (King Parīkṣit).

TRANSLATION

As a lion drags a dead elephant, the Lord then dragged Kaṁsa's dead body along the ground in full view of everyone present. O King, all the people in the arena tumultuously cried out, "Oh! Oh!"

PURPORT

Śrīla Viśvanātha Cakravartī explains that many people in the audience thought Kaṁsa had simply been knocked unconscious when thrown from the lofty dais. Therefore Lord Kṛṣṇa dragged his corpse so everyone would realize that the evil King was indeed dead. Thus the exclamation *hā hā* indicates how surprised the people were that the King was suddenly dead and gone.

The audience's astonishment is also mentioned in the *Viṣṇu Purāṇa:*

tato hāhā-kṛtaṁ sarvam
āsīt tad-raṅga-maṇḍalam
avajñayā hataṁ dṛṣṭvā
kṛṣṇena mathureśvaram

"Then the entire arena became filled with cries of astonishment as the people saw that the master of Mathurā had been contemptuously killed by Kṛṣṇa."

TEXT 39

स नित्यदोद्विग्नधिया तमीश्वरं
पिबन्नदन् वा विचरन् स्वपन् श्वसन् ।
ददर्श चक्रायुधमग्रतो यतस्
तदेव रूपं दुरवापमाप ॥३९॥

sa nityadodvigna-dhiyā tam īśvaraṁ
pibann adan vā vicaran svapan śvasan
dadarśa cakrāyudham agrato yatas
tad eva rūpaṁ duravāpam āpa

saḥ—he, Kaṁsa; *nityadā*—constantly; *udvigna*—anxious; *dhiyā*—with mind; *tam*—Him; *īśvaram*—the Supreme Lord; *piban*—while drinking; *adan*—eating; *vā*—or; *vicaran*—walking; *svapan*—sleeping; *śvasan*—breathing; *dadarśa*—saw; *cakra*—the disc weapon; *āyudham*—in His hand; *agrataḥ*—before himself; *yataḥ*—because; *tat*—that; *eva*—same; *rūpam*—personal form; *duravāpam*—very difficult to achieve; *āpa*—he achieved.

TRANSLATION

Kaṁsa had always been disturbed by the thought that the Supreme Lord was to kill him. Therefore when drinking, eating, moving about, sleeping or simply breathing, the King had always seen the Lord before him with the disc weapon in His hand. Thus Kaṁsa achieved the rare boon of attaining a form like the Lord's.

PURPORT

Although born out of fear, Kaṁsa's constant meditation on the Supreme Lord eradicated all his offenses, and therefore the demon was liberated upon his death at the Lord's hands.

TEXT 40

तस्यानुजा भ्रातरोऽष्टौ कंकन्यग्रोधकादयः ।
अभ्यधावन्नतिक्रुद्धा भ्रातुर्निर्वेशकारिणः ॥४०॥

tasyānujā bhrātaro 'ṣṭau
kaṅka-nyagrodhakādayaḥ
abhyadhāvann ati-kruddhā
bhrātur nirveśa-kāriṇaḥ

tasya—of him, Kaṁsa; *anujāḥ*—younger; *bhrātaraḥ*—the brothers; *aṣṭau*—eight; *kaṅka-nyagrodhaka-ādayaḥ*—Kaṅka, Nyagrodhaka and the others; *abhyadhāvan*—ran forward to attack; *ati-kruddhāḥ*—infuriated; *bhrātuḥ*—to their brother; *nirveśa*—repayment of the debt; *kāriṇaḥ*—doing.

TRANSLATION

Kaṁsa's eight younger brothers, led by Kaṅka and Nyagrodhaka, then attacked the Lords in a rage, seeking to avenge their brother's death.

TEXT 41

तथातिरभसांस्तांस्तु संयत्तान् रोहिणीसुतः ।
अहन् परिघमुद्यम्य पशूनिव मृगाधिपः ॥४१॥

tathāti-rabhasāṁs tāṁs tu
saṁyattān rohiṇī-sutaḥ
ahan parigham udyamya
paśūn iva mṛgādhipaḥ

tathā—in this manner; *ati-rabhasān*—running very swiftly; *tān*—they; *tu*—and; *saṁyattān*—ready to strike; *rohiṇī-sutaḥ*—the son of Rohiṇī, Lord Balarāma; *ahan*—beat down; *parigham*—His club; *udyamya*—wielding; *paśūn*—animals; *iva*—as; *mṛga-adhipaḥ*—the lion, king of animals.

TRANSLATION

As they ran swiftly toward the two Lords, ready to strike, the son of Rohiṇī slew them with His club just as a lion easily kills other animals.

TEXT 42

नेदुर्दुन्दुभयो व्योम्नि ब्रह्मेशाद्या विभूतयः ।
पुष्पैः किरन्तस्तं प्रीताः शशंसुर्ननृतुः स्त्रियः ॥४२॥

nedur dundubhayo vyomni
brahmeśādyā vibhūtayaḥ
puṣpaiḥ kirantas taṁ prītāḥ
śaśaṁsur nanṛtuḥ striyaḥ

neduḥ—resounded; *dundubhayaḥ*—kettledrums; *vyomni*—in the sky; *brahma-īśa-ādyāḥ*—Brahmā, Śiva and other demigods; *vibhūtayaḥ*—His expansions; *puṣpaiḥ*—flowers; *kirantaḥ*—scattering down; *tam*—upon Him; *prītāḥ*—pleased; *śaśaṁsuḥ*—they chanted His praises; *nanṛtuḥ*—danced; *striyaḥ*—their wives.

TRANSLATION

Kettledrums resounded in the sky as Brahmā, Śiva and other demigods, the Lord's expansions, rained down flowers upon Him with pleasure. They chanted His praises, and their wives danced.

TEXT 43

तेषां स्त्रियो महाराज सुहृन्मरणदुःखिताः ।
तत्राभीयुर्विनिघ्नन्त्यः शीर्षाण्यश्रुविलोचनाः ॥४३॥

teṣāṁ striyo mahā-rāja
suhṛn-maraṇa-duḥkhitāḥ
tatrābhīyur vinighnantyaḥ
śīrṣāṇy aśru-vilocanāḥ

teṣām—of them (Kaṁsa and his brothers); *striyaḥ*—the wives; *mahā-rāja*—O King (Parīkṣit); *suhṛt*—of their well-wishers (their husbands); *maraṇa*—because of the death; *duḥkhitāḥ*—sorrowful; *tatra*—that place; *abhīyuḥ*—approached; *vinighnantyaḥ*—beating; *śīrṣāṇi*—their heads; *aśru*—with tears; *vilocanāḥ*—their eyes.

TRANSLATION

My dear King, the wives of Kaṁsa and his brothers, aggrieved by the death of their well-wishing husbands, came forward with tearful eyes, beating their heads.

TEXT 44

शयानान् वीरशयायां पतीनालिंग्य शोचतीः ।
विलेपुः सुस्वरं नार्यो विसृजन्त्यो मुहुः शुचः ॥४४॥

śayānān vīra-śayāyāṁ
patīn āliṅgya śocatīḥ
vilepuḥ su-svaraṁ nāryo
visṛjantyo muhuḥ śucaḥ

śayānān—lying; *vīra*—of a hero; *śayāyām*—upon the bed (the ground); *patīn*—their husbands; *āliṅgya*—embracing; *śocatīḥ*—feeling sorrow; *vilepuḥ*—lamented; *su-svaram*—loudly; *nāryaḥ*—the women; *visṛjantyaḥ*—shedding; *muhuḥ*—repeatedly; *śucaḥ*—tears.

TRANSLATION

Embracing their husbands, who lay on a hero's final bed, the sorrowful women loudly lamented while shedding constant tears.

TEXT 45

हा नाथ प्रिय धर्मज्ञ करुणानाथवत्सल ।
त्वया हतेन निहता वयं ते सगृहप्रजाः ॥४५॥

hā nātha priya dharma-jña
karuṇānātha-vatsala
tvayā hatena nihatā
vayaṁ te sa-gṛha-prajāḥ

hā—alas; *nātha*—O master; *priya*—O dear one; *dharma-jña*—O knower of religious principles; *karuṇa*—O kind one; *anātha*—to those who have no protector; *vatsala*—O you who are compassionate; *tvayā*—by you; *hatena*—being killed; *nihatāḥ*—are killed; *vayam*—we; *te*—your; *sa*—together with; *gṛha*—the home; *prajāḥ*—and offspring.

TRANSLATION

[The women cried out:] Alas, O master, O dear one, O knower of religious principles! O kind and compassionate protector of the shelterless! By your being slain we have also been slain, together with your household and offspring.

TEXT 46

त्वया विरहिता पत्या पुरीयं पुरुषर्षभ ।
न शोभते वयमिव निवृत्तोत्सवमंगला ॥४६॥

tvayā virahitā patyā
purīyaṁ puruṣarṣabha
na śobhate vayam iva
nivṛttotsava-maṅgalā

tvayā—of you; *virahitā*—bereft; *patyā*—the master; *purī*—the city; *iyam*—this; *puruṣa*—of men; *ṛṣabha*—O most heroic one; *na śobhate*—does not appear beautiful; *vayam*—us; *iva*—just like; *nivṛtta*—ceased; *utsava*—festivity; *maṅgalā*—and auspiciousness.

TRANSLATION

O great hero among men, bereft of you, its master, this city has lost its beauty, just as we have, and all festivity and good fortune within it have come to an end.

TEXT 47

अनागसां त्वं भूतानां कृतवान् द्रोहमुल्बणम् ।
तेनेमां भो दशां नीतो भूतध्रुक्को लभेत शम् ॥४७॥

anāgasāṁ tvaṁ bhūtānāṁ
kṛtavān droham ulbaṇam

tenemāṁ bho daśāṁ nīto
bhūta-dhruk ko labheta śam

anāgasām—sinless; *tvam*—you; *bhūtānām*—against creatures; *kṛtavān*—have committed; *droham*—violence; *ulbaṇam*—terrible; *tena*—by that; *imām*—to this; *bho*—O dear one; *daśām*—condition; *nītaḥ*—brought; *bhūta*—to living beings; *dhruk*—causing harm; *kaḥ*—who; *labheta*—can achieve; *śam*—happiness.

TRANSLATION

O dear one, you have been brought to this state because of the terrible violence you committed against innocent creatures. How can one who harms others attain happiness?

PURPORT

Having expressed their sentimental grief, the ladies now speak practical wisdom. They are beginning to see things realistically because their minds were purified by the agony of the recent events and by the association of Lord Kṛṣṇa.

TEXT 48

सर्वेषामिह भूतानामेष हि प्रभवाप्ययः ।
गोप्ता च तदवध्यायी न क्वचित्सुखमेधते ॥४८॥

sarveṣām iha bhūtānām
eṣa hi prabhavāpyayaḥ
goptā ca tad-avadhyāyī
na kvacit sukham edhate

sarveṣām—of all; *iha*—in this world; *bhūtānām*—living beings; *eṣaḥ*—this (Śrī Kṛṣṇa); *hi*—certainly; *prabhava*—the origin; *apyayaḥ*—and disappearance; *goptā*—the maintainer; *ca*—and; *tat*—of Him; *avadhyāyī*—one who is neglectful; *na kvacit*—never; *sukham*—happily; *edhate*—prospers.

TRANSLATION

Lord Kṛṣṇa causes the appearance and disappearance of all beings in this world, and He is their maintainer as well. One who disrespects Him can never prosper happily.

TEXT 49

श्रीशुक उवाच
राजयोषित आश्वास्य भगवाल्ँ लोकभावनः ।
यामाहुर्लौकिकीं संस्थां हतानां समकारयत् ॥४९॥

śrī-śuka uvāca
rāja-yoṣita āśvāsya
bhagavāl̐ loka-bhāvanaḥ
yām āhur laukikīṁ saṁsthāṁ
hatānāṁ samakārayat

śrī-śukaḥ uvāca—Śukadeva Gosvāmī said; *rāja*—of the King (and his brothers); *yoṣitaḥ*—the wives; *āśvāsya*—consoling; *bhagavān*—the Supreme Lord; *loka*—of all the worlds; *bhāvanaḥ*—the sustainer; *yām*—which; *āhuḥ*—they (Vedic authorities) enjoin; *laukikīm saṁsthām*—funeral rites; *hatānām*—for the deceased; *samakārayat*—He arranged to be performed.

TRANSLATION

Śukadeva Gosvāmī said: After consoling the royal ladies, Lord Kṛṣṇa, sustainer of all the worlds, arranged for the prescribed funeral rites to be performed.

TEXT 50

मातरं पितरं चैव मोचयित्वाथ बन्धनात् ।
कृष्णरामौ ववन्दाते शिरसा स्पृश्य पादयोः ॥५०॥

mātaraṁ pitaraṁ caiva
mocayitvātha bandhanāt
kṛṣṇa-rāmau vavandāte
śirasā spṛśya pādayoḥ

mātaram—Their mother; *pitaram*—father; *ca*—and; *eva*—also; *mocayitvā*—releasing; *atha*—then; *bandhanāt*—from their fetters; *kṛṣṇa-rāmau*—Kṛṣṇa and Balarāma; *vavandāte*—paid obeisances; *śirasā*—with Their heads; *spṛśya*—touching; *pādayoḥ*—their feet.

TRANSLATION

Then Kṛṣṇa and Balarāma released Their mother and father from bondage and offered obeisances to them, touching their feet with Their heads.

TEXT 51

देवकी वसुदेवश्च विज्ञाय जगदीश्वरौ ।
कृतसंवन्दनौ पुत्रौ सस्वजाते न शङ्कितौ ॥५१॥

devakī vasudevaś ca
vijñāya jagad-īśvarau
kṛta-saṁvandanau putrau
sasvajāte na śaṅkitau

devakī—Devakī; *vasudevaḥ*—Vasudeva; *ca*—and; *vijñāya*—recognizing; *jagat*—of the universe; *īśvarau*—as the two Lords; *kṛta*—paying; *saṁvandanau*—full respects (by standing with joined palms); *putrau*—their two sons; *sasvajāte na*—they did not embrace; *śaṅkitau*—apprehensive.

TRANSLATION

Devakī and Vasudeva, now knowing Kṛṣṇa and Balarāma to be the Lords of the universe, simply stood with joined palms. Being apprehensive, they did not embrace their sons.

Thus end the purports of the humble servant of His Divine Grace A. C. Bhaktivedanta Swami Prabhupāda to the Tenth Canto, Forty-fourth Chapter, of the Śrīmad-Bhāgavatam, *entitled "The Killing of Kaṁsa."*

Appendixes

The Author

His Divine Grace Śrīla Hridayananda dāsa Goswami Ācāryadeva is one of the foremost spiritual leaders of the International Society for Krishna Consciousness. He enjoys the rare status of being among the first Western-born members of the authorized chain of disciplic succession descending from the Supreme Lord, Kṛṣṇa. In modern times, the most essential task of Kṛṣṇa conscious spiritual masters has been to translate the Vedic scriptures of ancient India into modern languages and distribute them widely throughout the world. Śrīla Ācāryadeva has made this mission his life and soul.

Śrīla Ācāryadeva appeared in this world on November 5, 1948, in Los Angeles, California. As an academically gifted student at the University of California, Berkeley, he attended a talk given by His Divine Grace A. C. Bhaktivedanta Swami Prabhupāda, the founder and spiritual master of the Kṛṣṇa consciousness movement. Impressed by Śrīla Prabhupāda's scholarship and saintliness, Śrīla Ācāryadeva became a member of the Kṛṣṇa consciousness community in Berkeley and, shortly thereafter, on February 8, 1970, was initiated as Śrīla Prabhupāda's disciple.

From the beginning, Śrīla Ācāryadeva distinguished himself by his oratorical skills, his spiritual dedication and his devotion to studying the writings of his spiritual master, through which he acquired a deep knowledge of Sanskrit. He quickly gained recognition from Śrīla Prabhupāda himself, who marked him as "a literary man" and in 1970 sent him to Boston to accept responsibilities with ISKCON's publishing activities there. Later, Śrīla Ācāryadeva served as president in ISKCON's centers in Gainesville, Florida, and Houston, Texas, and made a significant contribution to the rapid expansion of the Kṛṣṇa consciousness movement there in the early 1970s. In 1972, he adopted the renounced order (*sannyāsa*) in order to fully dedicate himself to serving the mission of his spiritual master: the propagation of the Kṛṣṇa consciousness movement throughout the world. For the next two years he traveled widely, speaking at colleges and universities throughout the United States.

In 1974, Śrīla Ācāryadeva was appointed to the Governing Body Commission of ISKCON and entrusted with the development of the Kṛṣṇa consciousness movement in Latin America. Over the following three years, he established twenty-five centers of the Society and attracted thousands of Latin Americans to the movement, as predicted by Śrīla Prabhupāda himself. In the course of his travels he met with numerous heads of state, government ministers and high religious leaders, conversing with them in fluent Spanish and Portuguese. He also founded the Spanish- and Portuguese-language divisions of the Bhaktivedanta Book Trust for the translation and publication of Śrīla Prabhupāda's books. At present, more than 20 million books in these two languages have been distributed throughout Latin America and abroad.

Shortly before his departure from this world in November, 1977, His Divine Grace Śrīla Prabhupāda chose Śrīla Ācāryadeva, along with ten other senior disciples, to accept the role of spiritual master and to initiate disciples. Currently, Śrīla Ācāryadeva serves as the Governing Body Commissioner for Brazil and the state of Florida and as one of the initiating spiritual masters for Latin America and the southern United States. His most challenging assignment came, however, in 1979, when the leaders of ISKCON, in recognition of his devotional scholarship, commissioned him to complete Śrīla Prabhupāda's monumental translation of and commentary on the *Śrīmad-Bhāgavatam*. For thousands of years in India, great spiritual masters have presented commentaries on the *Bhāgavatam* to make its urgent message clear to the people of their times. Śrīla Ācāryadeva is the first Westerner to be entrusted with this demanding task, and his success in communicating the essence of India's spiritual heritage to modern readers has already been noted by scholars and religionists around the world.

His Divine Grace
A. C. Bhaktivedanta Swami Prabhupāda

His Divine Grace A.C. Bhaktivedanta Swami Prabhupāda appeared in this world in 1896 in Calcutta, India. He first met his spiritual master, Śrīla Bhaktisiddhānta Sarasvatī Gosvāmī, in Calcutta in 1922. Bhaktisiddhānta Sarasvatī, a prominent religious scholar and the founder of sixty-four Gauḍīya Maṭhas (Vedic institutes), liked this educated young man and convinced him to dedicate his life to teaching Vedic knowledge. Śrīla Prabhupāda became his student, and eleven years later (1933) at Allahabad he became his formally initiated disciple.

At their first meeting, in 1922, Śrīla Bhaktisiddhānta Sarasvatī Ṭhākura requested Śrīla Prabhupāda to broadcast Vedic knowledge through the English language. In the years that followed, Śrīla Prabhupāda wrote a commentary on the *Bhagavad-gītā*, assisted the Gauḍīya Maṭha in its work and, in 1944, started *Back to Godhead*, an English fortnightly magazine. Maintaining the publication was a struggle. Singlehandedly, Śrīla Prabhupāda edited it, typed the manuscripts, checked the galley proofs, and even distributed the individual copies. Once begun, the magazine never stopped; it is now being continued by his disciples in the West and is published in over thirty languages.

Recognizing Śrīla Prabhupāda's philosophical learning and devotion, the Gauḍīya Vaiṣṇava Society honored him in 1947 with the title "Bhaktivedanta." In 1950, at the age of fifty-four, Śrīla Prabhupāda retired from married life, adopting the *vānaprastha* (retired) order to devote more time to his studies and writing. Śrīla Prabhupāda traveled to the holy city of Vṛndāvana, where he lived in very humble circumstances in the historic medieval temple of Rādhā-Dāmodara. There he engaged for several years in deep study and writing. He accepted the renounced order of life (*sannyāsa*) in 1959. At Rādhā-Dāmodara, Śrīla Prabhupāda began work on his life's masterpiece: a multivolume translation of and commentary on the eighteen-thousand-verse *Śrīmad-Bhāgavatam* (*Bhāgavata Purāṇa*). He also wrote *Easy Journey to Other Planets.*

After publishing three volumes of the *Bhāgavatam*, Śrīla Prabhupāda came to the United States, in September 1965, to fulfill the mission of his spiritual master. Subsequently, His Divine Grace wrote more than sixty volumes of authoritative translations, commentaries and summary studies of the philosophical and religious classics of India.

When he first arrived by freighter in New York City, Śrīla Prabhupāda was practically penniless. Only after almost a year of great difficulty did he establish the International Society for Krishna Consciousness, in July of 1966. Before his passing away on November 14, 1977, he guided the Society and saw it grow to a worldwide confederation of more than one hundred *āśramas,* schools, temples, institutes and farm communities.

In 1968, Śrīla Prabhupāda created New Vrindaban, an experimental Vedic community in the hills of West Virginia. Inspired by the success of New Vrindaban, now a thriving farm community of more than two thousand acres, his students have since founded several similar communities in the United States and abroad.

In 1972, His Divine Grace introduced the Vedic system of primary and secondary education in the West by founding the Gurukula school in Dallas, Texas. Since then, under his supervision, his disciples have established children's schools throughout the United States and the rest of the world, with the principal educational center now located in Vṛndāvana, India.

Śrīla Prabhupāda also inspired the construction of several large international cultural centers in India. The center at Śrīdhāma Māyāpur in West Bengal is the site for a planned spiritual city, an ambitious project for which construction will extend over the next decade. In Vṛndāvana, India, are the magnificent Kṛṣṇa-Balarāma Temple and International Guesthouse, and Śrīla Prabhupāda Memorial and Museum. There is also a major cultural and educational center in Bombay. Other centers are planned in a dozen important locations on the Indian subcontinent.

Śrīla Prabhupāda's most significant contribution, however, is his books. Highly respected by the academic community for their authority, depth and clarity, they are used as standard textbooks in numerous college courses. His writings have been translated into over fifty languages. The Bhaktivedanta Book Trust, established in 1972 to publish the works of His Divine Grace, has thus become the world's largest publisher of books in the field of Indian religion and philosophy.

In just twelve years, in spite of his advanced age, Śrīla Prabhupāda circled the globe fourteen times on lecture tours that took him to six continents. In spite of such a vigorous schedule, Śrīla Prabhupāda continued to write prolifically. His writings constitute a veritable library of Vedic philosophy, religion, literature and culture.

References

The purports of *Śrīmad-Bhāgavatam* are all confirmed by standard Vedic authorities. The following authentic scriptures are specifically cited in this volume. For specific page references, consult the general index.

Bhagavad-gītā

Bhakti-rasāmṛta-sindhu

Caitanya-caritāmṛta

Kṛṣṇa, the Supreme Personality of Godhead

Śrīmad-Bhāgavatam

Taittirīya Upaniṣad

Viṣṇu Purāṇa

Glossary

A

Ācārya—a spiritual master who teaches by example.

Aniruddha—one of the four expansions of Lord Kṛṣṇa in the spiritual world. He presides over the mind. *See also:* Vāsudeva; Saṅkarṣaṇa; Pradyumna.

B

Bali Mahārāja—one of the twelve *mahājanas,* or great authorities on devotional service. He surrendered the whole universe to Lord Vāmanadeva.

Brahmā, Lord—the first created being in the universe. He is a sub-creator under the supervision of the Supreme Lord.

E

Ekādaśī—the eleventh day after both the full and the new moon. On this day devotees abstain from grains and beans and increase their remembrance of Kṛṣṇa.

G

Garuḍa—the bird carrier of Lord Viṣṇu.

K

Karma—fruitive activities and their subsequent reactions.

Kṣatriya—a warrior or administrator; the second Vedic social order.

L

Lakṣmī—the goddess of fortune, Lord Nārāyaṇa's eternal consort.

M

Mahat-tattva—the total material energy, from which the material world is manifested.

Mānasa-gaṅgā—a sacred river that flows in Vṛndāvana along part of the base of Govardhana Hill.

Mantra—a transcendental sound heard and chanted to purify one's consciousness and raise it to the spiritual platform.

P

Pradyumna—one of the four original expansions of Lord Kṛṣṇa in the spiritual world. He presides over the intelligence. *See also:* Vāsudeva; Saṅkarṣaṇa; Aniruddha.

Purāṇa—a Vedic history of the universe.

Puruṣa—the supreme enjoyer; the Lord of the universe.

R

Rāsa Dance—Lord Kṛṣṇa's pleasure dance with the cowherd maidens of Vṛndāvana. It is a pure exchange of spiritual love between the Lord and His most advanced, confidential servitors.

S

Saṅkarṣaṇa—one of the four original expansions of Lord Kṛṣṇa in the spiritual world. He presides over the ego. *See also:* Pradyumna; Aniruddha; Vāsudeva.

Śūdra—a laborer; the fourth Vedic social order.

V

Vaiṣṇava—a devotee of Lord Viṣṇu, or Kṛṣṇa.

Vāsudeva—one of the four original expansions of Lord Kṛṣṇa in the spiritual world. He presides over consciousness. *See also:* Saṅkarṣaṇa; Pradyumna; Aniruddha.

Vedas—the original revealed scriptures; first spoken by Lord Kṛṣṇa.

Y

Yamarāja—the demigod in charge of judging and punishing sinners after death. He is also one of the *mahājanas,* leading authorities on devotional service.

Yogī—a person who practices any one of several processes for linking his consciousness with the Supreme.

Sanskrit Pronunciation Guide

Throughout the centuries, the Sanskrit language has been written in a variety of alphabets. The mode of writing most widely used throughout India, however, is called *devanāgarī*, which means, literally, the writing used in "the cities of the demigods." The *devanāgarī* alphabet consists of forty-eight characters: thirteen vowels and thirty-five consonants. Ancient Sanskrit grammarians arranged this alphabet according to practical linguistic principles, and this order has been accepted by all Western scholars. The system of transliteration used in this book conforms to a system that scholars in the last fifty years have accepted to indicate the pronunciation of each Sanskrit sound.

Vowels

अ a आ ā इ i ई ī उ u ऊ ū ऋ ṛ

ॠ ṝ ऌ ḷ ए e ऐ ai ओ o औ au

Consonants

Gutturals:	क ka	ख kha	ग ga	घ gha	ङ ṅa
Palatals:	च ca	छ cha	ज ja	झ jha	ञ ña
Cerebrals:	ट ṭa	ठ ṭha	ड ḍa	ढ ḍha	ण ṇa
Dentals:	त ta	थ tha	द da	ध dha	न na
Labials:	प pa	फ pha	ब ba	भ bha	म ma
Semivowels:	य ya	र ra	ल la	व va	
Sibilants:	श śa	ष ṣa	स sa		
Aspirate:	ह ha	Anusvāra: ं ṁ	Visarga: ः ḥ		

Numerals

०-0 १-1 २-2 ३-3 ४-4 ५-5 ६-6 ७-7 ८-8 ९-9

The vowels are written as follows after a consonant:

ा ā ि i ी ī ु u ू ū ृ ṛ ॄ ṝ े e ै ai ो o ौ au

For example: क ka का kā कि ki की kī कु ku कू kū

कृ kṛ कॄ kṝ के ke कै kai को ko कौ kau

Generally two or more consonants in conjunction are written together in a special form, as for example: क्ष kṣa त्र tra

The vowel "a" is implied after a consonant with no vowel symbol.

The symbol virāma (्) indicates that there is no final vowel: क्

The vowels are pronounced as follows:

a — as in but
ā — as in far but held twice as long as **a**
ai — as in aisle
au — as in how
e — as in they
i — as in pin
ī — as in pique but held twice as long as **i**

ḷ — as in lree
o — as in go
ṛ — as in rim
ṝ — as in reed but held twice as long as **ṛ**
u — as in push
ū — as in rule but held twice as long as **u**

The consonants are pronounced as follows:

Gutturals
(pronounced from the throat)

k — as in kite
kh — as in Eckhart
g — as in give
gh — as in dig-hard
ṅ — as in sing

Labials
(pronounced with the lips)

p — as in pine
ph — as in up-hill (not f)
b — as in bird
bh — as in rub-hard
m — as in mother

Cerebrals
(pronounced with tip of tongue against roof of mouth)

ṭ — as in tub
ṭh — as in light-heart
ḍ — as in dove
ḍh — as in red-hot
ṇ — as in sing

Dentals
(pronounced as cerebrals but with tongue against teeth)

t — as in tub
th — as in light-heart
d — as in dove
dh — as in red-hot
n — as in nut

Aspirate

h — as in home

Anusvāra

ṁ — a resonant nasal sound like in the French word *bon*

Palatals
(pronounced with middle of tongue against palate)

c — as in chair
ch — as in staunch-heart
j — as in joy
jh — as in hedgehog
ñ — as in canyon

Semivowels

y — as in yes
r — as in run
l — as in light
v — as in vine, except when preceded in the same syllable by a consonant, then like in swan

Sibilants

ś — as in the German word s*prechen*
ṣ — as in shine
s — as in sun

Visarga

ḥ — a final **h**-sound: **aḥ** is pronounced like **aha**; **iḥ** like **ihi**

There is no strong accentuation of syllables in Sanskrit, or pausing between words in a line, only a flowing of short and long (twice as long as the short) syllables. A long syllable is one whose vowel is long (**ā, ai, au, e, ī, o, ṝ, ū**) or whose short vowel is followed by more than one consonant (including **ḥ** and **ṁ**). Aspirated consonants (consonants followed by an **h**) count as single consonants.

Index of Sanskrit Verses

This index constitutes a complete listing of the first and third lines of each of the Sanskrit poetry verses of this volume of *Śrīmad-Bhāgavatam*, arranged in English alphabetical order. The first column gives the Sanskrit transliteration, and the second and third columns, respectively, list the chapter-verse reference and page number for each verse.

A

P

T

U

V

Y

General Index

Numerals in boldface type indicate references to translations of the verses of *Śrīmad-Bhāgavatam.*

A

Abhīyate defined, 65-66
Absolute Truth
  Kṛṣṇa as, 65
  See also: Kṛṣṇa; Supreme Lord
Ācārya(s) See: Spiritual master; *specific spiritual masters*
Ā-caturthād bhavet srāvaḥ
  verse quoted, 4
Acyuta, Lord. *See:* Kṛṣṇa
Āgacchateti vṛṣabhānu-sutā smitāsyā
  verse quoted, 16
Āgacchateti bhagavad-vacasā ta etya
  verse quoted, 13
Agṛhāṇām, 192
Ahaṁ hi sarva-yajñānām
  verse quoted, 135
Āhṛtya puṇya-salilaṁ śata-koṭi-kumbhaiḥ
  verse quoted, 15
Akrūra
  arrival of
    in Gokula (Vṛndāvana), **76-78**
    in Mathurā, **153**
  & austerities, **59**
  at Balarāma's house, **84-96**
  bewilderment of, **118**
  & Bhoja dynasty, **25**
  chariot used by, 26
  & charity, **59**
  cowherd men follow chariot of, **113**
  definition of name of, 103
  departure of
    from Mathurā, **58**
    from Vṛndāvana, **112**
  as descendant of Madhu, **95**
  desires of, fulfilled, **91**

Akrūra (*continued*)
  devotion for Lord felt by, **59**
  & dust from Kṛṣṇa's feet, **78**-79
  Dvārakā left by, 112
  ecstasy of, **78-79, 82-83, 125**
  as eminent Yadu, **24**
  enroute to Vṛndāvana, **58-77**
  entering Mathurā, **160**
  fast broken by, 85
  father of, **76, 153**
  fatigue forgotten by, **87**
  fear abandoned by, **79**
  gopīs condemn, **107**
  gopīs offended by, 112
  journey of, time of, 58
  Kaṁsa flatters, **24-26**
  Kaṁsa informed by, **160**
  Kaṁsa merciful to, **62**
  Kaṁsa selects new chariot for, 26
  Kaṁsa's order to, 58
  Kaṁsa summons, **24**
  Kṛṣṇa & Balarāma greeted by, **82**
  Kṛṣṇa & Balarāma requested to visit house of, **156-57**
  Kṛṣṇa & Balarāma seen by, **81**
  Kṛṣṇa & Balarāma seen in Yamunā by, **117**
  Kṛṣṇa asks about vision of, **151**
  Kṛṣṇa embraces, **83**
  Kṛṣṇa informed by, **95-96**
  Kṛṣṇa inquires from, **92-93**
  Kṛṣṇa instructs, to go home, **156**
  Kṛṣṇa separated from, 112
  Kṛṣṇa's & Balarāma's reception for, **84-86**
  Kṛṣṇa's footprints seen by, **77-79**
  Kṛṣṇa's Viṣṇu form disappears from sight of, **150-51**
  lamentation abandoned by, **79**

B

C

E

K

O

P

Q

R

S

T

W